ORGANIZATIONAL BEHAVIOUR

An Introductory Text

SECOND EDITION

STUDENT WORKBOOK

Andrzej A. Huczynski
Glasgow University Business School

David A. Buchanan
Loughborough University Business School

Prentice Hall

New York   London   Toronto   Sydney   Tokyo   Singapore

First published 1994 by
Prentice Hall International (UK) Limited
Campus 400, Maylands Avenue
Hemel Hempstead
Hertfordshire, HP2 7EZ
A division of
Simon & Schuster International Group

Typeset in 10/12 pt Times
by Columns Design and Production Services Ltd, Reading

Printed and bound in Great Britain
by Ashford Overload Services, Southampton

British Library Cataloguing in Publication Data

A catalogue record for this book is available from the British Library
ISBN 0–13–641077–4

1 2 3 4 5   98 97 96 95 94

Contents

PART III Technology in the organization

PART IV Structural influences on behaviour

Student's briefing

First a comment on spelling. Various colleagues and students have asked us over the years why we insist on using the American spelling for the title of our subject area. Wrong. We use the correct *English* spelling of this and other similar words. The 'z' is correct according to the *Oxford English Dictionary*; check with this source if you are not convinced, and check also with the *Oxford Dictionary for Writers and Editors*. Still not sure? Look up the entry under 'ize' in Fowler's *Modern English Usage*; or check the similar entry in Eric Partridge's *Usage and Abusage*. Organize and similar words come from a Greek root, and to use '-ise' is according to Partridge, 'to flout etymology and logic' as well as being inconsistent with pronunciation. So there. Language and usage are, of course, not static and one must accept change in this respect. However, change born of carelessness or ignorance must, in our view, merit some resistance.

This *Student Workbook* is designed to complement the book, *Organizational Behaviour: An Introductory Text*, Prentice Hall, 1991 (second edition). We will refer to that text as *ORBIT* for short. The purpose of this *Workbook* is to provide you with a comprehensive, integrated learning resource that will enable you to work through the subject matter of organizational behaviour in an interesting and challenging way. Several of the materials in this *Workbook* are designed to complement or replace more conventional lecture room techniques, and offer your organizational behaviour instructor a flexible and easy-to-use set of teaching materials. You should not attempt to read this *Workbook* like a conventional text. Your instructor will tell you when you are expected to have your copy available, and how he or she would like you to use it. If you do not have your copy with you as requested by your instructor for scheduled sessions, you will not be able to make best use of these materials, as they have not been designed solely for independent study.

We have designed the materials with four fundamental principles in view.

1. Complementarity

These materials are designed to complement (and not replace) both *ORBIT* and the other materials that your Instructor will use. Different instructors approach the subject of organizational behaviour in different ways, as you would expect, and have their own emphases and preferences. Your Instructor may use some of the materials in this *Workbook* and not others, and he or she may use some of these materials in a manner different from that offered here. A number of factors can affect the sequence in which material is covered, and it is not necessary to follow the sequence in the textbook. We recommend, therefore, that you remove pages and sections from this *Workbook* and punch them into your own ring binder for your particular course. In this way you can build up a systematic set of materials that relates specifically to your organizational behaviour course, and use this for revision.

2. Awareness

These materials seek to demonstrate that organizational behaviour can be observed and studied in many different settings, and not just in factories and offices. Together with the textbook, *ORBIT*, we hope to raise your awareness of the factors which influence human behaviour in all kinds of organizations. So examples are drawn from banks, pizza restaurants, schools, street gangs, shops, and a range of industrial organizations. The sources of these materials are similarly wide and unconventional.

3. Stimulation

The materials are designed to stimulate interest and debate. One criticism of existing (mainly American) workbooks is that they tend to be dull, as well as ethnocentric. We would like you, even if you never study our subject further, to remember organizational behaviour as stimulating and interesting. Many such workbooks deter student and instructor with conventional content and layout. We have in contrast tried to bring together material that we enjoy using, which our students find enjoyable, and which we hope will encourage you to study the subject further.

4. Ease of use

The materials are easy to use. All the exercises in this *Student Workbook* have been selected for maximum impact, to generate maximum classroom debate and learning. Moreover, the exercises are designed to be flexible, to fit different teaching time frames and the needs and preferences of different instructors. We have suggested ways in which each of the exercises in the *Workbook* can be used; the same materials can, however, be put to different uses according to how your instructor wants to deliver his or her own course.

Workbook structure

The *Student Workbook* is divided into twenty-two sections, each relating to the corresponding chapter in *ORBIT*. Each section contains four teaching activity types. These vary in length, but cover a wide range of interesting, provocative and varied activities suitable for undergraduate and postgraduate *ORBIT* users. The four teaching activity types are:

1. Large group activities (LGAs)

The distinguishing features of these activities are *student participation* (even in a large group), and *no preparation*. They typically focus on the introduction of key concepts and theories.

These are teaching activities which can be used with very large student groups (say, 60 to 300 students) in sessions of sixty to ninety minutes. The main constraints of this setting include the limited scope for physical student movement and syndicate work, and for student–instructor dialogue. Materials used in this context have to be short enough to run 'cold', without advance preparation. These activities can typically take from ten to twenty minutes. Large syndicate groups may be impractical, but students can discuss issues in 'buzz groups' made up of pairs and threes. So ten minutes of small group discussion can be followed by ten minutes of instructor's debriefing. The remainder of a teaching session in this mode may be devoted to a short lecture, perhaps combined with a video presentation. Such exercises can of course also be used in small group sessions if required.

2. Small group activities (SGAs)

The distinguishing feature of these activities is *small group discussion*. They are likely to focus on the operationalization of concepts or the application of theories in practical organizational settings.

These are teaching activities designed for small seminar, workshop or tutorial groups, and for larger classes where syndicate or 'break out' rooms are available. Syndicate group size may vary from four to fifteen students, and the exercise and debriefing together are likely to occupy from sixty to ninety minutes altogether

3. Prepared tasks (PREPs)

The distinguishing feature of these activities is that they require advance student preparation. They are likely to require data collection and depth of analysis, and the output may be some form of student preparation.

These are therefore activities that students carry out between scheduled lecture and tutorial sessions. You may be required to prepare a case, collect some data, analyse a problem situation and bring these materials with you to a session as specified by your Instructor.

4. Reviews (REVs)

Reviews are designed to provide students with opportunities for continuing feedback to allow you to assess your understanding and progress through the course material. They are not intended to be used as part of a formal assessment system. We have used a variety of approaches, including case studies, multiple choice questions, sentence completion, matching pairs, crosswords, true–false choice and short (one- or two-sentence) answer tests. Each section includes such review material, but this varies from section to section to maintain student interest.

In this *Student Workbook*, the LGAs, SGAs and PREPs each follow broadly the same sequence:

Objectives
Introduction
Procedure
The exercise, case or other material
Supplementary materials as appropriate
Notes (special features, sources, etc.)

The 'correct answers' to exercise questions are omitted for three reasons. First, in many organizational settings, there are no correct answers, there is no one best way. This is a feature of the subject which is reinforced in some of the early exercises in this *Workbook*. Second, as already indicated, your instructor may decide to use these materials in a manner different from that in which the authors would use them, depending on different needs and preferences. So look to your instructor for an appropriate debriefing. Third, we don't want you to be able to cheat and look up the 'correct answers' before carrying out the work.

In the REVs, the sequence is similar and includes:

Objectives
Procedure
The review materials

Once again, your instructor will provide you with an answer guide in each case; you may on occasion be required to grade or mark your own work, or that of a colleague.

Chapter 1
Introduction to organizational behaviour

1.1 LGA: Self-test

Objectives

❏ To explore the ways in which we as individuals construct explanations of human behaviour in organizations.

❏ To explore individual differences in our understanding of and assumptions about human behaviour in organizations.

❏ To explore the limits of 'common-sense' explanations of human behaviour in organizations.

Introduction

We are all experts in the subject of human behaviour – or at least we like to think we are. There must be some truth in this belief, given the rich base of personal and social experiences from which each of us can draw. However, this thinking leads to the claim that psychology, social psychology and sociology – the core subjects that underpin the study of organizational behaviour – are merely common sense wrapped in obscure jargon. Students with scientific, mathematical and engineering backgrounds are particularly likely to hold such a dismissive view. It is therefore useful at the beginning of a course of study in organizational behaviour to confront this issue, and not to avoid it. The underlying aim of this exercise is to ensure that, whatever students' backgrounds, and whatever view individual students hold or develop with respect to the study of organizational behaviour, their view is a considered one, based on evidence and argument, and not on unthinking prejudice.

Procedure

Step 1 Complete this step on your own, without discussion with colleagues. On the following page is a list of twenty statements. Your task is to indicate whether each statement is either true or false by writing a T or an F at the side. In some cases you will naturally want to answer, 'it depends'. However, you are asked here to take a stand and indicate whether you feel that, in your view, on the whole, in most circumstances, for most practical purposes, the statement is true or false. If you are still not happy with this you may put a circle round your response to indicate this.

Step 2 Compare your responses with at least two people sitting round about you. Identify responses where you have clearly disagreed, choose up to three disagreements that you find interesting, share your thinking, and establish *why* you have disagreed. If time allows, share your reasoning on items where you were particularly unhappy about making a clear commitment.

Step 3 Your Instructor will interrupt your discussion in step 2 when appropriate, and will take some examples from around the group, concentrating on disagreements with respect to the truth of these statements, and in particular identifying the *reasons* for such disagreements. It should become clear by this stage that there are a number of specific causes or sources of such disagreements.

Step 4   Instructor's debrief.

Self-test

Read each of the following statements carefully and determine, in the light of your experience, whether it is True or False, and write a T or an F beside each statement accordingly.

1. Men are naturally better when it comes to decisive managerial decision-making, compared with women.

2. People who are satisfied in their work are more productive than those who are not.

3. Resistance to new technology increases with age.

4. Alcohol in small amounts is a stimulant.

5. You can 'read' a person's emotional state by watching their facial expressions closely.

6. The more challenging the goals you face, the more you are likely to accomplish.

7. Selection interviews, handled correctly, are effective ways to assess candidates' suitability for a job.

8. When asked to rank features of their work in order of personal importance, the vast majority of people put pay at the top of their list.

9. Punishment is an effective way of eliminating undesirable behaviour.

10. When you have to remain working for several hours, it is better to take a small number of long rest periods than a larger number of short breaks.

11. When people can share their thinking in groups, they can come up with more original ideas than individuals working on their own.

12. Most people, if they are being honest with themselves, can tell you what their motives are.

13. People have a natural resistance to organizational change and managers always have to overcome this first.

14. Conflict in an organization is disruptive and should be avoided at all costs.

15. Some people are born leaders, and this is evident in their behaviour.

16. A reliable personality test is a good predictor of job performance.

17. People learn new tasks better when they are only told about their successes and their mistakes are overlooked.

18. It is not possible for individual managers to change their style because this reflects an innate aspect of their personalities.

19. Organizations always become ineffective when people do not have clear job descriptions that set out their responsibilities and define their place in the organization structure.

20. Extroverts invariably make better salespersons.

This exercise is based on and influenced by a similar exercise, with an interesting accompanying article: 'Social psychology as common sense', by Adrian Furnham, *Bulletin of the British Psychological Society*, 1983, vol. 36, pp. 105–9.

1.2 SGA: Incident analysis

Objectives

- ❑ To illustrate the nature and benefits of a systematic 'micro-analysis' of management behaviour in an organization.
- ❑ To give students an opportunity to experience the role of management consultant or adviser, giving practical advice on the basis of systematic analysis.
- ❑ To consider the extent to which an individual manager's style or approach can and should change.

Introduction

We each have our own preferred ways of dealing with the world and with other people. In an organizational context, this is often reflected in an individual's 'management style'. Given the differences in management style between individuals, two fundamental questions arise. First, is it possible to distinguish more effective and less effective styles? Second, can individual managers change their styles in practice, or do inherited and immutable personality traits prevent this? In this exercise, you are invited to consider a short report of a conversation between a superior and his subordinate, to consider what the superior is trying to achieve in this incident, and to offer practical advice as you feel appropriate to the manager concerned. The incident report is based on a real (of course disguised) conversation.

Procedure

Step 1 Complete this step on your own, without discussion with colleagues. Read the following *Incident report* which gives a verbatim account of a short conversation between a Project Leader, Jan van Beek, and one of the Project Managers who report to him, Peter Vermaat.

Step 2 In syndicate groups of three to five participants, complete the *Incident analysis* sheet which follows the *Incident report*. Here you are invited to consider, first, what the superior van Beek was trying to achieve. You are then asked to consider what his objective(s) in this meeting *should* have been. These two issues should be dealt with separately and in sequence. The two issues should not become confused. Appoint a spokesperson for your syndicate.

Step 3 Share your syndicate responses to the *Incident analysis* with the other groups. Agree on what the objective or objectives *should* have been.

Step 4 Returning to your syndicate groups, consider the *Incident replay* question concerning the advice you would like to offer to van Beek given that you are now agreed on what he is trying to achieve. Put a summary of this advice on an overhead foil, on a flipchart sheet, or on a whiteboard, depending on what is available, but this is not essential. Remember to nominate a spokesperson.

Step 5 Then share your advice with the whole class in a plenary session. When there is broad collective agreement on the advice to feed back, consider the following questions:

1. How easy, or how difficult, is it for someone to follow the kind of advice that you are giving?
2. To what extent can van Beek argue that you are trying to change his personality?
3. To what extent can van Beek argue that his subordinates will see him acting inconsistently if he follows your advice – and that this will damage his reputation?
4. On the basis of your analysis and advice, how would you now respond to the question – can a manager change his or her style?

Step 6 Instructor's debrief.

FUNNY BUSINESS

'If you want me Miss Timpson, I'll be in the general office throwing my weight around'

Incident report

Jan van Beek is a Project Leader in the research and development division of a plastics manufacturing company. Reporting to him are four Project Managers who coordinate the work of specialist staff whose project allocations change two or three times each year depending on client demand. At the planning and review meeting this morning, the Division Head was concerned about progress on one of Jan's major projects. He was clearly angry, and Jan was taken by surprise. It was not unusual for deadlines on large projects to 'slip', and nobody had complained about this project before. When Jan got back to his office, he telephoned his young Project Manager, Peter Vermaat, to tell him to come to his office as soon as possible to discuss the matter:

Peter: (Arrives at Jan's door looking glum and upset. Jan waves him into the room and he stands in front of Jan's desk.) Good morning, Mr van Beek. I believe you wanted to talk to me?

Jan: (Sitting at his desk.) Yes Peter, your electrofusion project, well I'm not surprised you look miserable, like your progress account on this one, eh! Well, what the hell's gone wrong here?

Peter: Gone wrong? I'm not sure that . . .

Jan: (Waving the papers from the planning and review meeting.) Look at the evidence. Three major deadlines missed in three months. Are your people working a three-day week now? (Laughs.) Things are going to pick up this month then?

Peter: Ah well, you remember that four months ago after the appraisal interviews you asked us to draw up action plans for individual staff development. You see, that has started to change the way in which we decide project allocations, and the problem since then that we've been trying to find a way around is that we seem to have been developing . . .

Jan: (Interrupting impatiently.) I don't want you to bring me problems, Peter. I want you to bring me solutions. (The telephone rings. Jan answers it. Peter stands for five minutes while Jan deals with a casual request for information from another project leader.) Where were we? That's it then. I want that project back on schedule. I want you to get on top of this and fix it, fast.

Peter: So, it's fast action you want?

Jan: Of course, Peter. I want you to sort this problem out immediately. That's what you're paid for, isn't it? And you're not going to fix it standing there pulling faces at me, are you? (Peter turns around and slams Jan's door shut as he leaves.)

Incident analysis

From this report, what would you say were the objectives of the superior, Jan van Beek?

1. _____

2. _____

3. _____

From a professional management point of view, what do you think the objectives of the superior, Jan van Beek, *should* have been?

To _____

Incident replay

Imagine that Jan van Beek has been given an opportunity to 'replay' this incident, and that you have an opportunity to give him some advice on how to achieve his management objective.

Be as detailed and specific as you feel you have to be, about what he should do and say differently this time to achieve his objective. What advice are you going to give him? Prepare a syndicate report summarizing and justifying your advice.

1.3 PREP: Resolving the dilemma

Objectives

❑ To collect specific practical examples of a key introductory concept – the *organizational dilemma*.

❑ To consider whether and how such organizational problems can be resolved.

❑ To offer an opportunity to relate a textbook concept directly to personal experience.

Introduction

Chapter 1 of *ORBIT* introduces the concept of the 'organizational dilemma' on page 10. This concept concerns the potential inconsistency and conflict between the goals of individuals and the purposes of organizations. We would like to invite students to consider this dilemma and its implications in more depth.

Chapter 1 of the text argues that organizations, as social arrangements, are not given but can be changed. The previous exercise sought to establish that management behaviour is similarly not constrained by personal or organizational factors but is also open to change. Does this mean that we do not need to accept the organizational dilemma – that we can challenge and effectively resolve such inconsistencies and conflicts?

You are thus invited to carry out the following analysis, in preparation for a tutorial, seminar or workshop session.

Procedure

Step 1 Identify three specific examples of the 'organizational dilemma' and write a description of each. These could be based on current or past personal experience. They could rely on accounts from relatives or friends. They could be based on media reports. Try asking a relative or friend (somebody not directly involved with your course of study) about this topic if you can; you could be surprised by the answers and illustrations you collect. Your write-up for this step should be around 1000 words long (at only 350 words an illustration, this is not going to be difficult).

Step 2 Recommend for each of the three instances the organizational changes or changes to management behaviour that would be required to resolve the problems you have described. The resolution may be obvious; on the other hand you may need to exercise some creative or lateral thinking here. Note that there is not necessarily 'one-best-way' to resolve these issues, and that several different approaches may all be effective in some respects. Your write-up for this step should again be around 1000 words long.

Step 3 Write a short concluding assessment on the practicality of dealing with such organizational dilemmas; can it be done, and if so is it worth the cost, time and effort?

Step 4 Prepare a 5-minute oral summary presentation of your illustrations, recommendations and assessment.

Step 5 Instructor's debrief: you may also be required to submit a written report for assessment.

1.4 REV: Sentence completion

Objectives

This test is designed deliberately to encourage you to pay attention to detail in your reading. It is based on the Foreword (by Derek Pugh) and Chapter 1 (Introduction) to *ORBIT*. If you have read and remembered these introductory chapters, this test will present few difficulties. However, if you have not absorbed those two chapters, there may be little point in proceeding with this Review.

Some students may be able to guess some of the correct responses, but most of these require a close reading of the material first. If somebody wants to claim that this is a test of memory and not of understanding – then they are correct. We simply wish to reinforce the point that attention to detail is *one* desirable learning discipline.

Procedure

Complete the following fifteen sentences with words chosen from the following list:

control	organizers
retention	organizational dilemma
diagnostic reading	social psychology
mental programming	archaeology
behaviourists	Goldsmith and Clutterbuck
convergence	standards
psychic prisons	culture interpretation
social	twelve
flexibility	flexible
political systems	sex discrimination
international trends	symphony orchestras
autonomous	sociology

classicists	trading conditions
recruitment	controlled
organizational factors	Peters and Waterman
collective	internationalization
ten	social
humanists	tired crew members

You get one point for each correctly completed sentence, irrespective of the number of blank words.

There are more items on the list than blanks in the following sentences; some are simply not relevant. Where you feel that you have two or more options for completing a sentence, choose the one that you think is best; the other choices could be wrong, but they could just be less appropriate.

1. Contemporary demographic trends have given management a _____ and _____ problem.

2. One key British contribution to the 'organizational excellence' debate comes from _____ and_____ .

3. According to a *Time* magazine analysis, _____ _____ were to blame for the tanker *Exxon Valdez* disaster.

4. The task of managing a modern organization has been made more difficult by the combination of _____ , demographics and studies of 'excellence'.

5. Derek Pugh in his Foreword to *Organizational Behaviour* divides organization theorists into two camps which he labels _____ and _____respectively.

6. It is the question of _____ that is at the heart of the debate between Pugh's two camps.

7. The view that organizations around the world are adopting similar structures and procedures, regardless of differences in national culture, is called the _____ thesis.

8. Geert Hofstede argues that, because of differences in _____ _____, managers in Greece have a different attitude towards risk-taking than, for example, managers in Singapore.

9. The study of organizational behaviour is multidisciplinary, drawing on, for example, _____ and _____ , among other subjects.

10. The Draft Social Charter published by the European Commission in 1989 covered _____ sets of proposals affecting working conditions in the Community.

11. Organizations can be defined as _____ arrangements for the _____ performance of _____ goals.

12. Organizational control means comparing actual outcomes with _____ .

13. The American management writer, Peter Drucker, argues that modern organizations can be compared with _____ _____ .

14. The management writer, Gareth Morgan, invites us to 'critically evaluate' organizations with the help of eight metaphors, which include organizations as _____ _____ , and as _____ _____ .

15. The problem of reconciling organizational and individual goals is called the _____ _____ .

Chapter 2

Natural and social science

2.1 LGA: Harry's problem

Objectives

❑ To provide experience in analysing the cause or causes of an organizational problem and in identifying an approach to resolving the problem.

❑ To demonstrate the uses and limitations of diagnostic frameworks for resolving organizational problems.

❑ To illustrate that problem-solving in this domain is not a straightforward mechanical exercise of simply linking solutions to problems.

Introduction

Ask any manager to tell you about the kinds of 'people problems' that he or she has had to deal with. The stories that they tell are likely to have a number of common characteristics. First, such problems can be extremely frustrating for the manager who has to deal with them, involving emotional stress and perhaps embarrassment. Second, these problems are usually 'messy' in that they can have a number of dimensions or aspects which may or may not be interrelated, but which all contribute to the problem in some way. Third, they often appear to be impossible or extremely difficult to resolve given the complexities of the situation, or because there are factors outside the direct control of the manager or the organization. Fourth, initial attempts to solve the problem are often only partially effective and can even expose further complications. Finally, effective solutions can take a long time to implement. For these reasons, 'people problems' in organizations are often not addressed, because action is considered too expensive, too time-consuming, or because the significant effort involved may be ineffective. It is difficult to convey these characteristics fully in a classroom exercise, so it is helpful to bear these points in mind when addressing the problem that follows.

Here is an account of a typical organizational problem, concerning the unsatisfactory performance of a branch manager working for a bank. The problem is a real one (but is of course disguised) and has the 'messy' characteristics just described. Many managers rely on past experience and intuition when confronted with issues such as those raised here. That approach can of course be effective in many settings. However, what is advocated here is a *systematic* approach which seeks to ensure that all or at least most of the possibilities have been explored, and that key issues are not overlooked. Why is this better than intuition? The individual manager does not always have all the relevant information to hand; people often do not reveal everything about their personal motives, aspirations or circumstances to senior figures in the organization. Some approaches to solving such problems are expensive, and some as we will see are free or low-cost. It is therefore useful to be confident about the diagnosis before spending time or money on a solutions package, and a systematic approach is more effective in building that confidence.

Procedure

Step 1   Read through *Harry's problem*, on your own and without discussion with colleagues. Then turn to the *Preliminary analysis* which follows it. Your task is to identify *possible* causes of this problem, and to identify for each cause potentially appropriate solutions. Base your analysis on the problem description, on personal or indirect experience of any similar settings, and on what you feel are reasonable assumptions about what is happening here. This is an 'ideas generation' phase, and your analysis does not have to be internally consistent.

Step 2   Working in buzz groups of two or three neighbours, compare your *Preliminary analysis* with that of colleagues. Use these comparisons to confirm and to add to your own analysis. Reasoning that is not clear should be challenged by your group until a satisfactory explanation is forthcoming.

Step 3   Then turn to the *Diagnostic framework*, which your Instructor will explain as necessary to make sure that the terminology is clear. This framework provides a comprehensive and systematic approach to the analysis and resolution of organizational performance problems. The analysis in steps 1 and 2 involves two of the central stages of the overall framework.

Step 4   Moving again into groups of two and three, look for aspects of the analysis that you have overlooked. Identify any potential causes and solutions that you have identified that do not appear in the framework. Note that the framework may therefore have some gaps.

Step 5   Instructor's debrief.

Harry's problem

Harry is in his early forties and has been working for the Anytown Bank for over twenty years. He has been a Branch Manager for the last nine years, and held a number of management posts in head office before that. It is now 1992, and Harry's Regional Manager has watched his performance deteriorate over the past eighteen months. All banks saw their businesses change dramatically in the late 1980s, with more competition, new technology and changes to organization structures and working practices. The traditional paternalistic culture that characterized banking until the 1980s was transformed into a more dynamic customer-oriented culture by the 1990s. The concept of 'selling financial products to customers', rather than providing professional services to clients, was reflected in new 'open plan' branch layouts.

Harry became Branch Manager at Bridgford in 1983, when it was a small branch with an assistant manager, two supervisors, and twelve well-trained and efficient staff. The branch was moved to larger premises in a more central location in the town in 1985 and the business grew. In 1986, the branch became a central site for handling some of the mortgage account administration of smaller branches in the region. A third supervisor was appointed and the staff rose to seventeen. In 1990, the branch was modernized with a new open plan layout, but the transfer of experienced personnel to a separate regional mortgage administration centre reduced Harry's staff to thirteen, with only a customer service manager and a specialist salesperson to replace the assistant manager and supervisors. The priorities of a Branch Manager were clear and included staff development, customer service, business results and use of resources. A manager's performance was judged against targets set in these four areas. From 1983 to 1990, Harry performed satisfactorily, demonstrating good leadership skills, but did not excel. From 1990, his performance deteriorated. Business results were poor, new customer-oriented working practices were not being introduced, and Harry appeared not to be using and developing his branch team. In 1991 Harry's performance fell further, and staff morale and motivation collapsed.

The Regional Manager visited Harry's branch regularly to discuss the problems. Harry admitted that things had not been going well, but blamed his inexperienced staff. He accepted advice, but did not implement it. Harry appeared harassed in meetings, missed deadlines and was late with branch returns. He seemed to be easily sidetracked by small problems and did not focus on priority tasks. He did not plan adequately. Staff were not clear about their targets, but found Harry sociable and friendly and always ready to listen sympathetically and help with personal problems. He carried out a lot of the administrative work of the branch himself without delegating it to staff. He did not spend much time with customers and was constantly in conflict with his Customer Service Manager who took a stricter line with the branch staff. The Regional Manager also discovered that Harry had misled him about actions that were supposed to have been implemented, and that he had falsified staff development records. Harry had been able to persuade staff to support him in hiding the fact that these records had been falsified.

Preliminary analysis

From your reading of the problem, drawing on your own experience, and making reasonable assumptions about aspects of the situation that may not be detailed here, what do you think might be the causes of this problem, and what then might be the appropriate solutions? Use this page to make notes of your analysis.

Possible causes   **Possible solutions**

Diagnostic framework

The analysis that you have just completed forms two of the central stages in the following seven-stage *diagnostic framework*. This is a structured approach to organizational problem-solving. It is designed to encourage a comprehensive and informed analysis of causes and solutions, and to ensure that action plans are based on reasoning and evidence rather than on hunch, habit or intuition. The causes are not always obvious, and often several causal factors are at work. Solutions have to take these issues into account. The seven stages of the framework are:

1. *Define the problem.* What is the problem? Problem definitions based on actions and outcomes are more appropriate than problem definitions in terms of personality traits, motives or attitudes. It is usually more effective to establish what the person is doing that should be avoided, or what they are not doing which they should be. It is usually not helpful to define these kinds of issues in terms of 'attitude problems', or 'personality defects'.

2. *Confirm the value.* We pointed out earlier that this kind of problem can be difficult and time-consuming to address, with no guarantee of an effective solution. So, is it likely to be worth the effort in this particular case?

3. *List the likely causes.* Establish possible causes behind the problem as defined in stage 1.

4. *List the possible solutions.* Establish possible solutions for each of the causes you have identified in stage 3. Exercise as much creative judgement at this stage as you feel appropriate in the circumstances.

5. *Finalize a solutions package.* Assuming that you are confident in your diagnosis (you may feel that you need more information), establish an effective solution, or a solutions package.

6. *Evaluate the solutions proposed.* Identify the costs and benefits of implementing your solution. The costs and benefits may be financial, performance-related, or psychological. If the costs appear to outweigh the benefits, abandon the attempt to resolve the problem, and either live with it or go back to stage 4.

7. *Implement.* Assuming that in your judgement the benefits outweigh the costs, implement your recommendations.

You have already carried out steps 3 and 4 in this framework. Your analysis, in outline, should look something like this:

Possible causes   **Possible solutions**

1.	Personal, family, or domestic factors	Advice and counselling, referral to professionals; compassionate leave
2.	Health problems	Refer to company doctor or to own doctor; compassionate leave
3.	Personal ability	Training, retraining, secondment, coaching
4.	Job difficulty	Simplify the job, reduce work load, relax pressures
5.	Job simplicity and lack of challenge	Job enrichment, special projects, promotion, increased responsibility
6.	Clarity of job goals	Guidance on targets and standards
7.	Extrinsic motivation	Improve financial reward, praise from superiors for good performance
8.	Feedback	Improve communications with superior about performance
9.	Resources	Improve equipment, staffing, space, etc.
10.	Working conditions	Improve lighting, heating reduce noise, distractions, improve layout, etc.
11.	Organization structure	Change reporting lines, redefine supervision

The format of this exercise and the diagnostic framework was inspired by the approach developed in *Improving Leadership Performance* by Peter Wright and David Taylor, Prentice Hall, Hemel Hempstead, 1984, Chapter 2.

2.2　SGA: Morale at Mouldswich

Objectives

❑ To explore the practical application of the research designs and methods introduced in Chapter 2 of *ORBIT*, with respect to an organizational setting.

❑ To consider the strengths and limitations of different research approaches.

❑ To establish criteria on which research work can be assessed.

Introduction

The organizational researcher has a range of available approaches and tools with which to answer research questions. Chapter 2 of *ORBIT* distinguishes between *research design* – the broad strategy – and *research methods* – specific ways of collecting data. These designs and methods can be applied in a wide variety of combinations. The designs and methods used very often depend less on theoretical considerations and more on the practical realities of the organizational setting in which they are applied. The line between organizational research for academic purposes and consultancy for purely managerial purposes is often blurred, as the goals and approaches can typically overlap. You are invited in the following exercise to design a research approach that will generate academic information about current trends in manufacturing work organization, and which will also help the company to address specific problems that it is experiencing with the introduction of these work organization changes.

Procedure

Step 1 First read the *Morale at Mouldswich* briefing that follows this section, on your own and without discussion with colleagues. As you do this, make preliminary notes on how you think you would begin to approach this task. The aim at this stage is not to produce a complete answer but to begin the decision-making process.

Step 2 Move into syndicate groups with three to five members. Decide as a group how you propose to tackle this research brief. Remember to nominate a spokesperson, and prepare a five-minute presentation that will explain and justify your recommendations.

Step 3 Present your summary to the class as a whole, concentrating on the four primary questions in the briefing. Allow five minutes for each presentation, and five to ten minutes for questions. Invite the 'listening' groups to assess critically the presentations from the other groups, to probe aspects which are not clear, and to challenge ideas with which they disagree. This can become boring and repetitive with a large number of syndicate groups (more than five or six). The alternative is for the first presenting group to deal with question one, the second group to deal with question two and so on.

Step 4 Optional: if you have time. Present your responses to the three secondary questions stated in the briefing. As in step 3, to avoid repetition over a large number of syndicate groups, have those syndicates that have still to present concentrate on the secondary questions. Note how different groups may have tackled these issues.

Step 5 In open discussion identify the criteria on which you now feel it appropriate to assess a piece of research work published in an academic journal. Record the points on a board or flipchart (you could nominate someone to do this for you). Individual students should keep a set of their own notes from this discussion; these may come in useful for a later exercise.

Step 6 Instructor's debrief.

Morale at Mouldswich

Your organizational research group has been approached by a Product Manager from a local engineering company which manufactures high precision, high value-added titanium fabrications (which sell for around £1000 each). He has been introducing some Japanese-inspired manufacturing methods, such as just-in-time scheduling, and giving the operators on the shop floor more discretion to determine their own work allocation. However, things don't seem to have been going as planned. Teamwork on the shop floor has not developed effectively, and although the first line supervisors were supposed to adopt a new 'facilitating' role, in contrast with their traditional 'policing' function, this does not seem to be happening. The new system does appear to be working quite well in many respects, and some very significant savings have been made. On the other hand, morale is low, and communications between management and the shop floor have become strained. The Product Manager would like to enlist your help to find out what is going on, what is going wrong, and to establish what might be done to improve the situation. He thought that some kind of attitude or opinion survey might be helpful, but these have not been welcomed in the company in the past (they've been conducted by company personnel), and he is looking to you for suggestions, ideas and professional advice.

The Mouldswich factory is one of several that the company operates around the country. The Mouldswich site is home to a number of the company's businesses. The Product Manager who has approached you is responsible for just one of the businesses at Mouldswich – the 'A Module' business. This business was chosen as the pilot for the implementation and testing of the changes to manufacturing work organization. In this respect, it is even more important that the changes are implemented smoothly, because the intention is to spread the changes first to other businesses on the Mouldswich site, and then to the company's other locations. The A Module business has an annual turnover of around £15 million, and employs sixty-nine skilled and semi-skilled men who each belong to one of seven skill groups: welders, resistance welders, millers, finishers, process operators, machinists and inspectors. These men are deployed over three shifts. There are in addition three Shift Supervisors who report to a Superintendent, who in turn reports to the Product Manager.

That is all the briefing you're going to get. The Product Manager is not sure what the problem is – he wants you to find that out for him – so you have to design your approach on this basis. In determining your approach, you are required to deal with the following four primary questions:

1. What are the aims of your research project?
2. Which research design(s) and which research method(s) do you recommend, and why?
3. How will the research be implemented and phased? Or put more crudely, how long is this going to take?
4. Be realistic about this: what are the strengths and limitations of the approach you are recommending?

Depending on the time allowed at this part of your course, and on your instructor's aims, consider the implications of the following issues:

5. Your Product Manager is in a hurry. He has to prepare a report for senior managers and wants to incorporate your findings. He has to do this by the end of next week. How does this affect your plans – if at all?
6. Your Product Manager is now not in a hurry, but other company managers are interested in your findings which could be of value to other sites. They have offered to finance a larger-scale study of the company's changes to manufacturing work organization. How does this development affect your plans – if at all?
7. The local Shop Stewards Convener has taken your proposals to a union meeting – and they have been rejected. The Shop Stewards don't want their members passing information to outsiders, and they have instructed their members not to cooperate with the research team. How does this development affect your plans – if at all?

This exercise is based on a piece of published research: D. Buchanan, and D. Preston, 'Life in the cell: supervision and teamwork in a "manufacturing systems engineering" environment', *Human Resource Management Journal,* 1992, vol. 2, no. 4, pp. 55–76.

The research design and methods are outlined in an appendix to the article, on pages 73–4. This is *not* the correct answer that your syndicate groups should have generated. This approach was conditioned by circumstances prevailing in the organization concerned at the time of the study, and by the resources available to the researchers at that time.

2.3 PREP: Is this any good?

Objectives

❑ To develop critical skills in evaluating published research output.
❑ To establish the criteria on which published research work can be assessed.

Introduction

If your group has worked through the previous exercise, *Morale at Mouldswich,* you will have already discussed the criteria on which a piece of published research can be assessed. If you have, then recover your notes from that discussion. If you do not have those notes, then you will need to spend some time now deciding what criteria are important in this respect. You are invited here to decide on your own criteria, using terms with which you feel comfortable, and under headings that you feel are important. You are also invited here to be *critical.* Just because it is published in an expensive journal by somebody with a prestigious title from a reputable institution does not mean that one has to accept every word of it without question. On the contrary, it is through rigorous criticism that our understanding, and our research activity, develops.

You must have an *assigned article* on which to base this exercise. Your instructor may indicate and supply an article. You may on the other hand choose one for yourself. The assigned article must report *empirical* research, in any aspect of personnel or human resource management, industrial relations or organizational behaviour. The article on which the previous exercise, *Morale at Mouldswich*, is based would be suitable. There are advantages in all members of your class each carrying out an independent assessment of the same article. The comparison of notes afterwards should prove interesting and instructive. However, this depends on your instructor's aims, and there are advantages in using a number of different assigned articles for this exercise. Selecting an appropriate article in the first place could be part of the task. You should not use an article that offers only a literature review, reports a theoretical development, or is a 'position statement' of some kind (such as a paper seeking to outline a new research agenda).

Procedure

Step 1   You are about to read and to assess critically a published account of a piece of organizational behaviour research. Is it any good? What criteria are you going to apply in order to reach a conclusion? Your first step is to decide what criteria you wish to apply. If you have already done this, remind yourself what these are. If not, spend some time thinking through this issue, and decide what criteria you are going to use.

Step 2   List your criteria down the left-hand margin of a sheet of A4 paper. Six or eight criteria should be enough, but take these figures as a guide. It's up to you. You are going to make comments against each of these criteria on the remainder of the page.

Step 3   Work through the assigned article making notes as you feel appropriate against each of your listed criteria. Note aspects of the publication that you find satisfactory and interesting as well as those you find unsatisfactory and wish to criticize.

Step 4   Write an evaluation report on the assigned article, using your listed criteria as sub-headings to organize the report. You may find that you have to add new headings, and perhaps drop some of those with which you began. Introduce your report with a brief summary of the content of the assigned article. End your report with your considered conclusions about the article: Was it any good?

Step 5   The report should be around the length indicated by your instructor. It may be submitted for grading, as part of your overall course or term assessment. You may also be required to present your report in class, perhaps to a tutorial group.

2.4 REV: Crossword

Objective

❑   To assess your familiarity with the language and concepts of Chapter 2 of *ORBIT*.

Introduction

This test is based on Chapter 2 of *ORBIT*. If you have read the chapter and understood it, you will find this exercise straightforward. This is a simplified crossword with only eight clues – seven across and one down. You have to locate the single down answer for yourself.

Procedure

Complete the seven across clues, then find the answer to the single down clue.

Across:

1. What's the meaning of this behaviour?
2. Studying people is no different in this view.
3. Explores self-interpretations.
4. The type of validity that makes findings applicable elsewhere.
5. The independent really did affect the dependent – that type of validity.
6. Not unless it's observable!
7. Just one step beyond description.

Down:

? There are moral constraints on the pursuit of this goal.

PART I
THE INDIVIDUAL IN THE ORGANIZATION

Chapter 3
Perception

3.1 LGA: Character assassination

Objectives

❏   To examine how we perceive other people.
❏   To identify factors influencing our judgement of other people's character.
❏   To identify factors that affect how other people might judge us.

Introduction

The way in which we perceive other people influences how we relate to them, how we deal with them, how we respond to them. Person perception thus plays a vital role in our social lives in influencing patterns of friendship. Person perception also plays a vital role in organizations, affecting such processes as staff selection and interdepartmental cooperation. Chapter 3 of *ORBIT*, 'Perception', explains the basic principles of the psychology of perception. It is often useful to relate material like this to one's own personal psychology. This exercise encourages an examination of the specific factors affecting one individual's judgement of the character of another. The way in which we as individuals perceive other people is only one side of the issue; it is also interesting and valuable to know how others make judgements about us.

One approach to the description of character useful for this exercise concerns identifying personality *traits*. The English language is rich in words that describe such traits: aggressive, warm, hostile, friendly, trustworthy, dishonest, introvert, outgoing, punctual, tough, unethical and so on.

We would like you to carry out this exercise with *care* and with *precision*: care with respect to your observation, and precision with respect to your inferences.

Procedure

Step 1   Divide into pairs. Select close neighbours, not necessarily pairs sitting next to each other, and preferably split into 'stranger' pairs rather than 'friendship' pairs.

Step 2   Look closely at your chosen partner, at every aspect of their appearance that you can see (this will depend on your seating arrangements; the more you can see the better). Without entering into any further conversation, what judgements or inferences can you make about their character? Use the space provided to record your judgements.

Observation: Character inference:

Step 3 Take about five minutes each to explain your observations and inferences to your partner. You may find it helpful, if it is possible, to change seats to bring you together for this step. Do this without comment or challenge from each recipient, other than questions designed to clarify and to explain the observations and inferences that have been made.

Step 4 Each member of the pair takes about another five minutes to give feedback to their observer on how they would rate the accuracy of the inferences.

Step 5 Each member of the pair then identifies one aspect of their appearance that they might consider changing as a result of this exercise, and why. This is shared with the other member of the pair.

Step 6 Instructor's debrief.

3.2 SGA: Impression management checklist

Objectives

❑ To help you to evaluate some critical aspects of the ways in which you relate to other people.

❑ To help you to evaluate whether and how you could improve your interpersonal effectiveness through appropriate behaviour change.

❑ To consider the practicalities and ethics of changing one's behaviour to suit different people and different social settings.

Introduction

We each have our own preferences with respect to the ways in which we deal with and relate to others. You could say that we each have our own 'comfort zone' which includes ways of behaving and interacting that we enjoy, and excludes ways of behaving and interacting that we dislike. Our individual comfort zones in this respect may be expected to overlap; there will also be differences. This is relevant to the subject of perception because the ways in which we behave affect how others perceive and respond to us – and vice versa. What can we do to make our interactions with others more effective, to make mutual perceptions of each other more accurate? These are the questions addressed by the following exercise.

Procedure

Step 1 Think about the ways in which you interact with other people across the range of social settings (work, leisure, domestic, romantic) in which you might find yourself. Eighteen short statements follow. We would like to ask you simply to give a 'yes' or 'no' response to each statement, depending on whether or not you think the statement applies to you. Write a Y or an N alongside each statement number.

You will, naturally, feel that you want to answer, 'sometimes' or 'it depends' in response to some of these statements. However, with this checklist, you do not have the option of sitting on the fence. In each case decide where your personal preferences, strengths and priorities lie and answer with a clear 'yes' or 'no' accordingly.

This is not a test with right or wrong answers. It is designed as a basis for personal reflection and group discussion.

Step 2 Compare your answers with those of one or two colleagues sitting around you. Note one or two items where you have responded differently. Briefly compare your thoughts and feelings about your different responses to those particular items.

Step 3 Score your responses, out of eighteen, using the scoring key provided. Compare your score with those of one or two colleagues sitting around you.

Step 4 Instructor's debriefing.

Step 5 In syndicate groups of four discuss the four Analysis questions provided. Nominate a spokesperson and prepare a short feedback report.

Step 6 Syndicate groups report back, the first group dealing with analysis question 1, the second dealing with question 2 and so on. Each group's report can be used to trigger a discussion of each set of issues in turn, drawing also on the other groups' different responses.

Impression management checklist

1. I have difficulty imitating the behaviour of other people.
2. When I attend social occasions, like parties, I do not try to say and do things just because others there will like that.
3. I can only argue for ideas in which I really believe.
4. I can make an 'on the spot' speech to an audience even on a topic on which I have very little information.
5. I often put on a show to impress or to entertain others.
6. I would probably make a good actor or actress.
7. I am rarely the centre of attention when I am with a group of other people.
8. I often act like a different person, in different situations and with different people.
9. I am not particularly good at making other people like me.
10. I am not always the person that I appear to be.
11. I do not change my views or the way I do things in order to please someone or win their favour.

12. I have considered being an entertainer.
13. I have never been good at acting, or at games like charades that involve improvisation.
14. I find it difficult to change my behaviour to suit other people.
15. At parties I let other people keep the jokes and stories going.
16. I often feel awkward with other people and do not present myself as positively as I should.
17. I can look someone in the eye and tell a lie with a straight face, if I have a good reason.
18. I can deceive people by being friendly with them, when I actually dislike them.

Analysis

Regardless of your individual responses, consider and be prepared to report on the following issues:

1. Can we learn impression management skills, or is this something with which we are either born with or not?
2. Is it immoral or unethical to adjust one's behaviour in order to manipulate the feelings and behaviours of others?
3. Regardless of your own impression management abilities, in what ways would it benefit you to be more aware of how other people use these skills?
4. In what ways would it benefit you to improve your own impression management skills – or to enhance your awareness of how you use them?

Scoring

You get either one point or zero for each statement, depending on your response. Simply add up the number of points you got, giving you a score out of 18.

Statement	Score		Your score
	Yes	No	
1.	0	1	_____
2.	0	1	_____
3.	0	1	_____
4.	1	0	_____
5.	1	0	_____
6.	1	0	_____
7.	0	1	_____
8.	1	0	_____
9.	0	1	_____
10.	1	0	_____
11.	0	1	_____
12.	1	0	_____

| Statement | Score | | Your score |
	Yes	No	
13.	0	1	_____
14.	0	1	_____
15.	0	1	_____
16.	0	1	_____
17.	1	0	_____
18.	1	0	_____
		Your total:	_____

This exercise is based on the work of Mark Snyder, *Public Appearances and Private Realities: The Psychology of Self-Monitoring*, W. H. Freeman, New York, 1987.

3.3 PREP: Waiting for interview

Objectives

❑ To examine how perception is influenced by knowledge and past experience.

❑ To demonstrate how our individual and unique perceptual worlds are shaped by these factors.

Introduction

You are about to go for a job interview, but you will be kept waiting in the interviewer's office for a time beforehand. During that time, you can observe clues about your interviewer and perhaps about the company. What clues do you consider to be significant and revealing? Can you identify your own personal experiences that affect how you observe and judge in this kind of setting? How does that past experience colour your perception today? These are the issues addressed in this exercise.

Procedure

This exercise is to be completed outside class time, but a report will be required. This report may be written or presented, depending on the aims of your instructor.

Step 1 Read *The manager's room description* that follows, to get a feel for the setting in which you find yourself.

Step 2 Complete the analysis sheet below.

In the Data column, record those observations that you find significant and revealing about the kind of person who occupies this room.

In the Experiences column, record past incidents or events, recent or distant, that you think influence your observation.

In the Perception column, note the conclusions that you reach from your data.

Data	Experiences	Perception

Step 3 Using that analysis, write a profile of your interviewer.

Step 4 Finally, record your answers to these questions:

1. Would you work for this person?

2. What would you expect this person's management style to be like?

3. How confident are you of your analysis, your profile and your responses to the last two questions?

4. Explain how the analysis that you have just completed can be used to illustrate the concepts of perceptual selectivity, perceptual organization, perceptual world and stereotyping.

Step 5 Present your findings, according to your instructor's directions.

The manager's room description

You are now in the Acme Holdings company offices for your job interview. It sounds like your ideal position, personal assistant to the managing director. You would be working for the managing director who has asked to interview you. You have reached the office on time and are met by the managing director's secretary who apologizes and tells you there will be some delay. The managing director has been called to an important meeting which will take up to fifteen minutes. The secretary tells you that you are welcome to wait in the managing director's private office, and shows you in.

You go into the private office. You know that you will be alone here for fifteen minutes. You look around the room, naturally curious about the person with whom you may be working.

The shallow pile carpet is a warm pink, with no pattern. You choose one of six high-backed chairs, comfortably upholstered in a darker fabric that matches the carpet and curtains, and with polished wooden arms. In the centre of the ring of chairs is a low glass-topped coffee table. On the table there is a large white ashtray, advertising a well known national brand of beer. There is no sign of cigarettes, but the ashtray holds two books of matches, one from a hotel in Geneva and the other from a local restaurant. On the wall behind you is a large photograph of a vintage motor car, accompanied by its driver in leather helmet, goggles, scarf and long leather coat; you can't make out the driver's face. The window ledge holds four plants arranged equal distances apart; two look like small exotic ferns and the others are a begonia and a geranium in flower.

On the other side of the room sits a large wooden executive desk, with a black leather chair. A framed copy of the company's mission statement hangs on the wall behind the desk, and below that sits a closed black leather briefcase with brass combination locks. The plain grey waste-paper basket by the wall beside the desk is full of papers.

You can see most of the objects on the desk from where you are sitting. At the front of the desk sits a pen-stand with a letter opener. To the side is an expensive programmable calculator and a desk lamp. In front of the lamp sits a metal photograph frame holding two pictures. One is of an attractive woman in her thirties with a young boy around 8 years old. The other photograph is of a retriever dog in a field to the side of some farm buildings. In front of the frame is a stack of file folders. Immediately in front of the chair, on the desk, is a small pile of papers and a Parker pen with the company's logo stamped on the barrel.

On the other side of the desk is a delicate china mug. In front of it lies what looks like a leather-covered address book or perhaps a diary, and a pad of yellow paper. Beside the pad there is a pile of unopened mail with envelopes of differing sizes. On top of the mail and behind are some half-folded newspapers: *The Guardian*, *The Independent* and the *Financial Times*. You note that there is no telephone on the desk.

Behind the desk and to one side is a small glass-fronted display case with three shelves. There are some books lined up on top of the case: *In Search of Excellence*, *The Oxford Dictionary of New Words*, *Dealing with Difficult People*, *You Are What You Eat* and *Shattering the Glass Ceiling: The Woman Manager*. Also on top of the case sits a small bronze statue, of a man sitting with his legs crossed in a Yoga position, but abstract. There is a cheese plant climbing up and out from the far side of the display case. Inside the case, behind the glass, you see some company computing systems manuals and on the bottom shelf books and pamphlets on employment law, some of which deal with race and sex discrimination issues.

The window is on the far wall, and you get up to go over and look out. There is a three-seater settee under the window, covered in the same fabric as the armchairs with two matching scatter cushions sitting in the corners. From the window you can easily see people shopping and children playing in the nearby park. You turn to another table beside the settee. Several magazines sit in front of a burgundy ceramic lamp with a beige shade. There are two recent copies of *The Economist*, and a copy each of *Asia Today*, *Vanity Fair* and *Fortune*.

As you head back to your chair, you notice that the papers on the desk in front of the chair are your application papers and curriculum vitae. Your first name, obviously indicating your sex, has been boldly circled with the Parker pen. As the Managing Director may return at any moment, you go back and sit in your chair to wait.

This exercise was inspired by and draws on 'Sherlock: an inference activity', in *A Handbook of Structured Experiences for Human Relations Training*, by J. W. Pfeiffer and J. E. Jones, University Associates Press, San Diego, 1974.

3.4 REV: Multiple-choice test

Objective

❑ To assess your knowledge of the concepts and ideas in Chapter 3 of *ORBIT*.

Introduction

This test is based on Chapter 3, 'Perception', of *ORBIT*, and concerns the psychology of perception. If you have read and understood the chapter you should find this test straightforward.

Procedure

This is a conventional multiple-choice objective test with fifteen questions. It takes about fifteen minutes to complete. *Ring the letter* of the answer which in each case you think is most appropriate.

HINT: each question has only *one* correct answer. If you have difficulty choosing an answer because the alternatives provided seem similar, remember that you are also asked for the *best* answer.

Multiple-choice test: the psychology of perception

1. People's behaviour is related to what goes on in the world around them. Which statement best summarizes this relationship?
    (a) Human behaviour is determined by environmental influences.
    (b) Human behaviour is influenced by environmental stimuli.
    (c) Human behaviour is a response to environmental information.

2. Which of these statements best defines the concept of 'perception'?
    (a) A mental event that filters out redundant environmental information.
    (b) The individual's decisions about the relative importance of various environmental stimuli.
    (c) A mental process that selects and organizes environmental stimuli in meaningful patterns.

3. Only one of these statements is correct: which one?
    (a) Environmental stimuli which are not perceived cannot directly influence behaviour.
    (b) Environmental stimuli which are perceived will directly influence behaviour.
    (c) Environmental stimuli which are misinterpreted cannot directly influence behaviour.

4. Which of the following statements best defines the concept of perceptual set?
    (a) The way in which an individual systematically misperceives some environmental stimuli.
    (b) The fixed pattern of an individual's perception that is established through time.
    (c) The individual's readiness to respond to some stimuli rather than to others.

5. Only one of these statements is true: which one?
    (a) The individual's perceptual set is acquired through experience over a long period of time.
    (b) The individual's perceptual set can be affected by instructions and by the context in which perception takes place.
    (c) The individual's perceptual set is innate and can only be influenced with difficulty.

6. An opinion poll in 1989 examined how Canadians and Americans perceived each other. Which of these statements best summarizes the findings of the poll?
    (a) Americans think Canadians are friendly, but Canadians think Americans are snobs.
    (b) Americans and Canadians don't understand and don't like each other.
    (c) Americans and Canadians had difficulty with the questions because they did not know enough about each other's culture.

7. When making judgements about a person, we often categorize them on the basis of one outstanding characteristic, such as hair length, skin colour, occupation, and so on. What is the term given to this phenomenon?

    (a) The halo effect.
    (b) Perceptual selectivity.
    (c) Stereotyping.

8. When making evaluations of a person, we often use only one trait (either a good or a bad one) as the basis for judgements of all the person's other traits. What is the term given to this phenomenon?

    (a) The halo effect.
    (b) Perceptual organization.
    (c) Stereotyping.

9. Only one of these statements is correct: which one?

    (a) Actions and objects possess meanings that are perceived differently by different people.
    (b) Different people attach different meanings to otherwise identical actions and objects.
    (c) Actions and objects cannot be given 'meanings'.

10. Only one of these statements is correct: which one?

    (a) The meaning associated with an action or object depends on its relationship with other actions and objects in the perceptual field.
    (b) The meaning associated with an action or object depends on the motives and personality of the perceiver.
    (c) Meanings cannot be associated with actions and objects.

11. Environmental stimuli that are below a given level of intensity (like a very quiet musical note) are normally ignored. What is the term given to this level?

    (a) Perceptual filter.
    (b) Perceptual screen.
    (c) Perceptual threshold.

12. Some stimuli actually stop being sensed if they are familiar and unimportant. Examples might be the sound of a clock, or the pressure of the shoes around your feet. What term is given to this phenomenon?

    (a) Habituation.
    (b) Screening.
    (c) Selectivity.

13. We gather and pattern the information received by our senses in meaningful ways. What is the term given to this psychological process?

    (a) Perceptual selectivity.
    (b) Perceptual organization.
    (c) Closure.

14. Only one of these statements is accurate: which one?

    (a) The 'halo effect' applies to person perception.
    (b) The 'halo effect' applies to the perception of objects and events.
    (c) The 'halo effect' can be applied to perception of both people and things.

15. Which of these statements best highlights the organizational issues raised by the phenomenon of cultural stereotyping?

    (a) Cultural stereotypes are useful in giving us a basic understanding of the personalities of foreigners.
    (b) Cultural stereotypes are potential barriers to effective interpersonal communication.
    (c) Multicultural project teams are more effective because they include a rich variety of perspectives.

Chapter 4

Motivation

4.1	Large group activity:	**Individual differences**
4.2	Small group activity:	**The Digital experience**
4.3	Prepared task:	**The Body Shop experience**
4.4	Review:	**Concepts, concepts**

4.1 LGA: Individual differences

Objectives

❑ To examine personal motives, and the link between motives and behaviour.

❑ To illustrate the concept of *individual differences* in motivation and to explore the reasons for such differences.

❑ To assess the organizational implications of differences in motivation at work.

Introduction

The subject of motivation has retained prominence in organizational and managerial thought throughout the second half of the twentieth century. If we understand what motivates people at work, and in particular if we understand what motivates people to work hard and to work well, we can arrange for those who turn up on time and who do perform well to receive more of what they value, and for the latecomers and poor performers to receive less. Unfortunately, establishing such simple links between desirable behaviour and rewards is not a straightforward matter.

Motivation can be *extrinsic* – concerning rewards provided by others, such as praise and money – or *intrinsic* – concerning the rewards we give ourselves, such as feelings of achievement and self-confidence. Organization structures, management style and behaviour, work design, reward systems and interpersonal relationships can all be manipulated to provide people with increased extrinsic and intrinsic motivation – if that is what is required. The distinction between extrinsic and intrinsic motivation leaves open the question concerning the motivating potential of monetary reward, which is usually considered an extrinsic motivator. The point we would like to make in the exercise that follows is that people at work are potentially motivated by a range of factors, and money is one of these. There can be little doubt that, at least in Western-style industrialized cultures and for at least most people, money is a factor in work motivation, but it is not the only factor, and for some people may not be the most significant element of working experience. Financial reward can also be related to the satisfaction of other intrinsic needs, as a symbol of personal accomplishment, for example. Organizations that ignore the potential of other intrinsic and extrinsic motivators are ignoring some useful and powerful motivating tools.

Procedure

Step 1 Read the briefing, answer the three individual job characteristics question, then complete the *Individual motivation* questionnaire.

Step 2 Complete the short *Group estimation* task that follows the questionnaire.

Step 3 Complete the *Scoring* procedure and compare responses with colleagues sitting round about you.

Step 4 Work through the five analysis questions, following your instructor's guidelines, and depending on the time you have available.

Individual motivation questionnaire

You are invited to complete the following questionnaire with respect to your current (full- or part-time) job, or with respect to a job that you have held recently, or if neither of these possibilities applies to you, to complete the questionnaire with respect to the kind of job you expect to have to do when you do start work. Before you do this, however, reflect on and write down the three main features of your *ideal* job – this may include easy money, challenge and excitement, extended leisure time, opportunities for travel – whatever you personally look for from work.

The three main characteristics of my ideal job would be:

1. _____

2. _____

3. _____

The questionnaire describes a number of attributes or characteristics of work. Simply rate the importance of each of these attributes, to you personally, using this scale:

1. Not important for me.
2. A little important for me.
3. Below average importance for me.
4. Moderately important for me.
5. Above average importance for me.
6. Quite important for me.
7. Very important for me.

--- 1. The opportunity to develop close relationships with others.

--- 2. The opportunity for me to develop further my personal capabilities.

--- 3. The feeling that all the basics in life are provided for.

--- 4. The feeling of achievement and reputation that comes with this job.

--- 5. The knowledge that my job is secure and that I can probably stay here for as long as I like.

--- 6. The feeling of working alongside a number of good, close friends.

--- 7. The prestige and importance with which other people view this job.

--- 8. The knowledge that I will not go without the things I really need the most.

--- 9. The feeling that I belong here.

--- 10. The feeling of self-fulfilment that comes from using my capabilities effectively.

--- 11. The predictability of that regular pay cheque.

--- 12. The knowledge that I am achieving something really worth while.

--- 13. The feeling of self-confidence that goes with doing the job well.

--- 14. The feeling that I will not go short of food and shelter.

--- 15. The feeling that things will be tomorrow pretty much as they are today.

Group estimation

This questionnaire is designed to explore and measure, approximately, the strength of your needs under the following five headings, drawn from the motivational theory of Abraham Maslow (see *ORBIT*, Chapter 4):

physiological needs	H	M	L
safety needs	H	M	L
affiliation needs	H	M	L
esteem needs	H	M	L
self-actualization needs	H	M	L

How do you think your *group* will have rated those five sets of needs? Given what you know about their ages, backgrounds and current circumstances, which of these needs will they rate as important, and which do you think will be less significant? Use the H for high, M for medium and L for low indicators above, and ring the letter that for each need reflects your estimation of its strength for your group.

Scoring

Now score your own responses by entering your rating on each item against the item numbers:

Physiological:

13 _____

8 _____

14 _____   total: divided by 3: _____   PHY

Security:

5 _____

11 _____

15 _____   total: divided by 3: _____   SEC

Affiliation:

1 _____

6 _____

9 _____   total: divided by 3: _____   AFF

Esteem

4 _____

7 _____

13 _____   total: divided by 3: _____   EST

Self-actualization:

2 _____

10 _____

12 _____   total: divided by 3: _____   SAC

Now write these needs down in order of importance, with your highest scoring or most important need as number 1, and your lowest scoring or least important need as number 5:

Most important need: 1. _____

                            2. _____

                            3. _____

                            4. _____

Least important need: 5. _____

Analysis

1. Compare the ranking of your needs with the characteristics that you identified for your ideal job. Are these consistent? In other words, if your most important need is affiliation, is that reflected in your ideal job characteristics or not? If not, why not?

2. Having completed this questionnaire, what would you say are the strengths and limitations of this approach to the *measurement* of human motives?

3. The scoring should reveal at least some (and occasionally some striking) differences in motivational priorities. How can you *explain* the differences found in your group?

4. From a show of hands, find out how many in your group rated physiological needs as most important, how many rated security needs as most important and so on. Any surprises in the revealed pattern of priorities in this particular group, or is it much as you estimated?

5. If different individuals have different needs and motives, should work be organized accordingly? Consider, for example, how work could be organized to match the needs of those with high security needs on the one hand and those with high esteem needs on the other.

4.2 SGA: The Digital experience

Objectives

❑ To examine the range of factors affecting decisions concerning the organization of work.
❑ To consider the relative merits of different approaches to work organization.
❑ To illustrate the potentially complex interrelationships between technical, organizational and change implementation decisions.

Introduction

Approaches to work design, such as the *job characteristics model* and *high performance teamworking*, appear straightforward in a textbook. What difficulties arise when these methods are applied in practice? This exercise is designed to illustrate many of those difficulties, by inviting you to work through the management decision process with respect to a particular company with a specific problem. The 'solution' may appear 'obvious'. However, what is proposed must be workable in the particular circumstances of the organization, and management decisions need also to be justified and supportable. The application of motivation theory to organization practice invariably implies risk-taking, creativity, judgement and trade-off.

You are invited in this case to consider yourself a member of the plant management team, to decide how you would act in the circumstances described and to justify why you would act that way. In reality, you have to defend your judgement under the scrutiny of other managers in the company, and not just support a case in a tutorial essay. The company and its circumstances are real; this is not a fictitious exercise.

Procedure

Step 1   Read the following description of the company, Digital Equipment, and the problem which it was facing in 1983.

Step 2   Read through the list of policy options that follow, concerning *technical decisions*, *organizational decisions* and *change implementation decisions*.

Step 3   Working on your own, consider under each of these three headings which option you would select as a member of the company's management team, establish why you would select that option and note also why you would reject the other options.

Step 4   Working in a syndicate group with three to five members (depending on total group size), compare your reasoning, produce a syndicate response and justification and nominate a spokesperson.

Step 5   In plenary session, compare analyses and justifications. Depending on the number of syndicate groups, it can save time and avoid repetition if one group explains and justifies its technical decisions, before throwing this issue open to wider discussion. Then a second group explains and justifies its organizational decisions, and a third covers change implementation issues.

The Digital experience: the company

Digital Equipment Corporation is the world's second largest computer manufacturer, in dollar revenues, and the largest manufacturer of minicomputers. It created the minicomputer market in 1966 with the PDP system: the DEC PDP is the most popular minicomputer ever made.

Digital has a production site in Britain, at Ayr in Scotland, opened in 1976. In 1986, it employed 670 people and shipped around $500 million worth of systems. The initial charter for the site was the final assembly and test of minicomputer systems for European markets. This finishing stage involved tailoring complex systems to customer specifications, testing, order consolidation and shipping.

In 1982, 75 per cent of Digital installations were in Europe where sales in 1985 accounted for 30 per cent of global revenue. Like other multinational electronics companies, Digital is under political and commercial pressure to increase 'local sourcing' of its components.

Due to the technically complex nature of the work at Ayr, and management's preferred styles of working, few people have clear job titles. The organization structure and individual jobs, on the shop-floor and among management, are in a constant state of transition.

The Digital experience: the problem

As computer systems became more reliable and easier for customers to set up and configure for themselves, the traditional final assembly and test operation became redundant. In 1980, 60 per cent of Digital's systems went through this stage; by 1985, only 5 per cent did so as the final test, order consolidation and shipping operations were moved back to American manufacturing plants. The Scottish plant had to change its products, or face serious business decline.

The management at Ayr secured in 1983 the charter to manufacture in volume small 'Micro PDP11' computer systems for the European business market, with an extra £4 million investment in the site. The product life of these systems was short – with sales peaking over about three years. This market was extremely competitive and sales volumes were difficult to forecast accurately.

To get this charter, Ayr had to show that they could manufacture at a 'landed cost' competitive with other Digital plants, particularly those in the Far East. The unit cost of these systems is roughly 80 per cent in materials, 15 per cent in overheads and 5 per cent in labour.

On the shop-floor, these new products meant a change from technical configuration and test work to volume manufacture with very short cycles on individual operations. Staff in final assembly and test could be retrained, and the company wanted, as a matter of policy, to avoid redundancies if possible. This business was to generate 30 per cent of manufacturing employment on the site by 1986, from zero in 1984. There are no trade unions on the site, pay and conditions are superior for the area, and management believe that they have a skilled and loyal workforce.

The Digital experience: policy options

It is January 1983. You are a member of the Ayr plant management team. You have to begin volume manufacture of small computer systems in January 1984. You are faced with a number of policy options. For each of these three areas, which option would you support, why would you support that option and why would you reject the other(s)?

Technical decisions

In the manufacturing process, you have the choice of using either:

1. The latest automated production systems, requiring heavy capital investment, and with little human intervention in the process, requiring mainly low grade machine operation skills; or

2. Mainly manual assembly and test, using skilled labour with individual items of automated equipment for chip insertion and test routines.

Organizational decisions

Line management are concerned about the move into mass production – a departure from the plant's previous experience. The following organizational options have been raised:

1. 'There are so many other changes going on, we need to make as few organizational changes as possible. Our people are accustomed to the status quo, so let's keep things that way – allocate individual people to individual jobs with their same supervisors.'

2. 'This is going to be low grade, unskilled assembly work. Balancing the manufacturing line will be our priority. We need closer supervision than before, with smaller spans of supervisory control.'

3. 'These changes are going to challenge a lot of our people, and we need their skill and commitment. We are more likely to get this if we relax supervision and encourage skill development through teamwork.'

Change implementation decisions

Someone in personnel asked how the changes would be communicated to the workforce. A management meeting generated the following reactions:

1. 'These changes are inevitable. Our professionally qualified process engineers will design the assembly system. We'll just tell the shop-floor what's happening. Systematic training can start a couple of months before we go into production.'

2. 'These changes are radical. We must have the full support of our people. We need to involve them right from the start. Let's set up a Manufacturing Planning Team with shop-floor, engineering and management representation now.'

3. 'These changes will affect everybody. We need to consult our workforce and incorporate their suggestions about the assembly process. We should set up a Consultative Committee in October.'

Consider these options on your own, for about five minutes. Then compare your analysis with that of colleagues in syndicate discussion. Nominate a spokesperson to present to the group as a whole your syndicate report explaining and justifying your decisions.

A short (4-page) account of the Digital experience with high performance teams can be found in: D. Buchanan, 'Job enrichment is dead: long live high performance work design!', *Personnel Management,* May 1987, pp. 40–3.

A teaching case based on Digital's VLSI operation at Ayr and the work organization approach used there, can be found in D. Buchanan and J. McCalman, *Cases in Organizational Behaviour and Human Resource Management,* D. Gowler, K. Legge and C. Clegg (eds), Paul Chapman Publishing, London 1993, Chapter 1.

The chapter on 'new design plants' in Edward Lawler's book, *High Involvement Management: Participative Strategies for Improving Organizational Performance* (Jossey Bass, San Francisco, 1986), is an interesting and valuable addition to required student reading on this subject. Lawler identifies many of the problems of 'new design plants', and some of these problems were encountered at Digital.

4.3 PREP: The Body Shop experience

Objectives

- ❑ To provide a structured opportunity to apply a particular theoretical framework to a practical organizational setting.
- ❑ To analyse critically the work organization approach of a specific company.
- ❑ To demonstrate the use of a critical, theoretical analysis as the basis for assessing organizational strengths and weaknesses.

Introduction

This exercise is based on the *job characteristics model* which is illustrated on page 72 of *ORBIT* and which is explained in detail on pages 71–4. Detailed reference to this model will be required to complete this prepared assignment. The model was published in the 1970s, but the thinking behind it remains current today. Can it be applied to the analysis of contemporary company practice? This exercise provides an opportunity to find out.

Procedure

Step 1   Read the following article, 'The managerless shop'.

Step 2   Write a report of around 1,500 words answering the following questions:

1. Which *implementing concepts* have been used in the organization of work in this shop, and in what ways?

2. Which *implementing concepts* have not been used, and how could they now be applied?

3. What evidence is there that the predicted *critical psychological states* have been achieved?

4. What would you expect would be the main organizational problems and disadvantages of such an approach to shop management (think, for example, of your own local supermarket)?

Step 3   According to your instructor's requirements, submit your report for grading, or come to your next class meeting prepared to present and discuss your analysis.

The Body Shop experience

Staff at the Body Shop's new Oxford Street branch have been managing themselves within a teamworking system

The managerless shop

An experiment in team-working without managers has been launched by the Body Shop at its latest branch in London's west end.

The 25 full-time and three part-time staff are split into four teams and will rotate between teams over the first year that the Oxford Street outlet is open.

They all receive the same salary – £10,100 a year for a 37½-hour week or pro rata for part-timers – and are described by the company as 'performers' in an attempt to draw parallels between retail and the theatre.

Each team looks after an aspect of the business: storeroom, personnel, front of shop or finance. There are no managers or team leaders, although elected press spokesperson Debbie Greenwood said leaders were emerging.

The idea for the staff structure came from Body Shop's central management group, but the day-to-day running of the store is being left entirely to the 'performers'. They make decisions, for instance, on type and volume of stock, training, discipline and shift patterns. They will also make recommendations on recruitment once the initial intake is in place.

Kerensa Sheen, the Body Shop's general manager looking after human resources and retail operations, said that the lack of management and the equal salaries were selling points in advertising the jobs and appeared to draw more applicants.

There were 1,000 initial inquiries, compared with a maximum of 600 on previous central London trawls.

She said that she had initiated the system because of 'a feeling that there was a lot more we could develop in the staff'.

This short article appeared in *Personnel Management Plus*, 1991, vol. 2, no. 11, November, p. 3.

4.4 REV: Concepts, concepts

Objective

❏   To test understanding of concepts relating to the theory and practice of motivation.

Introduction

It is essential to be clear about the way in which we use language in any social scientific context. Precision reduces confusion and dispute, and allows us to share and compare experience in a systematic manner. This review covers material introduced in Chapter 4 of the textbook.

Procedure

Write down the concept label attached to each of the following definitions. For example, the definition:

> The extent to which research findings from one setting can be applied to other broadly similar settings.

would be attached to the concept label:

> External validity.

The concept label may be a single word, or it could be a short phrase; you are given no indication which it might be. Complete this *review* without reference to the textbook. If you have read and understood the chapter, you will have no difficulties with what follows.

If you are working on your own, then it makes sense to ask you to complete this *review*, or to complete as much of it as you can, before you refer back to the text. If you complete it as part of a class test or exercise, your instructor will advise you of the scoring procedure (self-, peer- or syndicate-based).

Concepts, concepts

1. The extent to which an individual feels accountable for the results of their efforts.

2. The social character type whose dominant values include mastery, control and autonomy.

3. Breaking down a complex task into its simple component steps.

4. Work groups that have front-to-back responsibility and allocate their tasks themselves.

5. A supervisory style based on the use of punishment, profanity and threat.

6. Giving employees responsibilities normally carried out by supervisors or foremen.

7. A technique for changing the design of work to improve employee-need satisfaction and performance.

8. An influential theory of motivation that takes into account the different values that we each attach to the different outcomes of our behaviour.

9. The innate biological factors influencing our behaviour.

10. An approach to work organization that seeks to improve performance by manipulating critical psychological states.

11. Characteristics of the context of work, like salary and company policies.

12. Influences on our behaviour arising from social learning.

13. The individual's expectation that a particular behaviour will lead to a particular outcome.

14. The job dimension concerned with giving the individual independence and discretion.

15. A measure of how effectively a job has been designed with respect to its core dimensions.

16. The innate desire to know better who and what we are.

17. The term used to describe our desires for confidence, independence, reputation and achievement.

18. Motivation theories that assume the existence of a given internal 'package' of needs or desires.

19. The degree to which a job involves a 'whole' or meaningful piece of work.

20. Giving employees responsibility for making personal contact with others both within and outside the organization.

21. The social character type whose dominant values include balancing knowledge and achievement with fun and play.

Chapter 5

Learning

5.1	**Large group activity:**	**The learning curve**
5.2	**Small group activity:**	**Making modifications**
5.3	**Prepared task:**	**Induction or indoctrination**
5.4	**Review:**	**True or false?**

5.1 LGA: The learning curve

Objectives

❑ To identify factors affecting the process of learning.
❑ To identify ways of improving the effectiveness of the learning process.

Introduction

Learning can be measured in many different ways. The learning of subject matter in an educational context is traditionally measured using examinations, essays, projects or assignments, and oral presentations. The learning process unfolds through time, and we establish whether learning has taken place by identifying changes in behaviour. The ability to write a clear account of contemporary motivation theory and practice, for example, should be higher towards the end of your organizational behaviour course than at the beginning (assuming this subject matter has not been previously encountered on other courses). We can assess, realistically, our own individual rates of learning by considering the extent to which our behaviour in this respect may or may not have changed. This exercise asks you to assess your own learning process, to identify factors that inhibit your learning, and to identify what you, your colleagues, and your instructor could do to improve the effectiveness of your learning in this subject area. If you reached the *STOP* exercise on pages 93–4 of *ORBIT*, you may have already thought through some of these issues for yourself. This is an opportunity to share your thinking with colleagues, and to give critical and constructive feedback to your instructor.

Procedure

Step 1 Using the example of a learning curve on page 93 of the textbook, construct a graph that will plot your learning on this organizational behaviour course. On the vertical axis, put *percentage of course material read and understood*, on a scale from 0 to 100 per cent. The horizontal axis represents number of weeks into the course.

Step 2 Now consider your overall approach to this subject and to your personal studying methods and learning pattern. Draw a line on the graph that honestly and realistically portrays your learning curve. This will, of course, start at week one, and at 0 per cent. It may not, however, reach 100 per cent by the time the course is complete.

Step 3 Compare your learning curve with those of colleagues sitting next to you. Note similarities and discuss differences.

Step 4 Now consider an 'ideal' learning curve for you and for this particular course. Plot your ideal learning curve on the same graph, perhaps using a different pen or colour. Compare your ideal also with that of colleagues sitting next to you.

Step 5   In buzz groups of three people, compare your actual with your ideal learning and study patterns, and identify three things that you and fellow students could do to improve the effectiveness of your learning on this course:

1. _____

2. _____

3. _____

Step 6   Still in buzz groups of three people, identify three things that your instructor could do to improve the effectiveness of your learning on this course (be realistic):

1. _____

2. _____

3. _____

Step 7   Share your proposals and suggestions with the class as a whole, if time and circumstances allow.

5.2 SGA: Making modifications

Objectives

❑ To demonstrate the practical dimensions of applying behaviour modification techniques.

❑ To explore the benefits and limitations of behaviour modification techniques.

Introduction

The theory and practice of behaviour modification appears to have significant potential in organizational settings. Organizations are concerned with eliciting 'appropriate behaviours' from all employees, at all levels. Managers typically occupy positions from which a wide range of different kinds of rewards and punishments can be manipulated. The scope for changing working methods and practices through behaviour modification techniques thus appears to be wide. In this exercise, you are invited to design and assess a behaviour modification approach that deals with specific problems of organizational behaviour – problems with which you may be familiar. An understanding of Chapter 5, 'Learning', in the textbook is a precondition for tackling this exercise.

Procedure

Step 1   Ensure that you are familiar with the behaviour modification approach explained in Chapter 5 of *ORBIT*, including theoretical background and practical applications.

Step 2   Read the *Making modifications* brief which follows this and, working on your own, make preliminary notes in answer to the questions at the end.

Step 3   In syndicates with three or four members each, design a practical, realistic behaviour modification programme that addresses at least some of the issues in the brief; you may feel that you cannot tackle all of them. Your design must clearly define the target behaviour(s), the nature and pattern of reinforcement and the anticipated behaviour change(s). Think *creatively* with respect to appropriate reinforcement regimes.

Step 4   Now that you have completed your design, make a realistic practical assessment. What are the three main *strengths* of your behaviour modification approach that give it a chance of working as intended? What are the three main *weaknesses* in your approach that might make it less effective? Don't forget to nominate a spokesperson to present your approach and assessment to the whole group.

Step 5   Present solutions and assessments to the whole group for comparison. To avoid repetition, perhaps have only two groups present designs, with the third and fourth groups presenting their strengths and weaknesses respectively, and with the audience each time commenting only on differences between their analysis and that presented. In this manner, a class of, say, twelve members can quickly build an elaborate picture of behaviour modification design options and of the strengths and weaknesses in the approach.

Making modifications

Your organizational behaviour instructor, Lesley, has been experiencing some problems recently. She has asked you to design a behaviour modification programme to help her.

Lesley has become particularly concerned about the increase in undesirable behaviours in one of her large organizational behaviour student groups. There are around two hundred students in this class, and organizational behaviour is one of the first courses they take as part of their qualification. The problem this year seems to be worse than in the past, but things are running much the same as they always have been. Lesley is not sure what is causing the increase in undesirable behaviours.

Many students are arriving late for lectures, sometimes by as much as ten minutes. This is very disruptive, as Lesley has to stop for each noisy new bunch of arrivals. This also effectively cuts down the lecture duration, and some material has been covered more superficially than Lesley planned. There has also been an increase in students talking during lectures. This is not confined to the back rows, and there does not seem to be any acoustic problem; Lesley's voice can be heard clearly from all seats in the lecture theatre. The crosstalk is usually quiet, but it is loud enough to be distracting for Lesley and annoying for students listening to the lecture. The behaviours which students manifest in tutorial discussions – failure to prepare, reluctance to present ideas, staring out of the window and failing to get involved – are also disappointing. Lesley is accustomed to more positive attitudes; she regularly uses practical, interesting, stimulating tutorial exercises.

There are no explanations – or excuses – to be found in the conditions surrounding the course. Lecture rooms are all close to each other, so there is little delay in getting from one class to another. Lesley's sessions are not at awkward times (not first thing Monday or last thing Friday), so students are not particularly tired or preoccupied in her sessions. In summary, we can assume that the undesirable behaviours are within the control of the students themselves, and are thus amenable to behaviour modification.

1. What target behaviour(s) would it be realistic to consider modifying in this situation?

2. What reinforcement regime could be developed and applied to achieve the desired behaviour change(s)?

3. What behaviour changes would you hope to see?

5.3 PREP: Induction or indoctrination?

Objectives

❏ To illustrate the practical issues concerned in the design of a systematic organizational induction programme.

❏ To explore the benefits and limitations of socialization techniques used in an organizational setting.

Introduction

The previous exercise explored ways of eliminating undesirable behaviours and encouraging desirable behaviour through behaviour modification techniques. The purpose of this exercise, in contrast, is to consider how similar results can be achieved through techniques based on *social learning theory*. This is also described as *socialization*, and finds expression in organizational settings in the form of *induction programmes* for new employees. Consider Lesley's problems in the previous exercise. How could those problems be overcome with a systematic, planned socialization process? This exercise invites you to answer that question. In other words, we will be dealing again with the same instructor's problems, but from an entirely different perspective. An understanding of Chapter 5, 'Learning', in the textbook, particularly pages 106–11, is again a precondition for tackling this exercise.

Procedure

Step 1 Ensure that you are familiar with the socialization approach explained in Chapter 5 of *ORBIT*, including theoretical background and practical applications.

Step 2 Remind yourself of the instructor's problems explained in the briefing for the previous exercise, *Making modifications*. You are in this exercise invited to consider resolving these problems from a different perspective.

Step 3 Write a 1000-word report describing a systematic, planned induction programme for new students. Your report should describe the elements of your induction programme, explaining why these elements have been included, and what effect you expect them to achieve. Your report should in addition indicate any recommended changes in the behaviours of administrators, secretaries and instructors in the institution as you feel appropriate to support the induction programme. Your approach will affect the next student intake; consider briefly how this approach could be used to help solve Lesley's current problems. Conclude with a paragraph that weighs the costs of your programme against the anticipated benefits and answers the question, 'Is it worth doing this?'.

Step 4 Submit and/or present your report according to the directions of your instructor who may use this exercise for a number of different purposes.

5.4 REV: True or false?

Objective

❑ To test your understanding of the main arguments and concepts of Chapter 5 in *ORBIT* concerning the psychology of learning.

Procedure

Simply write T or F beside each statement number to indicate whether you believe that statement to be either true or false respectively.

_____ 1. The power of intermittent reinforcement is demonstrated by anglers and gamblers who continue to fish and to feed slot machines respectively despite only occasional success.

_____ 2. One difference between behaviour modification and other techniques of performance improvement is that it does not depend on an understanding of employee attitudes.

_____ 3. Behaviour modification methods fail to recognize that employee performance is influenced by contingent consequences.

_____ 4. Behaviours that are emitted in the absence of identifiable stimuli were termed _respondents_ by B. F. Skinner.

_____ 5. The law of effect states that people tend to repeat behaviours that have favourable consequences for them and to avoid behaviours that have unpleasant outcomes.

_____ 6. Negative reinforcement can be just as influential as positive reinforcement in changing behaviour at work.

_____ 7. Socialization in the norms and standards of an organization is a naturally occurring process with which managers cannot hope to interfere.

_____ 8. Fragmenting a task into meaningful segments for training purposes can cause boredom, lack of interest and low motivation to learn.

_____ 9. Once desirable behaviours have been demonstrably established using effective behaviour modification techniques, reinforcement can be withdrawn.

_____ 10. Punishment for poor work indicates to learners what they are doing wrong and what they have to do to improve.

_____ 11. Behaviourist methods for learning and conditioning are based on the assumption that human beings have an innate desire for discovery and competence.

_____ 12. The process through which employee behaviour at work is changed through carefully selected supervisory feedback is known as 'shaping'.

_____ 13. Learners need time to reflect on their experience, and delayed feedback from supervisors is thus more effective than concurrent feedback.

_____ 14. Punishment can effectively change human behaviour when it is perceived as socially legitimate by the victim.

_____ 15. Barbara Woodhouse invented the respondent conditioning method of dog training.

Chapter 6

Personality

6.1	Large group activity:	Personality profiling
6.2	Small group activity:	Measuring up
6.3	Prepared task:	DIY personality assessment
6.4	Review:	Short answer test

6.1 LGA: Personality profiling

Objectives

❏ To demonstrate how individual differences in personality traits can be characterized.

❏ To develop understanding of the links between personality and behaviour.

Introduction

In the English language, there are over 17,000 adjectives which we use to describe individual behaviour. We thus have a rich vocabulary with which to explore and document the concept of personality, and through which to examine individual differences. From the perspective of organizational behaviour, there are two overarching questions of interest in this area. First, how can we measure personality? Second, can we predict a person's job performance in the future from knowledge of their current personality? If we can measure personality, and if we can use that measurement to predict behaviour and performance, then we can use personality assessment as part of the selection process for new recruits. This has been the thinking behind the development of *psychometrics*, the topic discussed in Chapter 6 of *ORBIT*. In this exercise, we invite you to consider how personality can be described and characterized, and to consider further how personality profiles can be used to predict behaviour.

Procedure

Step 1 Read the *Personality profiling* brief which follows, and draw a personality profile for yourself across the sixteen personality traits listed. Compare your profile with one or two neighbours. Note and discuss similarities and differences.

Step 2 Work through the remaining analysis activities, identifying behaviours that illustrate some of your personality traits, and considering with colleagues the five 'prediction' questions.

Step 3 Consider what this analysis and discussion has revealed about the extent to which someone's behaviour can be predicted from knowledge of their personality profile.

Personality profiling

This is an opportunity for you to make a rapid self-assessment of your personality, on sixteen main *personality traits*. These are the kinds of traits measured by personality assessment questionnaires currently in use in organizational selection procedures. The assessment which this exercise is based on is known as the '16PF' – where PF stands simply for personality factors. These personality characteristics are described in terms of sixteen continua.

In each case, ask yourself first where on the continuum you lie, for example between reserved on the one hand and outgoing on the other. Be honest. There is no point in 'cheating'. There is no such thing as a good or a bad profile; the one that is correct is the profile that is correct for you. Put a dot on the line to represent where you feel your personality lies.

reserved, detached	outgoing, easygoing
concrete thinker	abstract thinker
emotional	emotionally stable
mild, accommodating	assertive, aggressive
serious, reflective	lively, happy-go-lucky
flexible, rule-breaker	conscientious, persevering
shy, restrained	venturesome, bold
tough-minded	tender-minded
trusting, adaptable	suspicious, self-opinionated
practical, conventional	imaginative, creative
forthright, unpretentious	astute, worldly
confident, complacent	worrying, insecure
conservative, traditional	experimenting, free-thinking
group-dependent 'joiner'	self-sufficient, resourceful
less controlled	controlled, exacting
relaxed, tranquil	tense, frustrated

Analysis

1. When you have worked your way down this list, join up the dots to construct your individual *personality profile*. Compare this with one or two neighbours sitting close to you. Note and discuss differences.

2. Now choose three traits on which you have given yourself a more or less 'extreme' score (very tense, very reserved, very conscientious, for example). For each of these three traits, think of an incident where your behaviour offers a good illustration of that personality characteristic 'in action'. Make brief notes on each of these three incidents, noting the behaviours which illustrate aspects of your personality.

3. When you have done this, compare your three examples with one or two neighbours sitting close to you.

4. Working in pairs, exchange profiles, and consider the following questions. Considering what you now know about your colleague's personality profile:

    (a) Can you predict whether or not they would make a good organizational behaviour instructor? Explain your judgement.

    (b) Can you predict whether or not they would make a good policeman or policewoman? Explain your judgement.

    (c) Can you predict how they would behave if given an opportunity to cheat in an examination with only a small chance of being discovered? Explain your judgement.

    (d) Can you predict how effective they are likely to be in a leadership role in a large organization? Explain your judgement.

    (e) What other aspects of their future behaviour do you feel you could confidently predict?

5. Share your predictions with your partner in this exercise.

6.2 SGA: Measuring up

Objectives

❑ To develop an understanding of how personality characteristics and other individual attributes can be assessed.

❑ To develop an understanding of the value of different assessment strategies.

❑ To identify the limitations of selection interviewing and to explore how other approaches can improve the validity and reliability of the organizational selection process.

Introduction

The decision to select somebody for a job is always a *prediction*. This is a prediction that this particular candidate will perform in this job well, and that this candidate will perform the job better than the competing candidates. On what information should this prediction be based? Virtually all organizations still rely on the selection interview, at least to make preliminary assessments of the suitability of candidates. Some organizations have introduced refinements to their interview process for particular occupations; these include 'life themes analysis' and 'situational interviewing' in which questions are researched and are geared to job-specific activities and behaviours. During the 1990s, the use of *psychometric assessment* became more widespread in the search for valid and more reliable predictors of job behaviour. The available evidence seems to show that *assessment centres*, which use a variety of behavioural observation, psychometric and interviewing methods, can generate the most valid and reliable evidence of all. So, should we recommend the general use of assessment centres in all selection contexts? Interviews are still quick to organize and cheap to conduct, and the candidate can meet and talk with the person or people with whom they will be working. Assessment centres can be extremely expensive, consume large amounts of costly professional time, and may use trained assessors instead of the candidates' superiors or colleagues who simply get a final report. In choosing an assessment strategy, therefore, there are typically a number of trade-offs to be considered. The choice is not simple.

In this exercise, we would like to invite you to consider a strategy for selecting five graduate management trainee recruits from a candidate pool of twenty. The company has specified the attributes required in these candidates. What methods are you going to use to find out which five candidates fit this requirement most closely?

Procedure

Step 1 Ensure that you are familiar with Chapter 6 on the subject of *Personality* in the *ORBIT* textbook. This chapter discusses the relative effectiveness of different selection approaches.

Step 2 Working in syndicates with three to five members, design a selection strategy according to the *Measuring up* brief. You will then be asked to evaluate the *validity* and the *reliability* of your methods and the confidence you are likely to place in the results. Nominate a spokesperson to give an account of your strategy, and of its strengths and limitations.

Step 3 Present your strategy and assessment.

Measuring up

You are a member of the personnel department of ScotSouth Bank plc, a medium-sized national bank. Each year, the bank recruits five graduate management trainees who will begin their career with the bank at the head office in Edinburgh, but who can be rotated through and posted to branches anywhere in the country. Like other financial services sector institutions, the bank is facing increasingly rapid change and this is forcing changes in the way in which the company is managed. The bank's research, influenced by some recent American thinking, has identified a number of 'high performance competences' which are believed to be required by managers now and into the future to enable them to operate effectively in a dynamic, turbulent organizational climate. These individual high performance competences are:

Information search	Uses a range of sources and a variety of information before reaching decisions
Concept formation	Uses information to detect patterns, form concepts, build models, to identify trends and cause and effect relationships
Conceptual flexibility	Seeks out and evaluates a range of options when planning and deciding
Interpersonal search	Effective in getting good information from others through appropriate questioning, and good at seeing others' viewpoints
Managing interactions	Builds effective, cooperative teams by involving and empowering others
Developmental orientation	Encourages others to develop by helping them become aware of their own strengths and limitations, and by providing appropriate coaching, training and resources
Impact	Uses a range of influencing techniques to get support for plans and ideas
Self-confidence	Willing to take a stand, willing to commit when required, expresses confidence in success
Presentation	Good at presenting ideas to others in interesting and persuasive manner
Proactive orientation	Takes responsibility, structures tasks for others, implements actions
Achievement orientation	Sets high personal standards, sets ambitious but realistic goals, wants to do things better, has targets against which progress is measured

Your task is as follows:

1. Design a selection strategy, using whatever combination of selection methods you consider appropriate, to identify the five candidates who measure up best against this list of competences. Design this strategy on the assumption that, as a central plank of current company policy, you are faced with no time or resource constraints.

2. Prepare a realistic evaluation of the main strengths and limitations of the selection strategy that you have now designed. Assess how *valid* and how *reliable* your methods are. In addition, indicate the level of confidence (high, medium, low) you will place on your assessment of your candidates on those competences using those methods.

3. You have just heard a leaked rumour about the company's next quarterly financial results, due to be published in about ten days' time. They are not good, you have been told, and your department's budget looks as if it will be a prime target. Assuming that you could be faced with severe resource constraints, design a fall-back selection strategy that would enable you to complete the selection procedures within a week at a fraction of the cost of your original plan.

4. Prepare a realistic evaluation of the main strengths and limitations of your fall-back strategy. Once again, consider the *validity* and *reliability* of your methods. Assess also the impact of these changes on the confidence you will place in your assessments.

5. Be prepared to present and justify your plans to your whole group in the plenary session.

This exercise draws on the following article: T. Cockerill, 'The kind of competence for rapid change', *Personnel Management*, September, 1989, pp. 52–6.

The author was management development adviser for the National Westminster Bank, and the article identifies eleven 'high performance managerial competences', based on some American research. The article defends vigorously the position that such competences can be assessed reliably through behavioural observation – using a range of approaches. Cockerill further argues that these are the competences required by managers operating in increasingly turbulent, dynamic, changing organizational environments.

This exercise could be based instead on an article in the same series: V. Dulewicz, 'Assessment centres as the route to competence', *Personnel Management*, November, 1989, pp. 56–9. This article introduces twelve 'independent performance factors' or 'supra competences'. Any similar list of management attributes, characteristics, capabilities or competences could serve in this case.

6.3 PREP: DIY Personality assessment

Objectives

❑ To develop understanding of the way in which nomothetic personality assessment methods are constructed.

❑ To illustrate the pitfalls and hazards of personality assessment using this approach.

Introduction

You too can design your own personality assessments. In this exercise, you are invited to do just that. Behind the theoretical façade and the statistical sophistication of most personality assessment instrumentation, there lies a creative process in which the statements or questions that find their way into the questionnaire are generated. In this exercise, you are invited to work through that process, to get a feel for what is involved, and to give you a better understanding of the sources and limitations of the assessments to which you are likely to be subjected in a job-hunting context.

Procedure

Step 1 Familiarize yourself with Chapter 6 in the textbook *ORBIT*. The section that begins on page 121 is particularly important, as it outlines the methods used in the construction of personality questionnaires.

Step 2 Identify *two* personality traits in which you have a particular interest. Choose traits the measurement of which would be of *practical value* to you, in choosing syndicate team members, for example, or in selecting the residents for a corridor in an accommodation block. You could use some of the traits identified by Hans Eysenck, such as self-esteem, impulsiveness, or sociability. You could use a couple of the scales found in the Occupational Personality Questionnaire, such as change-oriented, emotional control, or competitiveness. You could choose other personality characteristics that carry particular significance to you at this time for personal reasons. The choice is yours. Before you proceed, *define* the two traits whose labels you have now chosen.

Step 3 Following the instructions that begin at the bottom of page 127 of the textbook, think of between ten and twenty statements or questions that could be used to measure each of the two traits you are working with. This will give you a questionnaire of twenty to forty items. You can word items simply as statements which invite a yes or no, agree or disagree response. You can word items as questions, and invite responses on a three-, five- or seven-point scale, perhaps from 'strongly disagree' to 'strongly agree'. Note that this is a creative exercise, and that the scoring system and item wording have to be designed together.

Step 4 Design your questionnaire and its accompanying scoring system. You will have to choose whether to mix together the items which apply to the two traits, or to put them each into a separate section. If you mix them, will respondents get confused? If you separate them, will you 'give the game away'? Remember to have a cover page stating your name, the name of your institution, the title or name of the questionnaire you have designed and instructions for completing the questionnaire.

Step 5 Photocopy a neat (preferably typed) version of your questionnaire, and ask up to twenty friends, colleagues, fellow students and/or relatives to fill them in. Calculate their scores on their behalf once they have done this for you, and note their reaction to your conclusions about their personalities.

Step 6 Write a report for your organizational behaviour instructor, explaining the purpose of your personality questionnaire, and explaining its design and scoring system. Include in your report the (anonymous) scores of your twenty respondents, and indicate what changes you would make to the questionnaire to refine it further based on that trial experience. Conclude your report with an assessment of the practical value of your questionnaire in achieving its intended purpose, and identify what you now see as its main limitations.

6.4 REV: Short answer test

Objectives

❑ To check your understanding of concepts and ideas relevant to the psychology of personality and the application of that thinking to organizational selection procedures.

❑ To illustrate and offer experience in the assessment technique of *short answer testing*.

Introduction

This review of Chapter 6 of *ORBIT* invites you to complete a *short answer test*, which should be graded independently either by another member of your student group or by your instructor. You can of course grade this yourself, but the temptation and the opportunity artificially to inflate your score is likely to be high if you approach the exercise in this way. You should check your incorrect or partially correct responses for yourself afterwards in any circumstances.

This style of test is becoming more common either to replace conventional 'essay-style' examinations or to complement that traditional approach.

Traditional examination essays allow candidates to demonstrate knowledge of particular sections of a course of study, and to demonstrate also the ability to use material from the course to sustain a description, analysis or argument under pressure and within time constraints. Because conventional exam papers offer a choice of questions, candidates can 'escape' covering the whole course and target specific areas, knowing or guessing which topics will feature in the exam paper. This is usually the case, even when exam questions are designed to encourage candidates to combine knowledge from different areas in their answers (and this is difficult and thus rare). This approach cannot adequately assess a candidate's knowledge and understanding of the course as a whole. Another difficulty with the traditional essay-style question and answer technique lies in the subjectivity of the grading. In a subject area like organizational behaviour, candidates with a smattering of knowledge of the subject and its key concepts and theories, and with some significant work experience, can sometimes 'fluff' their way through an adequate answer. This combined with a reluctance to give very high or very poor grades leads to most candidates being awarded 'sixtysomething'. Traditional examining techniques are therefore not *discriminating*.

The short answer test allows an instructor to examine candidates' knowledge over large portions of the material of a course of study. The short answer test that follows is designed to cover the *whole* of Chapter 6. The trade-off lies in the shorter answers, so this cannot be a test of candidates' ability to sustain lengthy reasoned arguments. The short answer test can, however, examine conceptual understanding and concept discrimination, and it can examine the ability to précis accurately and to illustrate ideas and arguments. The grading involves a considerably lower element of subjectivity as you will see in this exercise. This means that the test takes less time to grade, that the score is more objective, and that the test is more *discriminating*; candidates who know the material can attract extremely high grades, while those who have not done their homework get lousy scores. The range of scores on a short answer test is thus typically much wider than on a conventional essay-style examination.

Procedure

Step 1   Here are twenty questions from the material on personality in Chapter 6 in *ORBIT*. Your answer to each question should be written in the space provided, which gives you an indication of the length of answer required. Do not attempt to offer more information in each answer than the question demands; that will not attract a higher grade. If you provide the information requested, accurately, you receive five points for that answer. You may answer in your own words; you are not expected to recall whole sentences and phrases from any of your reading, although you are expected to use technical terms as appropriate. If you leave the space blank, or if your answer is completely wrong, you will receive a score of zero. You get intermediate scores for partially correct answers.

Step 2   Give your test sheets and answers to your Instructor or to a colleague who will then calculate your test score out of 100.

Step 3   Discuss if necessary your score with the person who graded your answers to make sure you understand why you lost points on particular answers.

Step 4   Check your answers against the text, again concentrating on areas where your knowledge seems weakest.

Short answer test: twenty questions

1. Give a brief explanation followed by a brief illustration of the technique of *situational interviewing*.

2. List five common organizational applications of *psychometric* testing and assessment methods.

3. Research has revealed the relative effectiveness of different selection methods. What are currently thought to be the three least effective methods, used on their own? And what are currently believed to be the two most effective methods?

4. Define the concept of *personality*. What two assumptions do we need to make about this concept if it is to be a useful tool for understanding human behaviour?

5. Explain *The Barnum Effect*, with an appropriate illustration.

6. What is *stereotyping*? Identify one advantage that accrues to us from this phenomenon. Identify one problem that arises from this phenomenon.

7. Identify three reasons for the growing popularity of *psychometric assessment* in the context of organizational selection procedures.

8. Outline the main dimensions of the *nature–nurture debate* concerning the determination of individual personality.

9.   What is the difference between a personality *type* and a personality *trait*? Illustrate your answer with two examples of each.

10.   Identify three of the personality traits that characterize the personality type *extrovert*. Identify three of the personality traits that characterize the personality type *introvert*.

11.   Describe in brief three of the main characteristics of the *nomothetic* approach to personality assessment.

12. Describe in brief three of the main characteristics of the *idiographic* approach to personality assessment.

13. Describe five of the characteristics that typify the personality of the *neurotic* individual.

14. Describe five of the characteristics of the individual with a high *need for achievement.*

15. Explain briefly the technique of *thematic aptitude testing,* and illustrate how this method can be used to measure personality.

16. Identify two reasons why somebody with an *extrovert* personality could make an effective salesperson. Identify three reasons why they would make a lousy salesperson.

17. Explain the notion of *the looking-glass self.* Explain how this notion contributes to our understanding of personality formation.

18. Carl Rogers argued that our *self-concept* has two dimensions. What are they?

19. What is meant by the concept *unconditional positive regard,* and what effect is this treatment said to have on individual personality?

20. Give three reasons why thematic apperception testing is unpopular in contemporary psychometrics and in organizational selection settings.

PART II

GROUPS IN THE ORGANIZATION

Chapter 7
The formation of groups

7.1 LGA: Scavenger hunt

Objectives

- To introduce concepts relevant to an understanding of formal and informal organization.
- To highlight informal modes of group control on individual behaviour.
- To show the effect that work measurement schemes can have on the management process.
- To illustrate how behaviour can inhibit performance potential being reached.

Introduction

In contrast to the formal organization which is highly visible in terms of artefacts such as the organizational chart, job titles, job descriptions, rules and so on, the informal organization is more elusive. The purpose of this exercise is to sensitize students to some of the features of the informal organization and the effect that it has on employees and the organization as a whole.

Procedure

Step 1 Read the case, *Ice Cold plc*, and respond individually to the seven questions as directed by your instructor.

Step 2 Listen to the presentation given by your instructor to the concept of groups, distinguishing between the features of, and reasons for the formal and informal organization.

Step 3 Offer your suggestions to the seven questions if asked by your instructor.

Case: Ice Cold plc

(1) Graham Unwin was 20 years old. He had left school with good grades, and had been offered a place to study economics at a university. However, unlike his fellow schoolfriends, who had gone straight on to higher education, Graham decided to spend two years doing Voluntary Service Overseas in Africa before coming back to take up his university place. He had returned to Britain in January, too late for the start of the academic year. He was not bothered however, since he wanted to earn some money before going to university so that he didn't have to take out a loan.

(2) Graham had heard that the nearby manufacturing plant which made refrigerators was seeking temporary staff. He applied, took the aptitude tests and interview administered by the Personnel Department, and was offered a job starting the following Monday. The interviewer told him that his manual dexterity was excellent and, because of this, Graham was placed in a department where payment

was based on piecework (the more you produced, the more you earned). Graham was allocated to the third shift (10 p.m. to 7 a.m.) because he lacked seniority – experienced workers usually chose the first (6 a.m. to 2 p.m.) or the second (2 p.m. to 10 p.m.) shifts. He was pleased about this because the third shift carried an unsocial hours premium payment.

(3)   Graham approached his first night of work with apprehension. He had never before had a job that paid as much as this one did. The nature of the job also concerned him. He was to be an automatic spot-welder, even though he didn't know the first thing about welding.

(4)   Arriving at the factory's security office, he asked the guard to direct him to his department. He had arrived a little early, but entered an office and introduced himself. His shift supervisor, Brian Cousins, was there. Cousins explained what was done in the Refrigerator Assembly Area (RAA). RAA spot-welded all the individual parts of the refrigerator and then, in one final operation, combined all the parts together with more spot-welding. Cousins then explained the rules and procedures in the department, such as reporting for work on time, taking breaks, and how to report in when sick.

(5)   As Cousins concluded his discussion with Graham, another man entered the office and was introduced as the foreman, David Brook. Brook took Graham around the department, and showed him all the automatic welding machines, how they worked, and which refrigerator parts they welded. Graham met all the men, twelve in all, and noticed that about half of them looked as if they were in their early twenties. After the departmental tour, Brook explained how to fill in his timecard, and how to call for more materials when he needed them. He also explained what the piece-rates meant. Brook went on to explain that he should not worry about the rate for the first couple of weeks. In the early days, if a new worker didn't produce at least the standard rate, he would still be paid at day rate (equivalent to forty-seven units or 75 per cent performance). After all the preliminaries had been concluded, Graham was given his first assignment. He was to weld the base for the refrigerator. Cousins demonstrated how to take the four separate pieces and spot-weld them together. Additionally, he showed him how to clean the copper tips which would improve the quality of the weld. During the next four nights of work, Graham also inserted freezer units, coolant tubes and various caster assemblies.

(6)   During the main meal break, Graham noticed that a group of seven men ate together with the foreman, while the other five workers went somewhere else. On his fifth night at work, he was approached by one of the seven, Patrick Duffy. Duffy asked him if he would like to eat with the other workers. Graham agreed and went with Duffy. During discussions with others over meals, Graham learned that all had left school at 16, and none had received any further education. A couple of the men had attended some day-release classes, but had dropped out. Duffy asked Graham how he liked his job, and he replied that it was interesting. Duffy then casually remarked that it was best if operatives produced at or about the group's average production which was the piece-rate performance of 100 instead of attempting to turn out a high performance rating and busting a gut! The others in the group nodded in agreement

(7)   Graham's skill increased rapidly. Within four weeks he could achieve the 100 performance figure on all the assemblies to which he had been assigned. He felt that this was great because now he could attempt to work harder and faster, thereby earning more money to finance his future studies. Brook would come over every so often, and comment on what a good job he was doing, and to keep it up. It wasn't long before he was achieving output rates of 150 on all assemblies, and in some cases, rates of nearly 200 performance which, for all intents and purposes, should have been impossible. Some of Graham's fellow-workers in the department would come over and jokingly tell Graham that he was going to drop dead from exhaustion if he continued to work at that pace. When the weekly pay packets

were distributed, these same workers would ask him if it was worth working that hard, and then have the government take away so much of his earnings. But all this good natured kidding failed to deter Graham from working as hard as he could, and regularly turning out high performances.

(8) One day a team of work specialists came in to examine how Graham worked on his favourite door assembly. This was his favourite because he achieved performances of at least 240 on this work. The team's observations, frenzied stop-watch work calculations and writings did not bother Graham that much, who rather enjoyed being the centre of attention. However, it did irritate Duffy and his friends. Duffy came over after the time study had been completed and remarked to Graham, 'I told you that's what happens to a rate buster'. Another worker came over and said, 'we'll all be affected now by the change in the value for the job, and it'll be your fault!'

(9) After this incident, Graham continued to raise his output. However, he noticed something peculiar was happening. At the meal breaks, he felt that his fellow workers were ignoring him. During one break, there was a lengthy discussion about the impact that a 'rate buster' could have on the department as a whole. Graham got the distinct impression that they were talking indirectly about him. He didn't like the meal breaks becoming so serious because he valued the time away from the machines and enjoyed the jokes and stories of his fellow workers.

(10) Not too long after this, Duffy remarked that if he kept getting the targets changed by the work study engineers, the RAA would not be a very good department to work in. Graham did not know exactly how to take this comment. He also learned from a coworker that Brian Cousins had been a spot-welder himself, but had recently been promoted to shift supervisor.

(11) After these events, Graham ceased to produce at twice the daily target rate. In fact, his production dropped a bit below one and a half the daily target rate. Brook noticed this decrease in output. He was not concerned at first because he felt that Graham might be physically exhausted, or perhaps there were problems at home. But when his output failed to increase again, Brook began to wonder what was behind the drop-off. During a meal break one night, he called Cousins into his office. The following conversation took place:

(12) *Brook:* Hey, Brian, is there anything wrong with young Unwin.

Cousins: In what way, Mr Brook?

Brook: I've checked his production output. When he first came here, he was a heck of a worker. Now, his production has sort of tapered off. I wonder why? Doesn't he get along with the other men?

Cousins: Of course he does (pointing in the direction of where the men, including Graham, were eating). He's one of the lads.

Brook: (Noticing that Unwin was taking part in the conversation) Well, that doesn't seem to be a problem. Do you have an explanation?

Cousins: Well, some of these youngsters come in here, keen to change every thing around. But after a while, they come up against reality. Perhaps that's what's happened to Unwin.

Brook: That could be it. Thanks.

As the klaxon sounded to signal the end of the meal break, Cousins could see that the group did not get up immediately to get back to work. They were still talking, and Graham was as involved in the discussion as the rest.

Case questions: Ice Cold plc

1. Place asterisks before and after the name of the informal group leader
    _____.

2. Place single quotation marks around the name of the formal leader of Graham's
    department '_____'.

3. Underline those sentences which reflect position, expert, referent, reward or
    coercive power _____ .

4. Use square brackets to denote examples of company standards used to evaluate
    productivity [_____].

5. Use round brackets to highlight examples of informal group sanctioning
    (_____).

6. Place double quotation marks around the two sentences that contain examples of
    the grapevine being used as a network for interpersonal communication
    "_____".

7. Circle any evidence that supports the contention that the incentive scheme lowers
    attainable levels of workforce performance.

The original exercise idea and content was created by Dr Max Douglas, Indiana State University.
This material was developed and extended by Dr Richard Thorpe, Manchester Metropolitan
University.

7.2 SGA: Group issues

Objectives

❑   To allow students to examine the effect of social influences on their own behaviour.

❑   To highlight some of the group concepts to be addressed in the course.

❑   To give some students practice in public speaking.

Introduction

In your day-to-day activities, you come up against issues relevant to group functioning and
performance. The purpose of this exercise is to encourage you to draw upon your experiences
of organizations, and to select an incident which raises issues which relate to this part of your
organizational behaviour course.

Procedure

Step 1   Individually think about a past experience which you feel illustrates something about
'individuals in groups'. The groups concerned may be from your current job, weekend or
holiday employment, school, family, church, sports or social club. Think about an incident and
note down its main features. Then specify what you feel it says about individuals in groups.
You have 10 minutes for this.

Step 2   Form into groups of three. Members are identified as A, B and C (and possibly D). Taking
turns, A describes their incident to B who listens without interrupting, and C looks on. B then
paraphrases A's points as succinctly as possible. C notes any additions or omissions. Then B
describes to C, while A listens. Finally, C describes to A, while B listens. Divide twenty-five
to thirty minutes between yourselves.

Step 3   Each group selects one of its members to relate his or her case to the class. The instructor will
note down the key aspects of each account for later comparison and analysis.

7.3 PREP: Labour turnover

Objectives

❑ To apply Elton Mayo's human relations perspective in analysing a work problem.

Introduction

The human relations perspective that Elton Mayo and his colleagues at the Harvard Business School developed has had a profound effect on social science in general and management in particular. It meant that people-problems in organizations were perceived in particular ways; that some causes of employee behaviour were given greater weight than others; and that certain solutions were advocated in preference to others. This is a real case study taken directly from research carried out by Mayo and a colleague during the Second World War. You are invited to carry out an analysis of the case from Mayo's perspective.

Procedure

Step 1 Imagine you are a management consultant who adopts a human relations approach to consulting. Using this perspective, read the case and identify the main problems, decide on their likely causes, and propose possible solutions. Bring this case and your notes to the class as directed by your instructor.

Step 2 In the class, form groups of four to six students.

Step 3 As a team of consultants, you have twenty minutes to discuss the case as a group, and collectively highlight the causes of, and possible solutions for the high turnover in the factory.

Step 4 Your instructor will conduct a plenary session to elicit the views of different groups.

Case

Late in 1943, Elton Mayo and certain members of staff of the Harvard Graduate School of Business Administration were asked to study the problem of labour turnover in the aircraft industry in southern California. The social setting was full of dramatic changes. Small aircraft plants had grown into large industries in a period of a few years. The drafting of workers into the army was a constant drain on the labour force and necessitated the continuous induction of new workers. These new workers migrated to California in their thousands. The staff at the Los Angeles War Manpower Commission estimated that in every month of 1943 approximately 25,000 people moved into southern California, and between 12,000 and 14,000 moved out. With this level of migration, it was not surprising to discover that labour turnover in the industry was running at 70 to 80 per cent. Mayo, however, refused to believe that this unsettlement alone was sufficient explanation for the turnover.

Like other aircraft companies in the area, Company A had applied scientific-engineering knowledge to its production, and had systematized its operations. Analysing turnover of staff, it found that with 40,000 employees, there were more than 30,000 departures in a 12-month period, and 65,000 transfers of workers within the plant. In addition, there were approximately 150,000 'loans' or temporary transfers of a day or less from one department to another. Thus labour turnover was running at 75 per cent, transfers at 157 per cent and loans at 360 per cent. Comparable data from other industries in the state suggested that the unsettlement in itself was insufficient to explain this problem.

Ignoring the departmental and shift organization, Mayo directed his attention at the smaller groups of people who were in daily working contact with each other. Seventy-one such groups were identified, and these differed in terms of their attendance and turnover record from no absence at all to high absence and turnover. This confirmed Mayo's suspicion that the dislocation caused by employee movement in and out of the industry could only provide a partial answer of the problem.

Sociometric studies led to the identification of 'natural groups'. These were very small groups varying in size from three to seven workers (see diagram below). Twelve such groups were found, and each had a nearly perfect attendance record.

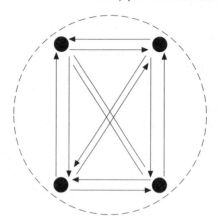

A researcher acting as a non-participant observer of one of the natural groups, submitted the following report:

> Group feature: excellent attendance record.
> Productivity: 25 per cent higher than average for plant.

Others' perception of this group:

- Reputation for 'working like beavers'.
- Considered somewhat clannish by other groups.

Report of participant observer:

- Group members made references to what 'we' are doing and 'our' efficiency.
- Commented that 'other groups were not performing'.
- Group received only very occasional visits from the departmental foreman, whose senior assistant popped his head in only once a day.
- One of the ordinary workers seemed to be actually in charge. This 'leadman' was a college graduate and had considerable experience of steel mills.
- He dealt with the minor hour-to-hour interruptions in the operations of the group.
- He introduced himself to new employees, and found them people they liked working with.
- After a few days he took new arrivals to the assembly line and showed them where the part that they had made fitted into the completed machine.
- He dealt with complaints, listening to what people said, and those he couldn't settle, he would discuss with the senior assistant foreman.
- He anticipated emergencies and shortages, and worked hard to get materials for his department.
- He dealt with inspectors and efficiency men who visited the group.
- Requests by group members for raises were channelled through him.
- He had the support of the senior assistant foreman in his actions.

This case is based upon Elton Mayo and George F. F. Lombard's book, *Teamwork and Labour Turnover in the Aircraft Industry of Southern California*, Graduate School of Business Administration, Harvard University, Boston, 1944.

7.4 REV: Word search

Objective

❑ To assess your familiarity with the language and concepts of Chapter 7 of *ORBIT* which deals with group formation.

Introduction

Read *ORBIT* Chapter 7 in detail. Remembering key social science concepts and the details of empirical research studies forms the basis for understanding organizational behaviour. The inability to identify correctly the name of a well-known organizational theorist or researcher indicates that you do not know the material well enough. It is important to define concepts accurately or identify the key thinkers in the field. This exercise is intended to make the point that it does matter.

Procedure

Find the answers to the thirteen questions that are hidden in the table. These may be presented horizontally, vertically, diagonally or backwards.

T	N	E	M	I	T	N	E	S
U	O	O	T	H	W	G	Q	W
C	E	B	R	O	O	U	I	T
K	T	E	O	M	E	Y	L	R
M	Y	C	W	A	I	F	A	E
A	H	R	B	N	E	N	O	K
N	W	E	T	S	L	T	G	I
B	R	F	I	A	O	R	R	L
E	T	A	G	E	R	G	G	A

	Clues	Answer
1.	Not a psychological group.	
2.	Developed a theory of how groups formed.	
3.	The boys' place (initials).	
4.	Feeling about a group.	
5.	Third stage of group development.	
6.	Tired plank at work? (initials).	
7.	Minimum required for a group.	
8.	Keen on linking the pins.	
9.	Ladies smell a Roland (initials).	
10.	Based on position in an informal group.	
11.	He said the group offered 'total integration'.	
12.	Can only be achieved if members work together.	
13.	He sells sweets as groups develop at school.	

Chapter 8
Group structure

8.1	Large group activity:	**Group process analysis**
8.2	Small group activity:	**Functional roles in groups**
8.3	Prepared task:	**Belbin's Team Role Theory**
8.4	Review:	**Norton Street Gang**

8.1 LGA: Group process analysis

Objectives

❑ To introduce students to a 'language' for describing and classifying different behaviours in a group.

❑ To get them to understand the difference between the content and process levels of a group's operation.

❑ To provide practice in using a framework to analyse behaviour in a group.

❑ To enable students to monitor their own as well as others' behaviour in a group, and thereby to plan and control their behaviour consciously in a particular situation.

Introduction

In order to study how people communicate and behave in groups, we need a precise and reliable way to describe what is going on. Psychologists have devised a procedure for describing and analysing behaviour which consists of a series of categories which are used to classify each group member's speech. This exercise gives you the opportunity to use a simplified classification system. You are asked to analyse and contrast the behaviour of two discussion groups.

Five university students engage in two discussions of ways of improving their tutorial system. Using the transcripts and record sheets, you will categorize each group member's contribution. The behaviour categories to be used are:

Category	Explanation
Proposing	Any behaviour which puts forward a new suggestion, idea or course of action.
Supporting	Any behaviour which declares agreement or support with any individual or their idea.
Disagreeing	Any behaviour which states a criticism of another person's statement.
Giving information	Any behaviour which gives facts, ideas or opinions or clarifies these.
Seeking information	Any behaviour which asks for facts, ideas or information or opinions from others.
Building	Any behaviour which develops or extends an idea or suggestion made by someone else.

Procedure

Step 1   Read the transcript of discussion A which reports part of a meeting between five university students. They are discussing their tutorial system. Try to get a general impression of what is happening, and how the group is behaving.

Step 2   Discuss the following two questions with the person next to you: (a) What did you conclude about the group as a whole? (b) What criteria did you use to make this judgement?

Step 3   Use record sheet A to analyse discussion A. Read the verbal contribution made by Alan (No. 1) to the discussion. At the end of it (marked by square brackets), decide into which of the first five behaviour categories (described in the introduction section) it fits best. Insert the initial of that category into the square brackets provided (P, S, D, GI or SI). Repeat this for the remaining sixteen contributions in discussion A. Put record sheet A aside for the moment.

Step 4   Listen to your instructor's comments.
   Repeat the procedure, but this time, use record sheet B to analyse discussion B. This sheet uses six behaviour categories ('Building' is an extra category to be included). Again, write the initial of the appropriate behaviour category in the square brackets (P, B, S, D, GI or SI) for the fifteen contributions that make up discussion B.

Step 5   Now total up your category codings for discussions A and B. Referring to your record sheets A and B, add up the totals for each of the different categories. That is, add up all the Ps (proposals made), Ss (statements of support) and so on. Insert these in record sheet C.
   Compare your scores to those produced by your instructor.

Discussion A

1.   *Alan:*   I really feel that, over the two years I've been a university student, one of the greatest deficiencies of the whole system has been the lack of clarity of roles between the personal student counsellor and the course instructor. I feel they've been rather confused. Counsellors have been advising academically, instructors are rather aloof, and kind of descend on you like some great sage. [   ]
   I would certainly prefer the two roles to be combined in future years. I don't know what other people think? [   ]

2.   *Peter:*   You don't feel then that the instructor has been playing solely an academic role? As students, we go to tutorials to learn, in depth, a particular item from the course content. I think that there is a specialized role for the tutor, and that the counsellor is a separate unit completely. [   ]
   So I tend to disagree there with you there Alan, and don't see the two roles as synonymous at all, and feel they should be kept separate. [   ]

3.   *Sue:*   No, I would disagree up to a point. I still think that there should be two roles. [   ]
   But the tutors and counsellors should coordinate what they are doing more and work together. [   ]
   They don't seem to do this at the moment. If you've got problems, you go to a counsellor, if you're worried about something academic, you go to your instructor. I'm not sure how much feedback there is between the two. [   ]

4.   *Kate:*   I think that the personal counselling should be expanded rather than reduced, especially when you get beyond the first year. Because I think the problems become greater . . . [   ]

5.   *Sue:*   After the first year, I never saw my counsellor. [   ]

6.   *Kate:*   I think the counsellor has a very specific role, which really should not be academic, they should be a personal adviser. [   ]

7.   *Alan:*   Some students have problems, others don't. Obviously everybody has

problems, but some have more than others. What I'm concerned with is that the counsellor won't have enough work entirely solving personal problems [   ]

After the first year, I think the counselling role should be undertaken by the tutor and there should be contact between the instructor and the student [   ]

8. *Kate:*   But the tutor has a formal structure to follow in his tutorial sessions, hasn't he? [   ]

9. *Jackie:*   I don't think you feel that you can waste everybody's time by bringing up your personal problems in an hour's session. [   ]

10. *Alan:*   Maybe there should be time afterwards. [   ]

11. *Peter:*   As a group, we seem to be saying, you know, that there is a separate identity between the counsellor and the tutor. And your particular point Alan, may be one that goes along university lines, but down at student level isn't necessarily a viable situation. [   ]

12. *Jackie:*   I think that most students would like to see more liaison between their own counsellors and tutors. [   ]

We tend to think that the tutor and counsellor have separate views of the student, and that their only contact in relation to the student is in the passing of papers about assignments. [   ]

Perhaps an extension of the tutorial session, to include a discussion of personal problems with the students' own counsellors present would be helpful in creating a congenial atmosphere. [   ]

13. *Sue:*   The situation as it stands, leads to this argument and disagreement between these two roles because students are drawn in different directions, particularly with regard to academic work. If you want to quibble about that, you often go to the counsellor because you often know them better, they're more approachable, they've built up a relationship with you, and as you say, the two should come together more and have joint sessions probably lasting much longer. [   ]

14. *Peter:*   One of the main problems is that students often miss tutorials. They're just not getting out of the course what they could. [   ]

15. *Sue:*   Yes, but why don't people attend? Maybe they've been unable to attend, they think they missed something last time, and think, 'I won't bother going'. If tutors took the initiative to tell students what happened at the last tutorial, and outline what will happen next, I think that there would be better group interaction, people would get together more, there'd be more group identity, and there wouldn't be splinter cliques which I think destroy the set-up. [   ]

16. *Kate:*   I think that smaller tutorial groups would be a good idea as well, then you could relate better to your tutor and other students. It would give the opportunity for the more timid ones to come in. [   ]

17. *Jackie:*   There are disadvantages with small groups. I have personal experience of where a personality clash between a student and a tutor, or between two students, can entirely disrupt a tutorial session. [   ]

Discussion B

18. *Alan:*   I think that one of the main problems of the university courses is the division between the tutor and the counsellor and the fact that you often get different advice from each. [   ]

19. *Sue:*   Well, I agree. [   ]

I think it would be a good idea if there was more liaison between tutors and counsellors. If students go to one or other of those people, they should tell each other what was said, so that they can work together. [   ]

20. *Peter:* I think that this can be taken a little further. Perhaps after the meeting of the tutor and the counsellor there should be more feedback to the student, because often they are left in a total vacuum. [   ]

21. *Jackie:* Do you think what we need are a series of more informal meetings between counsellors, tutors and the students themselves, to keep the students aware of how the tutors are reacting to their written assignments, and keep the tutors aware of the students' problems? [   ]

22. *Peter:* At the moment the communication between the tutor and the counsellor is done mainly by correspondence. I'd like to be a little bit more positive and suggest that these two meet face-to-face so that there is an exchange of information between them. [   ]

23. *Sue:* Yes. [   ]
    Possibly too, there could be a facility for there to be meetings other than formal tutorials. I know these happen in the first year, but later, when you speak to people, they feel very much in isolation. [   ]
    Perhaps there could be meetings between tutorials, involving both the tutor and the counsellor. [   ]

24. *Jackie:* I support Sue's proposal and can visualize the situation. [   ]
    I think we need to avoid imposing an increased workload on our counsellors and tutors who already have a heavy student commitment. Should we suggest that students themselves form meaningful self-help groups? [   ]

25. *Alan:* I think that's exactly right Jackie. [   ]
    I think it's absolutely essential that the university develops the concept of self-help groups, and give more publicity to their advantages as so much learning, I think, can be gained by students from other students. [   ].

26. *Peter:* Are we thinking of increasing the value of the self-help situation itself? [   ]
    In these self-help groups, why not have a tutor there in an advisory capacity, rather than in a tutorial capacity. [   ]

27. *Kate:* Do you mean on a regular basis? [   ]

28. *Alan:* Yes. [   ]

29. *Kate:* Yes. [   ]
    If students could help to choose some of the tutorial topics, then we would be incorporating the self-help concept. [   ]

30. *Sue:* Talking about the groups, do you think we should advocate they should be smaller? [   ]
    In these smaller groups, the two roles could be combined with one staff member doing both the counselling and tutoring. Do you think that would have any value? [   ]

31. *Jackie:* If we are considering smaller groups and specialist advice from tutors and counsellors, let's add an element of student mobility so that students can move between groups to gain the specialist advice they need at any particular time.[   ]

32. *Sue:* Yes, I think that's a very good point. [   ]
    I think it would be useful if students were allowed to consult other tutors. I think this could be done easily if all tutorials were held on the same day, and if students were told what each individual tutor's speciality was, and actually told that if they had a problem, they could consult that person. [   ]

Record sheet A

Category	Participants' names				
	Jackie	Alan	Sue	Peter	Kate
Proposing					
Supporting					
Disagreeing					
Giving information					
Seeking information					

Record sheet B

Category	Participants' names				
	Jackie	Alan	Sue	Peter	Kate
Proposing					
Supporting					
Building					
Disagreeing					
Giving information					
Seeking information					

Record sheet C

Category	Discussions		
	A	B	
Proposing			
Building	—		
Supporting			
Disagreeing			
Giving information			
Seeking information			

This excercise is based upon the Open University Course D 101, *Understanding Society* course programme, 'Analysing social interaction'.

8.2 SGA: Functional roles in groups

Objectives

❑ To give group members practice in observing the role behaviour of individuals in a group.
❑ To practise carrying out a variety of role functions in a group.

Introduction

The textbook (*ORBIT*, Chapter 8) distinguished between the task and maintenance roles played by individuals in groups. The former related to achieving the group's task objectives. The latter concerned keeping the group together as a working unit. The purpose of this role play is to allow students to observe 'behaviour in action', so as to be able to identify the behaviours which go towards making a role definition.

Procedure

Step 1 Review the concept of task and maintenance activities in a group, and the associated group member roles as directed by your instructor (see Chart A).

Step 2   Form one or more groups of five to eight people. Groups need not to be of equal size. Note down the names of the other group members in the left hand column of chart B 'Group Member Role Identification Form' for Discussion 1 (p. 74).

Step 3   On chart C of this workbook, 'Group role to be played' and Discussion 2 (p. 75,) print in capitals the task or maintenance role that you would like to practise playing in group discussion 1 (do not let anyone see what you write).

Step 4   Each group then spends five to ten minutes discussing the topic they will be given by the instructor.

During this discussion, each group member will try to display the role activity that they have selected. This should be done repeatedly, but not to such an extreme so as to appear obvious or ridiculous (e.g. the Initiator will give ideas or direction).

Step 5   When your instructor stops your discussion, the members of your group have to guess what specified role each person was playing.

Using chart B on page 74, opposite the names of the group members in the left-hand column, write in the role you think they played, in the right-hand column.

Going round in turn, each individual totals up the guesses from the other group members, then shows the role printed on their paper. This procedure is repeated until all group members have revealed their roles.

Step 6   The procedure is repeated for discussion 2, and once again each group member privately records the role that they will take in this discussion.

This time, however, members pick roles that they tend to avoid, find difficult, or have had little experience of playing.

Step 7   Repeat step 4. Your instructor provides a new topic for discussion.

Step 8   Repeat step 5.

When group members have all shared the nature of their roles they were trying to carry out, the others in the group offer helpful feedback about their role-playing. For each group member, the others highlight:

(a) What was effective about the way they played their roles

(b) What could be modified, or done differently

Comments should be as specific as possible, and focus on what the group member said and did.

Step 9   The class reassembles for a final discussion under the direction of the instructor.

Chart A: Functional roles in groups

Task roles

Initiator   Gives ideas or directions; proposes goals; defines problems; suggests procedures for solving problems.

Information seeker Asks other group members to provide information for the group.

Diagnoser   Analyses the problems and issues confronting the group.

Opinion seeker   Asks other group members for their opinions on the issue being discussed.

Evaluator setter   Makes critical judgements of ideas or suggestions of group members.

_____

_____

Maintenance roles

Encourager   Gives praise, provides acceptance of group members' ideas, as well as of the group members' themselves.

Compromiser   Looks for areas of common interest; negotiates differences between group members.

Peacekeeper   Helps to relieve tensions; assists working through conflicts to arrive at agreements among group members.

Clarifier   Makes comments which simplify and place into focus the problem which the group is trying to solve, or a decision it wants an agreement on.

Summarizer   Periodically summarizes what the group has discussed and agreed, and identifies what still has to be done.

Standard setter   Helps to define the norms of group members' behaviour, that is, sets the standards which everyone will adhere to when working together.

_____

_____

Chart B: Group Member Role Identification Form

Discussion 1

Group member   Role played

_____   _____

_____   _____

_____   _____

_____   _____

_____   _____

_____   _____

_____   _____

_____   _____

_____   _____

_____   _____

_____   _____

_____   _____

_____   _____

_____   _____

Discussion 2

Group member   Role played

_____   _____

_____   _____

_____   _____

_____   _____

_____   _____

_____   _____

_____   _____

_____   _____

_____   _____

_____   _____

_____   _____

_____   _____

_____   _____

Chart C   *Group role to be played*

Group Discussion 1

Selected Role (capitals)

Group Discussion 2

Selected Role (capitals)

Chart C   *Group role to be played*

8.3 PREP: Belbin's Team Role Theory

Objectives

❏ To analyse which roles individuals play in groups and teams.
❏ To introduce Belbin's Team Role Theory.

Introduction

A great deal of work in organizations is now carried out through team effort. Technical change projects, marketing task forces, appointments committees are just a few examples. In these circumstances, the composition of the team is crucial, and it cannot be guaranteed that members will always work together well, and succeed in the task that they have been set. The research of Meredith Belbin into effective team performance suggested that the chances of successful team performance could be increased if eight group member role behaviours were covered in a team. This exercise will allow you to assess the roles in a team that you tend to play.

Procedure

Step 1 *Before* the next session complete the team role inventory on pages 78–9 of this workbook, and bring it with you to the class.

Step 2 *At the class*, read Table 8.1 below, where you will find a brief summary of the strengths and a few weaknesses that tend to characterize each of the group roles.

From your understanding of these different roles, identify the ones that you feel that you play most often and next often in groups and teams of which you are a member:

Most often: _____

Next often: _____

Step 3 Score your team role inventory as directed by your instructor, using the scoring sheet in Table 8.2.

Table 8.1: Summary of Belbin's eight group roles

Type	Symbol	Typical features	Positive qualities	Allowable weaknesses
Company worker	CW	Conservative dutiful, predictable	Organizing ability, practical common sense, hard-working, self-discipline	Lack of flexibility, unresponsiveness to unproven ideas
Chairman	CH	Calm, self-confident, controlled	A capacity for treating and welcoming all potential contributors on their merits and without prejudice. A strong sense of objectives	No more than ordinary in terms of intellect or creative ability
Shaper	SH	Highly strung, outgoing, dynamic	Drive and a readiness to challenge inertia, ineffectiveness, complacency or self-deception	Proneness to provocation, irritation and impatience
Plant	PL	Individualistic, serious-minded unorthodox	Genius, imagination, intellect, knowledge	Up in the clouds, inclined to disregard practical details or protocol

Resource Investigator	RI	Extroverted, enthusiastic, curious, communicative	A capacity for contacting people and exploring anything new. An ability to respond to challenge	Liable to lose interest once the initial fascination has passed
Monitor–Evaluator	ME	Sober, unemotional, prudent	Judgement, discretion, hard-headedness	Lacks inspiration or the ability to motivate others
Team-worker	TW	Socially oriented, rather mild, sensitive	An ability to respond to people and to situations, and to promote team spirit	Indecisiveness at moments of crisis
Completer–Finisher	CF	Painstaking, orderly, conscientious, anxious	A capacity for follow-through. Perfectionism	A tendency to worry about small things. A reluctance to 'let go'

Table 8.2: Points table for team role inventory

Section									Total
I	g	d	f	c	a	h	b	e	= 10
II	a	b	e	g	c	d	f	h	= 10
III	h	a	c	d	f	g	e	b	= 10
IV	d	h	b	e	g	c	a	f	= 10
V	b	f	d	h	e	a	c	g	= 10
VI	f	c	g	a	h	e	b	d	= 10
VII	e	g	a	f	d	b	h	c	= 10
Total									= 70

Step 4 In your small groups:

(a) Compare and contrast your own role scores (predicted and actual) with those of the other members of your group.

(b) Reflect on experiences of participation in group/teams in the past. How well do scores reflect preferred group roles?

(c) Decide to what extent your preferred group roles reflect your personality.

(d) Identify which roles in this group are preferred and which are avoided, rejected or are missing? If this was a real management or project team, what could be done to cover the avoided or rejected roles?

(e) Decide whether certain roles are more important in certain phases of a team's operation? For example, which two team member roles are likely to be crucial in the getting-started phase, generating-ideas phase, developing-the-ideas phase, and implementing-the-decision phase?

Team role inventory

Instructions

For each section, distribute a total of ten points among the sentences which you think best describe your behaviour. The points may be distributed among several sentences: in extreme cases they might be spread among all the sentences or ten points may be given to a single sentence. Enter the points alongside each sentence in the space provided.

I.   What I believe I can contribute to a team:

   (a) _____ I think I can quickly see and take advantage of opportunities.

   (b) _____ I can work well with a very wide range of people.

   (c) _____ Producing ideas is one of my natural assets.

   (d) _____ My ability rests in being able to draw people out whenever I detect they have something of value to contribute to group activities.

   (e) _____ My capacity to follow through has much to do with my personal effectiveness.

   (f) _____ I am ready to face temporary unpopularity if it leads to worthwhile results in the end.

   (g) _____ I can usually sense what is realistic and likely to work.

   (h) _____ I can offer a reasoned case for alternative courses of action without introducing bias or prejudice.

II.   If I have a possible shortcoming in teamwork, it could be that:

   (a) _____ I am not at ease unless meetings are well structured and controlled and generally well conducted.

   (b) _____ I am inclined to be too generous towards others who have a valid viewpoint that has not been given a proper airing.

   (c) _____ I have a tendency to talk too much once the group gets on to new ideas.

   (d) _____ My objective outlook makes it difficult for me to join in readily and enthusiastically with colleagues.

   (e) _____ I am sometimes seen as forceful and authoritarian if there is a need to get something done.

   (f) _____ I find it difficult to lead from the front, perhaps because I am over-responsive to group atmosphere.

   (g) _____ I am apt to get too caught up in ideas that occur to me and so lose track of what is happening.

   (h) _____ My colleagues tend to see me as worrying unnecessarily over detail and the possibility that things may go wrong.

III.   When involved in a project with other people:

   (a) _____ I have an aptitude for influencing people without pressurizing them.

   (b) _____ My general vigilance prevents careless mistakes and omissions being made.

   (c) _____ I am ready to press for action to make sure that the meeting does not waste time or lose sight of the main objective.

   (d) _____ I can be counted on to contribute something original.

   (e) _____ I am always ready to back a good suggestion in the common interest.

   (f) _____ I am keen to look for the latest in new ideas and developments.

   (g) _____ I believe that my capacity for judgements can help to bring about the right decisions.

   (h) _____ I can be relied upon to see that all essential work is organized.

IV.   My characteristic approach to group work is that:

   (a) _____ I have a quiet interest in getting to know colleagues better.

   (b) _____ I am not reluctant to challenge the views of others or to hold a minority view myself.

   (c) _____ I can usually find a line of argument to refute unsound propositions.

(d) ____ I think I have a talent for making things work once a plan has to be put into operation.

(e) ____ I have a tendency to avoid the obvious and I come out with the unexpected.

(f) ____ I bring a touch of perfectionism to any job I undertake.

(g) ____ I am ready to make use of contacts outside of the group itself.

(h) ____ While I am interested in all views, I have no hesitation in making up my mind once a decision has to be made.

V. I gain satisfaction in a job because:

(a) ____ I enjoy analysing situations and weighing up all the possible choices.

(b) ____ I am interested in finding practical solutions to problems.

(c) ____ I like to feel I am fostering good working relationships.

(d) ____ I can have a strong influence on decisions.

(e) ____ I can meet people who may have something new to offer.

(f) ____ I can get people to agree on a necessary course of action.

(g) ____ I feel in my element when I can give a task my full attention.

(h) ____ I like to find a field that stretches my imagination.

VI. If I am suddenly given a difficult task with limited time and unfamiliar people:

(a) ____ I would feel like retiring to a corner to devise a way out of the impasse before developing a line.

(b) ____ I would be ready to work with the person who showed the most positive approach.

(c) ____ I would find some way of reducing the size of the task by establishing what different individuals might best contribute.

(d) ____ My natural sense of urgency would help ensure that we did not fall behind schedule.

(e) ____ I believe that I would keep cool and maintain my capacity to think straight.

(f) ____ I would retain a steadiness of purpose in spite of the pressures.

(g) ____ I would be prepared to take a positive lead if I felt the group was making no progress.

(h) ____ I would open up discussions with a view to stimulating new thoughts and getting something moving.

VII. With reference to the problems to which I am subject when working in groups:

(a) ____ I am apt to show my impatience with those who are obstructing progress.

(b) ____ Others may criticize me for being too analytical and insufficiently intuitive.

(c) ____ My desire to ensure that work is properly done can hold up proceedings.

(d) ____ I tend to get bored rather easily and rely on one or two stimulating members to spark me off.

(e) ____ I find it difficult to get started unless the goals are clear.

(f) ____ I am sometimes poor at explaining and clarifying complex points that occur to me.

(g) ____ I am conscious of demanding from others the things I cannot do myself.

(h) ____ I hesitate to get my points across when I run up against real opposition.

The team role inventory was developed by Dr Meredith Belbin. It is reprinted, with permission, from R. M. Belbin, *Management Teams: Why They Succeed or Fail*, Butterworth-Heinemann, London, 1981. pp. 153–6.

8.4 REV: Norton Street Gang

Objectives

❑ To assess your understanding of informal group structure.

❑ To test your understanding of leadership in a group.

Introduction

This case relates to Chapter 8 of *ORBIT* and is based on the book, *Street Corner Society*, by William F. Whyte (1943). The numbers on the left hand side of the case are intended to differentiate the paragraphs and thus assist in the discussion session.

Procedure

Read the case, *Norton Street Gang* and then:

(a) Depict the 'hierarchy' of the Norton Street Gang by drawing its organizational chart and the interpersonal channels of influence. Your chart should answer the questions: Who is the leader? Who are the deputy leaders? Where are the subgroups within the gang? Who leads these and who are the members? What is their relationship to the other parts of the gang?

(b) Identify the key traits of, and functions performed for the gang, by its leader.

Norton Street Gang

(1) The Norton Street Gang took its name from where its members always met – at the corner of Norton Street. It consisted of thirteen young men: Alec, Angelo, Carl, Danny, Doc, Frank, Fred, Joe, Long John, Lou, Mike, Nutsy and Tommy. All of them had lived in the neighbourhood as children and had attended the same school. Many of them had belonged to other gangs in their youth. The oldest, Doc, Nutsy and Mike were 29 years old; Tommy, the youngest, was only 20. Only two members of the gang, Carl and Tommy, had regular jobs working in a factory. Danny and Mike owned an amusement arcade. The others were permanently or occasionally unemployed.

(2) Doc, who was unemployed, had been the first to return to Norton Street. Nutsy, Joe, Frank, Alec, Carl and Tommy – all old friends – joined up with them. Then Angelo, Fred and Lou arrived. Danny and Mike joined as old friends of Doc's because of the amusement arcade that they had opened. Long John joined Doc because of them. As soon as their number became complete, they became organized.

(3) From the start, their meetings took place in Norton Street. They had a cafe there where they always met. They always went ten pin bowling on Saturday evenings. If Doc wanted the gang to do something, he would talk it over with Mike and Danny beforehand, and sometimes also with Long John. Even if Long John made an important suggestion, it was rarely adopted. Long John had no influence with the group. If a suggestion came from Mike or Danny, it was passed on to Nutsy, who in turn involved Frank, Joe and Alec, as well as Carl and Tommy (who were inseparable). However, if the decision came through Danny, it could be passed on to Angelo, and then involved Fred and Lou. Doc, however, influenced Nutsy and Angelo directly. Incidentally, if Tommy had an idea about something the gang should do, this could get to Doc by way of Carl and Nutsy. Tommy's status, together with that of Alec and Lou, was the lowest in the group while Doc's was the highest. Mike and Danny enjoyed a great deal of prestige and influence, and they were exactly one step down from Doc. Although owning an amusement arcade prevented Danny and Mike from attending meetings as frequently as Doc, it did confer prestige on them within the gang. They were businessmen, while the rest just lived at the expense of others.

(4) Doc, Mike and Danny enjoyed the highest status in the eyes of the gang members. All three were known for their skill in discussions. Above all, it was Doc who distinguished himself in such debates. Long John enjoyed a special position. Although he had little influence on the rest of the group, and although his suggestions were not accepted, he was the one who got on best with the group's leaders. He always supported them.

(5) Whenever the leader was away, the gang split into two opposing camps headed by Nutsy and Angelo respectively. However, when the leader was present, the situation changed radically, and the whole group stuck together, with all members talking to one another and getting things done. During the meetings, a member of the group might begin to talk, but would fall silent if the leader did not listen to him. The member would not resume speaking until the leader paid attention to him. Both in discussions as a group, and in person-to-person conversations, the communication was concentrated on the leader.

(6) Gang members turned to him with their problems and confidences. He was the one who was best informed about what was going on in the gang. If arguments arose between the men, he knew the reasons for them, and was in the best position to calm them down. This was because each combatant came to him with his version of events and asked for his judgement and decision. However, he had to be proper and fair in his behaviour towards his closest friends, because not all the members of the gang were absolutely loyal to him.

(7) It was usual for him to make the decisions about what the group did and this was expected of him. The others could make suggestions, but had to have his approval for any action. His method of making a decision followed a firmly established procedure. He delayed the group's proposed course of action until he had consulted those who took his place when he was absent. The leader's standing depended, in the final analysis, on how his decisions were assessed by the other group members. It was 'favourable' if the group had expected these decisions and accepted them. The members of the gang on the 'bottom rung of the ladder', could deviate from the norms of the group with relative impunity. The leader, however, could not permit himself to do this.

This case was prepared with the assistance of David Andrews, University of Glasgow

Chapter 9

Social control through groups

9.1	Large group activity:	Glasgow gangs
9.2	Small group activity:	Departmental Course Committee
9.3	Prepared task:	Discovering the norms
9.4	Review:	Essay marking

9.1 LGA: Glasgow gangs

Objective

❑   To sensitize students to the key concepts relevant to understanding group control.

Introduction

The dynamics of group control of individual behaviour are similar whether one is considering the members of a board of management of a major company, or a gang of youths. This exercise offers students who have no previous experience with the subject of group control, an opportunity to identify some of the key elements which will be examined in greater depth in the course.

Procedure

Step 1   Turn to the appropriate page in your workbook. There you will find a short article from the *Glasgow Evening News* of 1929. Read it through quickly now on your own.

Step 2   Working with the person next to you, answer the ten questions below. You have fifteen minutes for this.

1.   Were the Glasgow gangs 'psychological groups' or 'aggregates'?

2.   Were the gangs formal or informal groups?

3.   List the objectives of the gangs.

4.   Give an example of a gang norm.

5.   Give an example of a gang sanction to enforce that norm.

6.   On what criteria were gang leaders chosen?

7.   What enhanced the status of individuals in the gang?

8.   What contributed to each gang's unique identity?

9.   What features distinguished gang members?

10.   What could happen to the most effective gang member?

NTS

UAL

SALE

have already been furnished . . . made
prices and on terms well within the

eally good furniture at greatly reduced
Grant's *now* . . . while these amazing
he Showrooms and compare prices and

e but a *few examples* of the
ing at present. There are
aiting your inspection.

CREDIT

rnish out-of income, on our famous "No
thly instalment, all the furniture you have
The account can be cleared by weekly or
years, according to your requirements. In
difficult for you to continue payments you
siderate treatment that has made our name

12/6 with Order and 12 6 monthly secures delivery of
this luxurious Three-Piece Suite,

xurious Three-Piece Suite, covered in best quality Hide effect
finished a richly toned Brown colour, and complete with
some Brown Velveteen Cushions, filled feathers. This Suite is
and very comfortable, and being soundly constructed of good
materials, is eminently suited for hard wear. Usual Price,
Gns.

ALE £17 15/- Or N6 Deposit
RICE and 12/6 monthly

10/- with Order and 10 monthly secures delivery of
this Handsome Living-Room Suite.

some Living Room Suite made of figured Oak, beautifully
a rich Brown colour, comprising 4ft. wide Sideboard with
drawers tone knob with Green baize for cutlery) and two roomy
boards below: 5ft. by 3ft extending Dining Table and four
built small chairs with loose seats covered in Rexine.
al Price, 19 Gns.

LE £14 12/6 Or No Deposit
ICE and 10/- monthly.

GLASGOW GANGSTERS.

Youthful Hooligans Terrorise Small Shopkeepers.

BID TO RIVAL CHICAGO.

GIRL MEMBERS LEAD TO MANY DISPUTES

A special investigation into the activities of the Glasgow gangs was conducted by a representative of The Evening News. The inquiry revealed that these gangs constitute a serious menace to the community.

Their activities are not confined to one city area, but they are specially and notoriously active in Bridgeton and in Govan. The "Nudie Boys" of Bridgeton almost rival the gangsters of Chicago in their threats to the safety of the citizens.

BOTTLES BETTER THAN RAZORS.

The blackmailing activities of some of the Glasgow gangs were revealed to an Evening News representative who carried out an investigation in the areas principally affected. They terrorise the whole community, and particularly the small-shopkeeping class, in order that they may make an easy livelihood without doing any work themselves.

Most of the members of such gangs are unemployed or unemployable youths between 17 and 22. The leader is generally a few years older than his followers, and is chosen principally for his weight and fighting ability. A system of transfers (similar to that which obtains in the football world) is in operation, and when two rival gangs are about to stage a battle good fighters are transferred from one gang to another. Heavy fees are reported to be paid, and as much as £20 has been paid for a single "transfer."

GIRLS OR "MOLLS."

A girl is known to the gangsters as a "Moll." Each gang has a number of such girls attached to it and over these "fair" followers many disputes arise.

For example: Not long ago the sweetheart of the leader of one gang went off to a certain picture house with a member of another gang. They were discovered by the outraged leader, who also happened to attend the cinema that night, and he immediately remarked: "That gang can have the leavings of our gang any time they want." There was no verbal reply, but he woke up to find himself in the infirmary with a terrible slash, inflicted with a razor.

THEIR METHODS.

It is not to be thought that these gangs are formed for the mere purpose and from the love of fighting. That is not the case. They are formed in order that they may obtain an easy livelihood at the expense of their more peaceful neighbours.

The small shopkeeper they hold in a state of terror, and they extract from him a weekly payment of two shillings. Should he fail to pay, the gang burgle his premises or smash the shop window. Publicans are also victims, although they do not usually pay in cash.

AFRAID TO COMPLAIN.

To complain to the police would seem the obvious course, but this they are afraid to do, because (so effective is the organisation of the gangs), if they do, the gangs immediately take reprisals, smash a window, and loot the premises.

One reason why it is very difficult to deal with these gangs is that a rival gangster never gives the members of an opposing gang away. There is honour among gangsters. One member of a gang who did turn on his erstwhile companions not so long ago went soon after to hospital—as the result of an "accident"—and he is still there. His former colleagues seized him, broke his ribs, and left him lying on the street unconscious.

THE LEADING GANG.

The leading and by far the worst gang is that which operates in Bridgeton under the somewhat inexplicable title of "The Nudie Boys." Other well-known gangs are the "Pikers," and the "Billy Boys." A good fighter (a man who carries a big transfer fee) is one who can "gouge," and who is an expert bottle-thrower. "Gouging" is the most fiendish activity of the gangs. It is an operation whereby one damages an opponent's eye by using the pressure of the forefinger and the thumb.

A bottle-thrower is a particularly useful member of a gang. He throws a bottle in order to strike, and the experts can use two bottles at a time. A member of one gang stated that bottle-throwing was more effective than razor slashing. "Besides," he pointed out, "one only gets a bigger sentence if one is found in possession of a razor."

MENACE TO THE COMMUNITY.

It will be readily seen that these gangs constitute a serious menace to the community. They are particularly a menace to the young people in the district in which they operate. Very often a young man who has refused to join a gang is seized upon by members and mauled to such an extent that he finally agrees to become one of the desperadoes.

The police—who are known in the terminology of the gangs as "splits"—find great difficulty in suppressing these gangs. Even when a fight takes place in the public streets it is difficult to draw batons and lay around them because of the danger of innocent bystanders being involved.

There appears to be only one remedy. A fine is not enough. Very often the necessity of paying a fine is just another reason for further terrorism against the small shopkeepers. Imprisonment is not enough. Most of the members rather glory in the fact of having been in prison.

The use of the "cat" would appear to be the only remedy. If legislation is needed to allow of its use, that legislation should be passed, and passed as quickly as possible.

The article appeared in the *Glasgow Evening News*, 10 May, 1929

9.2 SGA: Departmental Course Committee

Objective

❑   To explore the effects of group pressure on individuals.

Introduction

This is a role-playing exercise set in the context of a university course. It will give you the opportunity to experience some of the dynamics to be found in groups.

Procedure

Step 1   Read the briefing note for the role that you have been allocated by your instructor, and think yourself into it.

The meeting will begin without two of the group members who will join the group a little late.

Group members' brief

General brief

You are one of the student members of the Departmental Course Committee (DCC). Each member represents one of the tutorial groups from the year class. The DCC meets regularly to hear student complaints and receive suggestions for improvements. It is attended by the course director, members of the departmental lecturing staff, and the head of department.

You and your fellow student members hold preliminary meetings, to set the agenda and agree an approach, before bringing matters to the DCC. In the past, your group has brought up matters at the DCC which have been swiftly resolved by the course director. At other times, your group has got into unproductive and acrimonious discussions on trivial matters, while important issues were neglected. You and your colleagues have looked silly in front of the teaching staff, and you have been criticized by those whom you represent.

You and your fellow student representatives are meeting today to decide whether or not to invite the course director to your future preliminary meetings (ahead of the DCC). You need a consensus before an invitation can be issued.

Brief (excluding latecomers)

Your view is that the course director should NOT be invited to your preliminary discussions, and that the arrangements should remain as they are. Your arguments are listed below. Feel free to refer or consult them during the role play.

1.   Your recent embarrassment was a one-off failure of planning and is unlikely to re-occur.

2.   It is bad practice to reveal student complaints ahead of time, as it will give departmental staff time to prepare excuses, and fudge the issue.

3.   In practice it will be impossible to isolate 'trivial' items with the course director and the full range of complaints will have to be revealed.

4.   Departmental staff on the DCC already do not give a high priority to student concerns, being preoccupied with financial matters. This change might give them an excuse for further neglect.

5.   Specifically, they might see the preliminary meetings as a viable alternative to the DCC which might be discontinued.

6.   The student members of the DCC may thus lose their only opportunity to raise issues directly with the head of department.

9.3 PREP: Discovering the norms

Objectives

❏ To raise students' understanding of the effect of group norms on behaviour in a non-university and a university environment.

❏ To demonstrate the link between behaviour in groups and the creation of group norms.

❏ To enable students to identify group norm enforcement strategies.

Introduction

Often group norms are implicit rather than explicit, and are difficult to identify. Nevertheless, individuals' behaviour may be influenced by norms which they may not be fully conscious of. When people become aware of the norms that affect them, the more they are able to understand their own behaviour. This activity seeks to make group norms explicit.

Procedure

Step 1 Before the class, write down in the space below, the THREE most salient norms that operate in a group of which you are a member. This should be a non-university group.

Norm A

Norm B

Norm C

Step 2   For each of the three norms, respond to the three sets of questions below:

    (a)   How was this group norm communicated to newcomers to the group including yourself?

    (b)   What happens to people who violate this norm? How did the group 'police' itself? How does any individual feel who 'goes against' this group norm?

    (c)   Is this norm still relevant to the group? What purpose does it serve for the group members?

     Bring your notes to class, and be ready to discuss them with your fellow students in syndicates.

Step 3   At the class, in your syndicates, compare and discuss the answers to the three questions about the operation of norms of groups of which you are a member outside of the university.

Step 4   The focus now switches to the class group itself. Within the same syndicate groups, identify three student behaviours which may provide the basis of class or group norms. Your instructor will provide you with some examples if you get stuck. A norm is usually based on an actual behaviour experienced by the class or the group about which they have feelings. For each behaviour, insert below the norm that operates. Example:

    Behaviour: absence from class

    Associated norm: ask fellow student to apologize to instructor for your absence

    Behaviour:

    Norm:

    Behaviour:

    Norm:

    Behaviour:

    Norm:

Step 5   After you and your group have identified three behaviours and their associated norms:

    (a)   Agree a rank order of importance for these norms to the group. Insert the ranking in the spaces on the right of each norm.

    (b)   Discuss how you would feel if you broke the norms? Would different group members have the same feelings?

    (c)   Discuss how this group might react if one of its members behaved in a way that broke these norms. What would the others do?

9.4 REV: Essay marking

Objective

❑ To assess your understanding of factual information group research contained in Chapters 2, 7, 9 and 10.

Introduction

This review exercise gives you the opportunity to check your understanding of research methodology from Chapter 2 with research on group behaviour in Chapters 7, 9 and 10. Additional factual errors are included. You are put into the position of an instructor marking an essay, and are asked to identify the mistakes.

Procedure

Assume that the student who wrote this essay began with twenty marks. Deduct one mark for each factual error, highlight it in the space on the right hand side of the page, and write in the correction. What mark out of twenty should this essay receive?

Essay question

What empirical evidence is there to suggest that the behaviour of individuals is influenced by the group to which they belong?

Student answer

Error

Through its studies, social psychology has conclusively demonstrated the effect on the individual of the group to which they belong. Prior to the First World War, studies documented the phenomena of social facilitation, that is, the altering of individual behaviour by the presence of others. Additionally, British industrial psychologists discovered that a person's boredom level while at work doing a repetitive task could be reduced if that individual worked in a group. Earlier, Frederick Winslow Taylor, the 'father of scientific management', realized that workers had feelings and associated with others in the factory, but felt that these were irrelevant to the issue of worker productivity.

Most research, however, was carried out in the post-1945 period. Much of this was focused on individuals and groups in organizations. Before addressing the question, some of the key terms will be defined. The question refers to the group. Social scientists reserve the term 'social group' to denote two or more people who regularly interact and are aware of each other, irrespective of whether they perceive themselves to be a group. Large social groups possessing these characteristics (of twelve or more people) are designated 'aggregates'. It is because group members share common goals and a common communication network, that enables the group to influence its individual members.

Such an informal group always meets both the work and the social needs of its members. Group members will comply with group demands because they want to satisfy their love and esteem needs. These were highlighted by the motivation theorist Frederick Herzberg. His hierarchy of needs theory located these needs in the middle of the pyramid. Both personal experience and anecdotal accounts suggest the individual behaviour is influenced by groups in this way. However, the question asks for empirical evidence to confirm such beliefs. Since empirical evidence is obtained from properly conducted research investigations, it is to these that we turn for supporting evidence.

Perhaps the best-known studies in the behaviour of groups at work were carried out in the 1940s by Elton Mayo, an industrial psychologist and employee of the Western Electric Company's Research Division. Mayo's study was of the women assembling electrical relays. In this laboratory-type research study, changes were introduced to the dependent variables – the rest and lunch breaks and work stopping times. The effects of these modifications on the independent variable – the women's output – were measured. Although these results were not conclusive, Mayo suspected that by being allowed to select coworkers, the positive internal relations between the women translated themselves into improved productivity.

More convincing evidence of group effects on the individual were obtained by Mayo's studies of the men working in the Bank Wiring Observation Room. This research revealed that three separate informal groups existed. Each one had its own norms, and applied sanctions to enforce individual behaviour to the norm. These related to acceptable production output limits, how to dress while at work, what you were allowed to tell a supervisor about a fellow worker, and how to behave if you were an inspector.

The research studies of Asch are also relevant to our understanding of group influence on the individual. His findings revealed the speed of norm formation in a group. Using the illusion of the autokinetic effect, he discovered that initially wide estimates of movement by a group of experimental subjects soon narrowed to form an acceptable group norm. In a related experiment, Sherif demonstrated how group pressure led individuals to distort their perception, judgement or action. His matching-the-length-of lines experiment revealed that 55 per cent of those studied succumbed to group pressure.

The work of Stoner on risk-taking in groups represents yet another empirical demonstration of group influence on individual behaviour. He asked subjects to read hypothetical scenarios described in a questionnaire and to indicate how much risk they were prepared to accept. Subjects first completed the instrument on their own, and then produced a group decision. Stoner found that groups made riskier decisions than individuals. The explanations offered to explain this include that younger group members were swayed by more experienced older ones; that in a group, individuals had the opportunity to compare and reassess their level of caution *vis-à-vis* others; that risk-taking was culturally accepted and esteemed behaviour; and that in a group, the responsibility for a risky course of action was diffused among several members.

The studies quoted so far, those of Mayo, Asch, Sherif and Stoner represent the most often cited empirical evidence for the proposition that groups do influence individual behaviour. However, the findings of these studies have not gone unchallenged by their critics. The entire Hawthorne studies have been criticized for the unsystematic way in which they were conducted.

The research of Asch and Sherif were conducted on random individuals who were prepared to participate in the study. The subjects therefore did not represent real groups or teams. Similarly, Stoner's research was carried out on liberal arts students. Apart from the respondents not constituting real groups, the questionnaire required respondents to select a 1-in-10, 1-in-20 or 1-in-30 chance level. This does not represent the way people normally evaluate risk. Since the findings cannot be applied to other groups, the internal validity of this research is highly suspect.

In conclusion, one might mention a field study carried out by Stanley Milgram. In a set of experiments aimed at testing the extent to which people will obey the instructions of an authority figure, one version of Milgram's set-up involved two stooges refusing to administer the electric shocks required by the white-coated 'professor'. On seeing the two refuse, all the real subjects also refused. The design of Milgram's experiment suggested that external variables in the test situation had been controlled, and that the stooges' refusal could be considered to be the cause of the subject's behaviour. The external validity of this study could therefore be claimed to be high.

In conclusion, one can say that personal experience and observation confirm the contention that groups influence individual behaviour, and this is supported by the empirical psychological research. However, some of this research on which this finding is based could be improved. Specifically, more experimentation should be done with real groups in companies, who have to live with the consequences of their decisions, and where the personal and political realities of organizations play a part.

Mark out of 20: _____

Chapter 10
Group effectiveness

10.1 LGA: Nightingale Hospital

Objective

❏ This exercise will consider how group effectiveness is influenced by organizational and managerial decisions.

Introduction

Research suggests that group cohesiveness has a major effect on group productivity and group member satisfaction. Actions that are taken by management, whether consciously or unconsciously, can damage cohesiveness, and result in lower productivity and a drop in morale.

Procedure

Step 1   Read the case on your own, and then make brief responses to the two parts of the question that follows.

Step 2   Once you have done that, compare your responses with those of the person next to you.

Nightingale Hospital

The domestic service arrangements in a large hospital had, for many years, been based on the permanent allocation of domestic staff to specific wards. When staff shortages occurred (due to sickness or leave), these were made up from a reserve pool of staff, or by overtime working. Permanent allocation to a ward thus carried status among the domestic staff. New entrants to the hospital's domestic department would begin as 'reliefs', and would then be 'promoted' to a permanent ward position on completion of a satisfactory probationary period. Domestic supervisors also operated an unofficial sanction system whereby staff off sick frequently, or for long periods of time, were penalized for their absences by being 'demoted' to the reserve pool, only returning to the permanent ward position when their record of attendance proved to be satisfactory.

The domestic staff had a permanent placement within a particular ward or two adjacent wards. Over time, the staff working on the same ward got to know each other well. They had their tea and lunch breaks together, during which time they discussed the patients on 'their' ward. Working in the same wards, these domestic staff also got to know the regular nursing personnel who had been assigned to their ward.

Getting the work done was achieved by group effort. Each domestic was expected to warn the others of the impending approach of a supervisor. Group members were required to support each other in the event of any 'harassment' by management. Bragging about the happenings on their ward was expected and acceptable. Different ward teams tried to outdo each other in terms of the dramas they had seen on their wards.

Shortly after the hospital had achieved Trust status, the hospital management called in Organization and Methods (O & M) consultants to review the working practices of these domestic staff. The consultants conducted numerous time and motion studies, and noted all the results. They recommended that efficiency could be increased, and overtime reduced, by changing work patterns, and the type of equipment used. Following these recommendations, the hospital management purchased the new equipment. Meanwhile, the changes in work patterns resulted in the dissolution of the reserve pool, and the allocation of staff to ward areas on a rotational basis. Each morning, domestic staff were allocated to different ward areas, to work alongside other staff. This was intended to increase flexibility in the transfer of staff on an *ad hoc* basis to any areas of shortage. These two changes resulted in the replacement of the old labour intensive system which depended on staff cooperation and coordination.

Much to the surprise of management, problems began to arise as soon as the revised system was put into operation. The levels of sickness and absenteeism among the domestic staff rose, their productivity and efficiency fell, and problems of liaison between domestic and nursing staff increased at ward level. Generally, a deterioration in working relationships between all concerned was observed.

1. Identify the causes of the problem and recommend a solution, based on your knowledge of group theory and motivation.

This case is based on research reported in A. A. Huczynski and M. J. Fitzpatrick, *Managing Employee Absence for a Competitive Edge*, Pitman, London, 1989.

10.2 SGA: Supersew Ltd

Objectives

❑ To apply research and theoretical findings to a given work problem.

❑ To make recommendations for managerial actions which are supported by data.

❑ Using your understanding of organizational behaviour, to highlight gaps in knowledge.

Introduction

Knowing a theory is one thing, being able to apply it to a concrete situation is another. This case study gives you an opportunity to apply what you have learned on the course so far to a real management problem. However, difficulties of this nature do not come neatly parcelled and wrapped up. It is important to be able to use your knowledge to identify what you don't know (but need to find out). This case provides you with an opportunity to do this.

Procedure

Step 1 Divide into groups of five to six students, and select a leader.

Step 2 All groups are to put themselves in Trevor's shoes, and solve the problem described in the case. You are to do two things:

(a) Limiting yourself to the facts presented in the case, agree on three recommendations that you feel will solve the problem.

  The recommendations should be in the form of specific actions for Trevor to take. Each recommended action should be supported by theoretical or empirical research evidence.

(b) Move beyond the facts given, and identify what additional information Trevor might obtain in order to implement an even more effective solution. Suggest how this information might be obtained.

Your group has thirty minutes for this task.

Supersew Ltd

For the past six months Trevor has been the supervisor of a sewing room of twenty-five women in a garment factory which produces underwear and T-shirts. The firm's output is bought by two large chains of retail stores. The share of their orders that they place with Supersew depends largely upon the company's past record for high quality and punctual delivery. For this reason, output to target and a low reject rate are crucial.

Sewing room layout

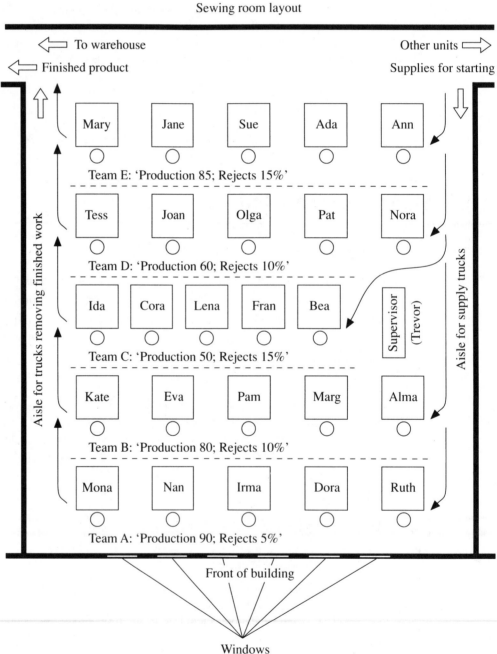

The manufacture of T-shirts involves eleven operations. Predominantly, these involve cutting the material to shape, and then sewing the bits together. The material is cut by hand with scissors, after which the sewing is done on electrically powered machines. Resembling domestic ones, these machines are more heavy-duty types which are built for long life, and can remain in service for a dozen years or even more. The old machines operate satisfactorily, but tend to become unreliable with age.

The women doing the cutting and sewing are all union members. They are organized into five teams (A, B, C, D and E) of five workers (see sewing room layout). For the simpler operations, there is little loss of production when operators move from one type of garment to another. However, it takes about three months for a machinist doing one of the more complicated operations such as lockstitching, to achieve the performance standard assigned for the garment that she is working on.

Some of the women, Mary, Jane, Sue, Ada and Ann, had been working together at Shirtail Ltd before it closed down, and was taken over by Supersew. The managing director of Supersew, Mr Henderson, was keen to expand production facilities, and acted quickly to take advantage of the available skilled labour. The girls agreed to be recruited after being given an assurance that they could continue to work together.

Until recently, Trevor's problem had been getting out enough production. Three months ago, however, payment for all sewing machine operations was changed from an hourly-rate to a team piece-rate, and production output became fairly satisfactory. Quality now became the main problem. Not only were there too many rejects, but serious complaints had begun to come in from both the salesmen in the field, and from the chain store buyers. Since the women were not paid for rejected items, it was difficult to understand why they were not being more careful. Trevor has been called in by his department foreman, Mr Preston to discuss the matter.

Mr P: Trevor, I want to talk to you again about the kind of work your unit is turning out. What's the matter down there anyway?

Trevor: Heaven knows! On the old hourly rate the girls weren't turning out anything, and now, on this new group piece-rate, a lot of the work that they do isn't any good. When I make them do it again, they say I'm picking on them.

Mr P: Sylvia and Eddie aren't having the trouble with their girls that you are having with yours.

Trevor: Well, I'm not having trouble with all of mine. There is just this small group of five or six who are the real problem. They all want to be finishers or anything but what they are. I've moved them near to my desk where I can keep an eye on them, and I've told them that I won't move them until they've improved their work. Even so, I'd like to see Sylvia or Ed or anybody else get any work out of them.

Mr P: You're not trying to tell me that just a few girls out of more than two dozen make your department look that bad.

Trevor: No, but they are the worst ones. I called all the girls in the 'C' and 'D' teams together last week and gave them a good talking to about how much worse they've become. Production and quality are both down.

Mr P: I'm beginning to think that you don't have any workers that are any good.

Trevor: No, that's not true. I'll take the girls in my 'A' team and put 'em up against any we've got in the factory. As a matter of fact, all of my finishers are a pretty decent bunch.

The 'B' team has a couple of good workers in it, and there is nothing wrong with the 'E' team.

Mr P: Yeah, but their rejects are too high.

Trevor: Well, that might be true, but those girls certainly produce. Maybe if I can get them to slow down a bit, their quality may rise. It's going to annoy them, though.

Mr P: That's your problem. You're not afraid of them, are you?

Trevor: No, but they didn't even like it the other day when I bawled them out for talking on the job. Come to think of it, all that chattering may be the reason they don't pay any attention to quality.

Mr P: Well, tell them that if they don't stop talking, you'll break up their little club. You're the boss down there, aren't you?

Trevor: Well, you've kind of got me there. Under Mr Henderson's instructions, I hired everybody in team 'E' in one batch with the understanding that they could stay together, and I hate to go back on my word.

Mr P: Well, give them a good lecture and threaten to do it.

Trevor: I know, but it's a headache. Those girls stick together and you can't locate the troublemaker. Even when they don't get on with one another, they still gang up on you. For example, I gave these girls in team 'C' a safety lecture the other day after one of them got her hands caught in the machine, and all they did was gripe and pick on me about everything under the sun. I never saw such a bunch of sour hens before in my life.

Mr P: What's bugging them anyway? There must've been something if they felt picked on?

Trevor: Oh, it was just the same old moaning about all of them wanting to be finishers. After they've been on the job a few weeks, they think they know everything.

Mr P: Sounds like you've been giving some of those new girls a lot of half-baked ideas about the jobs around here. What's so special about being a finisher anyway? The pay is the same.

Trevor: I don't know. I think its just a silly idea that they've got into their heads. You and I know the end job's no easier.

Mr P: Was that all they moaned about, or do they want us to install a staff swimming-pool?

Trevor: No, quite a few of them are annoyed because they said they couldn't make the standard. Most of the girls think it is too hard to hit anyway.

Mr P: I haven't heard complaints from any other departments about it. After all, eighty isn't so high. Why should your girls complain when none of the rest of them do?

Trevor: All I know is that they do. Except for team 'A' and a few others who really turn the stuff out, they're just about the worst bunch of operators I've ever seen. I don't know why I have to have all of them in my department.

Mr P: Trevor, we've been over all this before and I'm tired of listening to you feeling sorry for yourself. Either get those girls on the ball, or we'll have to put somebody else down there who knows how to run things. I don't want to be tough about it, but that's the way it is. I'll give you thirty days to get that mess straightened out, and I'll back you up on anything that seems reasonable. If you can show me some results by the end of that time you can stay; if you don't, we'll have to find someone to replace you. Is that clear?

Trevor: I suppose so. But after racking my brains for the past six months I don't know what you or I or anybody else can do with those girls. I've tried everything.

10.3 PREP: 'The Destructors'

Objective

❑   To apply the concepts of group formation, stucture, control and effectiveness to a fictional case study.

Introduction

Some novels can tell us a great deal about individuals and groups. This short story by Graham Greene is set in the post-war London of the 1950s. As a fictional account, it provides great scope for the consideration of group behaviour in general, and that of George Homans's theory in particular. Homans is important because he offers us an explanation of how a group forms and internally structures itself.

Procedure

Step 1   Before the session, read in your own time, the short story, 'The Destructors' by Graham Greene, twice. Then, referring to the *ORBIT* textbook chapters indicated, write short answers in response to the questions below. Each answer should be one or two paragraphs in length.

'The Destructors': questions

1. Why does the Wormsley Common Gang constitute a psychological group (Chapter 7)?

2. Using Homans's theory, describe the formation of the gang, specifying the factors which comprise the 'external' or formal system. Specifically, the group's (a) physical environment; (b) cultural environment; (c) technological environment. How were the sentiments of the group members strengthened (Chapter 7)?

3. Using Tuckman and Jensen's model, describe the stages of the gang's development from the point when T joins them and the original gang has to reform. Use the headings: (a) forming; (b) storming; (c) norming; (d) performing (Chapter 7).

4. What is group structure? Analyse the Wormsley Common Gang's structure on the following dimensions: (a) status; (b) power; (c) liking; (d) role (Chapter 8).

5. What is group process? Identify the gang's (a) mode of decision-making; (b) T's leadership style; (c) communication structure (Chapter 8).

6. How does the gang control the behaviour of its members? Specifically list the norms and sanctions used by the gang (Chapter 9).

7. What personal (psychological benefits) does each group member gain by adhering to the gang's norms (Chapter 9)?

8. Suggest how a gang of twelve highly spirited youngsters come to agree unanimously to carry out an action which breaks both criminal and moral laws (Chapter 9).

9. Assess the gang's effectiveness and its members' satisfaction (Chapter 10).

Step 2   Bring your notes to the class.

'The Destructors'

I

(1)   It was on the eve of the August Bank Holiday that the latest recruit became the leader of the Wormsley Common Gang. No one was surprised except Mike, but Mike at the age of 9 was surprised by everything. 'If you don't shut your mouth,' somebody once said to him, 'you'll get a frog down it.' After that Mike kept his teeth tightly clamped except when the surprise was too great.

(2)   The new recruit had been with the gang since the beginning of the summer holiday, and there were possibilities about his brooding silence that all recognized. He never wasted a word even to tell his name until that was required of him by the rules. When he said 'Trevor' it was a statement of fact, not as it would have been with the others a statement of shame or defiance. Nor did anyone laugh except Mike, who finding himself without support and meeting the dark gaze of the newcomer opened his mouth and was quiet again. There was every reason why T, as he was afterwards referred to, should have been an object of mockery – there was his name (and they substituted the initial because otherwise they had no

excuse not to laugh at it), the fact that his father, a former architect and present clerk, had 'come down in the world' and that his mother considered herself better than the neighbours. What but an odd quality of danger, of the unpredictable, established him in the gang without any ignoble ceremony of initiation?

(3)   The gang met every morning in an impromptu car-park, the site of the last bomb of the first blitz. The leader, who was known as Blackie, claimed to have heard it fall, and no one was precise enough in his dates to point out that he would have been 1 year old and fast asleep on the down platform of Wormsley Common Underground Station. On one side of the car-park leant the first unoccupied house, No. 3, of the shattered Northwood Terrace – literally leant, for it had suffered from the blast of the bomb and the side walls were supported on wooden struts. A smaller bomb and incendiaries had fallen beyond, so that the house stuck up like a jagged tooth and carried on the further wall relics of its neighbour, a dado, the remains of a fireplace. T, whose words were almost confined to voting 'Yes' or 'No' to the plan of operations proposed each day by Blackie, once startled the whole gang by saying broodingly, 'Wren built that house, father says.'
        'Who's Wren?'
        'The man who built St Paul's.'
        'Who cares?' Blackie said. 'It's only Old Misery's.'

(4)   Old Misery – whose real name was Thomas – had once been a builder and decorator. He lived alone in the crippled house, doing for himself: once a week you could see him coming back across the common with bread and vegetables, and once as the boys played in the car-park he put his head over the smashed wall of his garden and looked at them.

(5)   'Been to the lav,' one of the boys said, for it was common knowledge that since the bombs fell something had gone wrong with the pipes of the house and Old Misery was too mean to spend the money on the property. He could do the redecorating himself at cost price, but he had never learnt plumbing. The lav was a wooden shed at the bottom of the narrow garden with a star-shaped hole in the door: it had escaped the blast which had smashed the house next door and sucked out the window-frames at No.3.

(6)   The next time the gang became aware of Mr Thomas was more surprising. Blackie, Mike and a thin yellow boy, who for some reason was called by his surname Summers, met him on the common coming back from the market. Mr Thomas stopped them. He said glumly, 'You belong to the lot that play in the car-park?'
        Mike was about to answer when Blackie stopped him. As the leader he had responsibilities. 'Suppose we are?' he said ambiguously.
        'I got some chocolates,' Mr Thomas said. 'Don't like 'em myself. Here you are. Not enough to go round. I don't suppose. There never is,' he added with sombre conviction. He handed over three packets of Smarties.
        The gang was puzzled and perturbed by this action and tried to explain it away. 'Bet someone dropped them and he picked 'em up,' somebody suggested.
        'Pinched 'em and then got a bleeding funk,' another thought aloud.
        'It's a bribe,' Summers said. 'He wants us to stop bouncing balls on his wall.'
        'We'll show him we don't take bribes,' Blackie said, and they sacrificed the whole morning to the game of bouncing that only Mike was young enough to enjoy. There was no sign from Mr Thomas.

(7)   Next day T astonished them all. He was late at the rendezvous, and the voting for that day's exploit took place without him. At Blackie's suggestion the gang was to disperse in pairs, take buses at random and see how many free rides could be snatched from unwary conductors (the operation was to be carried out in pairs to avoid cheating). They were drawing lots for their companions when T arrived.
        'Where you been, T?' Blackie asked. 'You can't vote now. You know the rules.'
        'I've been *there*,' T said. He looked at the ground, as though he had thoughts to hide.
        'Where?'

'At Old Misery's.' Mike's mouth opened and then hurriedly closed again with a click. He had remembered the frog.

'At Old Misery's?' Blackie said. There was nothing in the rules against it, but he had a sensation that T was treading on dangerous ground. He asked hopefully, 'Did you break in?'

'No. I rang the bell.'

'And what did you say?'

'I said I wanted to see the house.'

'What did he do?'

'He showed it me.'

'Pinch anything?'

'No.'

'What did you go for then?'

The gang had gathered round: it was as though an impromptu court was about to form and try some case of deviation. T said, 'It's a beautiful house,' and still watching the ground, meeting no one's eyes, he licked his lips first one way, then the other.

'What do you mean, a beautiful house?' Blackie asked with scorn.

'It's got a staircase 200 years old like a corkscrew. Nothing holds it up.'

'What do you mean nothing holds it up. Does it float?'

'It's to do with opposite forces, Old Misery said.'

'What else?'

'There's panelling.'

'Like in the Blue Boar?'

'200 years old.'

'Is Old Misery 200 years old?'

(8) Mike laughed suddenly and then went quiet again. The meeting was in a serious mood. For the first time since T had strolled into the car-park on the first day of the holidays his position was in danger. It only needed the use of his real name and the gang would be at his heels.

'What did you do it for?' Blackie asked. He was just, he had no jealousy, he was anxious to retain T in the gang if he could. It was the word beautiful that worried him – that belonged to a class world that you could still see parodied at the Wormsley Common Empire by a man wearing a top hat and monocle, with a haw-haw accent. He was tempted to say, 'My dear Trevor, old chap,' and unleash his hell hounds. 'If you'd broken in,' he said sadly – that indeed would have been an exploit worthy of the gang.

'This was better,' T said, 'I found out things.' He continued to stare at his feet, not meeting anybody's eye, as though he were absorbed in some dream he was unwilling – or ashamed – to share.

'What things?'

'Old Misery's going to be away all tomorrow and Bank Holiday.'

Blackie said with relief, 'You mean we could break in?'

'And pinch things?' somebody asked.

Blackie said, 'Nobody's going to pinch things. Breaking in – that's good enough, isn't it? We don't want any court stuff.'

'I don't want to pinch anything,' T said. 'I've got a better idea.'

'What is it?'

T raised his eyes, as grey and disturbed as the drab August day. 'We'll pull it down,' he said. 'We'll destroy it.'

(9) Blackie gave a single hoot of laughter and then, like Mike, fell quiet, daunted by the serious implacable gaze. 'What'd the police be doing all the time?' he said.

'They'd never know. We'd do it from inside. I've found a way in.' He said with a sort of intensity, 'We'd be like worms, don't you see, in an apple. When we came out again there'd be nothing there, no staircase, no panels, nothing just walls, and then we'd make the walls fall down – somehow.'

'We'd go to jug,' Blackie said.

'Who's to prove? And anyway we wouldn't have pinched anything.' He added without the smallest flicker of glee, 'There wouldn't be anything left to pinch after we'd finished.'

'I've never heard of going to prison for breaking things,' Summers said.

'There wouldn't be time,' Blackie said. 'I've seen housebreakers at work.'

'There are twelve of us,' T said. 'We'd organize.'

'None of us know how . . .'

'I know.' T said. He looked across at Blackie. 'Have you got a better plan?'

'Today,' Mike said tactlessly, 'we're pinching free rides ...'

'Free rides,' T said. 'Kid stuff. You can stand down, Blackie, if you'd rather . . .'

'The gang's got to vote.'

'Put it up then.'

Blackie said uneasily. 'It's proposed that tomorrow and Monday we destroy Old Misery's house.'

'Here, here,' said a fat boy called Joe.

'Who's in favour?'

T said, 'It's carried.'

'How do we start,' Summers asked.

(10) 'He'll tell you,' Blackie said. It was the end of his leadership. He went away to the back of the car-park and began to kick a stone, dribbling it this way and that. There was only one old Morris in the park, for few cars were left there except lorries: without an attendant there was no safety. He took a flying kick at the car and scraped a little paint off the near mudguard. Beyond, paying no more attention to him than to a stranger, the gang gathered around T; Blackie was dimly aware of the fickleness of favour. He thought of going home, of never returning, of letting them all discover the hollowness of T's leadership, but suppose after all what T proposed was possible – nothing like it had ever been done before. The fame of the Wormsley Common car-park gang would surely reach around London. There would be headlines in the papers. Even the gangs that ran the betting at the all-in wrestling and the barrow boys would hear with respect of how Old Misery's house had been destroyed. Driven by the pure, simple and altruistic ambition for fame for the gang, Blackie came back to where T stood in the shadow of Old Misery's wall.

(11) T was giving his orders with decision: it was as though his plan had been with him all his life, pondered through the seasons, now in his fifteenth year crystallized with the pain of puberty. 'You,' he said to Mike, 'bring some big nails, the biggest you can find, and a hammer. Anybody who can, better bring a hammer and a screwdriver. We'll need plenty of them. Chisels too. We can't have too many chisels. Can anybody bring a saw?'

'I can,' Mike said.

'Not a child's saw,' T said. 'A real saw.'

Blackie realized he had raised his hand like any ordinary member of the gang.

'Right, you bring one, Blackie. But now there's difficulty. We want a hacksaw.'

'You can get 'em at Woolworth's,' Summers said.

The fat boy called Joe said gloomily, 'I knew it would end in a collection.'

'I'll get one myself,' said T. 'I don't want your money. But I can't buy a sledge-hammer.'

Blackie said, 'They are working on No. 15. I know where they'll leave their stuff for Bank Holiday.'

'Then that's all,' T said. 'We meet here at nine sharp.'

'I've got to go to church,' Mike said.

'Come over the wall and whistle. We'll let you in.'

II

(12) On Sunday morning all were punctual except Blackie, even Mike. Mike had a stroke of luck. His mother fell ill, his father was tired after Saturday night, and he

was told to go to church alone with many warnings of what would happen if he strayed. Blackie had difficulty in smuggling out the saw, and then in finding the sledge-hammer at the back of No. 15. He approached the house from a lane at the rear of the garden, for fear of a policeman's beat along the main road. The tired evergreens kept off a stormy sun: another wet Bank Holiday was being prepared over the Atlantic, beginning in swirls of dust under the trees. Blackie climbed into Misery's garden.

There was no sign of anybody anywhere. The lav stood like a tomb in a neglected graveyard. The curtains were drawn. The house slept. Blackie lumbered nearer with the saw and the sledge-hammer. Perhaps after all nobody had turned up: the plan had been a wild invention: they had woken wiser. But when he came close to the back door he could hear a confusion of sound hardly louder than a hive in swarm: a clickety-clack, a bang bang, a scraping, a creaking, a sudden painful crack. He thought: it's true, and whistled.

(13) They opened the back door to him and he came in. He had at once the impression of organization, very different from the happy-go-lucky ways under his leadership. For a while, he wandered up and down the stairs looking for T. Nobody addressed him: he had a sense of great urgency, and already he could begin to see the plan. The interior of the house was being carefully demolished without touching the walls. Summers, with hammer and chisel, was ripping out the skirting boards in the ground floor dining room: he had already smashed the panels of the door. In the same room Joe was heaving up the parquet blocks, exposing the soft wood floorboards over the cellar. Coils of wire came out of the damaged skirting and Mike sat happily clipping the wires.

(14) On the curved stairs two of the gang were working hard with an inadequate child's saw on the bannisters – when they saw Blackie's big saw they signalled for it wordlessly. When he next saw them a quarter of the bannisters had been dropped into the hall. He found T at last in the bathroom – he sat moodily in the least cared for room in the house, listening to the sounds coming up from below.

'You've really done it,' Blackie said with awe. ' What's going to happen?'

'We've only just begun,' T said. He looked at the sledge-hammer and gave his instructions. 'You stay here and break the bath and the wash-basin. Don't bother about the pipes. They come later.'

Mike appeared at the door. 'I've finished the wires, T,' he said.

'Good. You've just got to go wandering around now. The kitchen's in the basement. Smash all the china and glass and bottles you can lay hold of. Don't turn on the taps – we don't want a flood – yet. Then go into all the rooms and turn out the drawers. If they are locked get one of the others to break them open. Tear up any papers you find and smash all the ornaments. Better take a carving knife with you from the kitchen. The bedroom's opposite here. Open the pillows and tear up the sheets. That's enough for the moment. And you Blackie, when you've finished in here crack the plaster in the passage up with your sledge-hammer.'

'What are you going to do?' Blackie asked.

'I'm looking for something special,' T said.

(15) It was nearly lunch-time before Blackie had finished and went in search of T. Chaos had advanced. The kitchen was a shambles of broken glass and china. The dining room was stripped of parquet, the skirting was up, the door had been taken off its hinges, and the destroyers had moved up a floor. Streaks of light came in through the closed shutters where they worked with the seriousness of creators – and destruction after all is a form of creation. A kind of imagination had seen this house as it had now become.

Mike said, 'I've got to go home for dinner.'

'Who else?' T asked, but all the others on one excuse or another had brought provisions with them.

They squatted in the ruins of the room and swapped unwanted sandwiches. Half an hour for lunch and they were at work again. By the time Mike returned they were on the top floor, and by six the superficial damage was completed. The doors were all off, all the skirtings raised, the furniture pillaged and ripped and smashed – no one could have slept in the house except on a bed of broken plaster. T gave his orders – eight o'clock next morning, and to escape notice they climbed singly over the garden wall, into the car-park. Only Blackie and T were left: the light had nearly gone, and when they touched a switch, nothing worked – Mike had done his job thoroughly.

(16)   'Did you find anything special?' Blackie asked.

T nodded. 'Come over here,' he said, 'and look.' Out of both pockets he drew bundles of pound notes. 'Old Misery's savings,' he said. 'Mike ripped out the mattress, but he missed them.'

'What are you going to do? Share them?'

'We aren't thieves,' T said. 'Nobody's going to steal anything from this house. I kept these for you and me – a celebration.' He knelt down on the floor and counted them out – there were seventy in all. 'We'll burn them,' he said, 'one by one,' and taking it in turns they held a note upwards and lit the top corner, so that the flame burnt slowly towards their fingers. The grey ash floated above them and fell on their heads like age. 'I'd like to see Old Misery's face when we're through,' T said.

'You hate him a lot?' Blackie asked.

'Of course I don't hate him,' T said. 'There'd be no fun if I hated him.' The last burning note illuminated his brooding face. 'All this hate and love,' he said, 'it's soft, it's hooey. There's only things, Blackie,' and he looked round the room crowded with the unfamiliar shadows of half things, broken things, former things. 'I'll race you home, Blackie,' he said.

III

(17)   Next morning the serious destruction started. Two were missing – Mike and another boy whose parents were off to Southend and Brighton in spite of the slow warm drops that had begun to fall and the rumble of thunder in the estuary like the first guns of the old blitz. 'We've got to hurry,' T said.

Summers was restive. 'Haven't we done enough?' he asked. 'I've been given a bob for slot machines. This is like work.'

'We've hardly started,' T said. 'Why, there's all the floors left, and the stairs. We haven't taken out a single window. You voted like the others. We are going to *destroy* this house. There won't be anything left when we've finished.'

(18)   They began again on the first floor picking up the floor boards next the outer wall, leaving the joists exposed. Then they sawed through the joists and retreated into the hall, as what was left of the floor heeled and sank. They had learnt with practice, and the second floor collapsed more easily. By the evening an odd exhilaration seized them as they looked down the great hollow of the house. They ran risks and made mistakes: when they thought of the windows it was too late to reach them. 'Cor,' Joe said, and dropped a penny down into the dry bubble-filled well. It cracked and spun among the broken glass.

(19)   T was already on the ground, digging at the rubble, clearing a space along the outer wall. 'Turn on the taps,' he said. ' It's too dark for anyone to see now, and in the morning it won't matter.' The water overtook them on the stairs and fell through the floorless rooms.

It was then that they heard Mike's whistle at the back. 'Something's wrong,' Blackie said. They could hear his urgent breathing as they unlocked the door.

'The bogies?' Summers asked.

'Old Misery,' Mike said. 'He's on his way,' he said with pride.

'But why?' T said, 'He told me . . . ' He protested with the fury of a child he had never been, 'It isn't fair.'

'He was down at Southend,' Mike said, 'and he was on the train coming back. He said it was too cold and wet.' He paused and gazed at the water. 'My, you've had a storm here. Is the roof leaking?'

'How long will he be?'

'Five minutes, I gave Ma the slip and ran.'

'We better clear,' Summers said. 'We've done enough, anyway.'

'Oh no, we haven't. Anybody could do this.' 'This' was the shattered hollow house with nothing left but the walls. Yet walls could be preserved. Facades were valuable. They could build inside again more beautifully than before. This could again be a home. He said angrily. 'We've got to finish. Don't move. Let me think.'

'There's got to be a way,' T said. 'We couldn't have got this far . . .'

'We've done a lot,' Blackie said.

'No, no, we haven't. Somebody watch the front.'

'We can't do any more.'

'He may come in at the back.'

'Watch the back too.' T began to plead. 'Just give me a minute and I'll fix it. I swear I'll fix it.' But his authority had gone with his ambiguity. He was only one of the gang. 'Please,' he said.

'Please,' Summers mimicked him, and then suddenly struck home with the fatal name, 'Run along home, Trevor.'

T stood with his back to the rubble like a boxer knocked groggy against the ropes. He had no words as his dreams shook and slid. Then Blackie acted before the gang had time to laugh, pushing Summers backward. 'I'll watch the front, T,' he said, and cautiously he opened the shutters of the hall. The grey wet common stretched ahead, and the lamps gleamed in the puddles. 'Someone's coming, T. No, it's not him. What's your plan, T?'

'Tell Mike to go out to the lav and hide close beside it. When he hears me whistle he's got to count ten and start to shout.'

'Shout what?'

'Oh, 'Help', anything.'

'You hear, Mike,' Blackie said. He was the leader again. He took a quick look between the shutters, 'He's coming, T.'

'Quick, Mike. The lav. Stay here, Blackie, all of you, till I yell.'

'Where are you going, T?'

'Don't worry. I'll see to this. I said I would, didn't I?'

(20) Old Misery came limping off the common. He had mud on his shoes and he stopped to scrape them on the pavement's edge. He didn't want to spoil his house, which stood jagged and dark between the bomb-sites, saved so narrowly, as he believed, from destruction. Even the fanlight had been left unbroken by the bomb's blast. Somewhere somebody whistled. Old Misery looked sharply round. He didn't trust whistles. A child was shouting: it seemed to come from his own garden. Then a boy ran into the road from the car-park. 'Mr Thomas,' he called, 'Mr Thomas.'

'What is it?'

'I'm terribly sorry, Mr Thomas. One of us got taken short, and we thought you wouldn't mind, and now he can't get out.'

'What do you mean, boy?'

'He's got stuck in your lav.'

'He'd no business . . . Haven't I seen you before?'

'You showed me your house.'

'So I did. So I did. That doesn't give you the right to . . .'

'Do hurry Mr Thomas. He'll suffocate.'

'Nonsense. He can't suffocate. Wait till I put my bag in.'

'I'll carry your bag.'

'Oh no, you don't. I'll carry my own.'

'This way Mr Thomas.'

'I can't get in the garden that way. I've got to go through the house.'

'But you *can* get in the garden this way, Mr Thomas. We often do.'

'You often do?' He followed the boy with a scandalized fascination. 'When? What right . . .?'

'Do you see . . .? the wall's low.'

'I'm not going to climb walls into my own garden. It's absurd.'

'This is how we do it. One foot here, one foot there, and over.' The boy's face peered down, an arm shot out, and Mr Thomas found his bag taken and deposited on the other side of the wall.

'Give me back my bag,' Mr Thomas said. From the loo a boy yelled and yelled. 'I'll call the police.'

'Your bag's all right, Mr Thomas. Look. One foot there. On your right. Now just above. To your left.' Mr Thomas climbed over his own garden wall. 'Here's your bag Mr Thomas.'

'I'll have the wall built up,' Mr Thomas said, 'I'll not have you boys coming over here, using my loo.' He stumbled on the path, but the boy caught his elbow and supported him. 'Thank you, thank you, my boy,' he murmured automatically. Somebody shouted out again through the dark. 'I'm coming, I'm coming,' Mr Thomas called. He said to the boy beside him, 'I'm not unreasonable. Been a boy myself. As long as things are done regular. I don't mind you playing round the place Saturday mornings. Sometimes I like company. Only it's got to be regular. One of you asks leave and I say Yes. Sometimes I'll say No. Won't feel like it. And you come in at the front door and out at the back. No garden walls.'

'Do get him out, Mr Thomas.'

'He won't come to any harm in my loo,' Mr Thomas said, stumbling slowly down the garden. 'Oh my rheumatics', he said. 'Always get 'em on Bank Holiday. I've got to be careful. There's loose stones here. Give me your hand. Do you know what my horoscope said yesterday? "Abstain from any dealings in first half of week. Danger of serious crash". That might be on the path,' Mr Thomas said. 'They speak in parables and double meanings.' He paused at the door of the loo. 'What's the matter in there?' he called. There was no reply.

'Perhaps he's faint hearted,' the boy said.

(21) 'Not in my loo. Here, you come out.' Mr Thomas said, and giving a great jerk at the door he nearly fell on his back when it swung open easily. A hand first supported him and then pushed him hard. His head hit the opposite wall and he sat heavily down. His bag hit his feet. A hand whipped the key out of the lock and the door slammed. 'Let me out,' he called, and heard the key turn in the lock. 'A serious crash' he thought, and felt dithery and confused and old.

A voice spoke to him softly through the star-shaped hole in the door. 'Don't worry Mr Thomas, we won't hurt you, not if you stay quiet.'

(22) Mr Thomas put his head in his hands and pondered. He had noticed that there was only one lorry in the car-park, and he felt certain that the driver would not come for it before the morning. Nobody could hear him from the road in front, and the lane at the back was seldom used. Anyone who passed there would be hurrying home and would not pause for what they would certainly take to be drunken cries. And if he did call 'Help', who, on a lonely Bank Holiday evening, would have the courage to investigate? Mr Thomas sat on the loo and pondered with the wisdom of age.

(23) After a while there seemed to him to be sounds in the silence – they were faint and came from the direction of his house. As he stood and peered through the ventilation hole – between the cracks in one of the shutters he saw a light, not the light of a lamp, but the wavering light that a candle might give. Then he thought he heard the sound of hammering and scraping and chipping. He thought of burglars – perhaps they had employed the boy as a scout, but why should burglars engage in what sounded more and more like a stealthy form of carpentry? Mr Thomas let out an experimental yell, but nobody answered. The noise could not even have reached his enemies.

IV

(24) Mike had gone home to bed but the rest stayed. The question of leadership no longer concerned the gang. With nails, chisels, screwdrivers, anything that was sharp and penetrating, they moved around the inner walls of the house worrying at the mortar between the bricks. They started too high and it was Blackie who hit on

the damp course and realised the work could be halved if they weakened the joints immediately above. It was a long, tiring, unamusing job, but at last it was finished. The gutted house stood there balanced on a few inches of mortar between the damp course and the bricks.

(25)   There remained the most dangerous task of all, out in the open at the edge of the bomb-site. Summers was sent to watch the road for passers-by, and Mr Thomas, sitting on the loo, heard clearly now the sound of sawing. It no longer came from the house, and that a little reassured him. He felt less concerned. Perhaps the other noises had no significance.

A voice spoke to him through the hole. 'Mr Thomas.'

'Let me out,' Mr Thomas said sternly.

'Here's a blanket,' the voice said, and a long grey sausage was worked through the hole and fell in swathes over Mr Thomas's head.

'There's nothing personal,' the voice said. 'We want you to be comfortable tonight.'

'Tonight.' Mr Thomas repeated incredulously.

'Catch,' the voice said, 'Penny buns – we've buttered them, and sausage rolls. We don't want you to starve, Mr Thomas.'

Mr Thomas pleaded desperately. 'A joke's a joke, boy. Let me out and I won't say a thing. I've got rheumatics. I've got to sleep comfortable.'

'You wouldn't be comfortable, not in your house, you wouldn't. Not now.'

'What do you mean, boy?' But the footsteps receded. There was only the silence of night: no sound of sawing. Mr Thomas tried one more yell, but he was daunted and rebuked by the silence – a long way off an owl hooted and made away again on its muffled flight through the soundless world.

(26)   At seven next morning, the driver came to fetch his lorry. He climbed into the seat and tried to start the engine. He was vaguely aware of a voice shouting, but it didn't concern him. At last the engine responded and he backed the lorry until it touched the great wooden shore that supported Mr Thomas's house. That way he could drive right out and down the street without reversing. The lorry moved forward, was momentarily checked as though something were pulling from behind, and then went on to the sound of a long rumbling crash. The driver was astonished to see bricks bouncing ahead of him, while stones hit the roof of his cab. He put on his brakes. When he climbed out the whole landscape had suddenly altered. There was no house beside the car-park, only a hill of rubble. He went round and examined the back of the lorry for damage, and found a rope tied there that was still twisted at the other end round a part of a wooden strut.

(27)   The driver again became aware of somebody shouting. It came from the wooden erection which was the nearest thing to a house in that desolation of broken brick. The driver climbed the smashed wall and unlocked the door. Mr Thomas came out of the loo. He was wearing a grey blanket to which flakes of pastry adhered. He gave a sobbing cry. 'My house,' he said. 'Where's my house?'

'Search me,' the driver said. His eye lit on the remains of a bath and what had once been a dresser and he began to laugh. There wasn't anything left anywhere.

'How dare you laugh,' Mr Thomas said. 'It was my house. My house.'

'I'm sorry,' the driver said, making heroic efforts, but when he remembered the sudden check of the lorry, the crash of falling bricks, he became convulsed again. One moment the house had stood there with such dignity between the bomb-sites like a man in a top hat, and then, bang, crash, there wasn't anything left. He said, 'I'm sorry. I can't help it, Mr Thomas. There's nothing personal, but you got to admit it's funny.'

1954

'The Destructors' appears in Graham Greene, *Twenty-One Stories*, Penguin Books, Harmondsworth, 1975, pp. 7–23 and is used with permission. The story analysis for the workbook was prepared by C. Ritchie Graham.

10.4 REV: Groupthink in PC Support

Objectives

❑   To identify the symptoms of groupthink.

❑   To provide practice in applying a groupthink framework to the analysis of a work situation.

❑   To assess the relevance and potential usefulness of the groupthink framework for improving the performance of teams at work.

Introduction

This review exercise gives you the opportunity to apply your understanding of the concepts of groupthink to a work situation. Janis's eight symptoms of groupthink are:

1. Illusion of invulnerability – members display excessive optimism that past successes will continue and tend to take extreme risks.

2. Collective rationalization – members collectively construct rationalizations that allow them to discount negative information about the assumptions upon which they base their decisions.

3. Illusion of morality – members believe that they, as moral individuals, are unlikely to make bad decisions.

4. Shared stereotypes – members dismiss disconfirming evidence by discrediting its source (e.g. stereotyping other groups and its leaders as evil or weak).

5. Direct pressure – imposition of sanctions on individuals who explore deviant positions (e.g. who express doubts or question the validity of group beliefs).

6. Self-censorship – members keep silent about misgivings about the apparent group consensus and try to minimize their doubts.

7. Illusion of unanimity – members conclude that the group has reached a consensus because its most vocal members are in agreement.

8. Mind-guards – members who take it upon themselves to screen out adverse information supplied by 'outsiders' which might endanger the group's complacency.

Procedure

Step 1   Form into groups as directed by your instructor. Read the definitions of Janis's eight symptoms of groupthink contained in the Introduction.

Step 2   Read the Introduction and case A individually. Enter your answers in the space provided. Then compare and discuss your answers to it with fellow group members.

Step 3   Continue with cases B and C. Again, write in your individual decisions to both. When all syndicate members have finished, compare your group answers for both.

The groupthink virus in PC Support

The PC Support Unit at Universal Life Assurance offered advice and support to staff throughout the company. The members of the team were largely responsible for managing their unit (e.g. problem-solving, making technical adjustments). In consequence, there was a high level of interaction between members, and support from other members in order to make the necessary decisions and perform the required tasks that the unit was confronted with. Under these circumstances, there was a great potential for high group cohesion. The likelihood of individuals conforming to the general group view was also high. Group members worked as a unit on a daily basis, and depended on each other for the effective completion of group tasks. This increased the attractiveness of conforming in order to be accepted by the group. All these factors made the unit vulnerable to being infected by groupthink.

Case A

Twelve staff were present at one of the unit's weekly meetings. Peter raised the issue of changing the working hours. Other members responded quickly by giving reasons why these should stay as they are. One objector said that anyone wanting to start at 8 a.m., 'must be mad'. The proposal involved having 'core' attendance hours of 10–3, and allowing members to arrive early or work late as they chose. Jane, a software engineer, said that such an arrangement would help her to organize the childcare facilities for her daughter. Brian retorted that she shouldn't put personal convenience ahead of company requirements. It was stated that a vote was 'the best way' of deciding, and that the group had previously voted against such a change. Maggie, the unit leader, then pointed out that the issue of working hours had been discussed at the last meeting and that 'nobody' disagreed with keeping the times as they were, so she had assumed that everybody was in agreement.

As the meeting progressed, it became clear that the flexitime proposal had been lost by a single vote at the last meeting. Peter added that, 'it doesn't seem fair because almost half of us want the change'. He suggested that perhaps a flexible attendance pattern could operate on alternating weeks allowing all the unit's members preferences to be met some of the time. However, Peter received little support from the others in the room, and with pressure from the unit leader and the opposing group members, the subject was finally dropped. An observation of the body language of a number of the staff present indicated that they were not happy with the outcome, but that they were not expressing their views.

Identify the symptoms of groupthink which the behaviours illustrate.

Symptom   Behaviour

Symptom	Behaviour

Case B

The primary task of the six members of the unit's software support team is to help insurance staff who have difficulty in getting their software to function properly. During one of their meetings, one member informed the others that there had been a lot of complaints made about them. The ensuing discussion revealed that the Pensions Department had been dissatisfied with the length of time they had had to wait for assistance, and blamed it on them. Pensions felt that they were unable to achieve their customer care targets because they had to wait for their software to be rectified.

Various group members made comments which defended and supported their own position. One person said that few of the other company departments had complained. Another stated that, 'Pensions expect us to drop everything every time they whistle', and 'they don't understand how long it takes to de-bug the problems'. In the end, the topic was dropped and no solutions suggested to the problems raised. The group members were confident that they were in the right, and that the complaints they had received from Pensions were both unreasonable and unjustified.

Identify the symptoms of groupthink which the behaviours illustrate.

Symptom   Behaviour

_____

Case C

The eight members of the unit's hardware support group had a meeting which was attended by the Services Manager to whom Maggie, the unit leader, reports. The discussion concerned the quality of the hardware repairs that the group was carrying out. Participation in the problem-solving discussion was evenly spread, and most members appeared to be making a contribution. After a few minutes, however, the Services Manager made the statement, 'this is what I think you should do', and took charge of the rest of the meeting. From that point, the involvement of the support group became limited. The manager outlined the steps he wanted them to take, and the meeting ended once his instructions had been announced. As members left the meeting, their facial expressions indicated that although they would comply with the manager's instructions, they felt that they had neither contributed to the solution nor agreed with it.

Identify the symptoms of groupthink which the behaviours illustrate

Symptom   Behaviour

_____

_____

PART III

TECHNOLOGY IN THE ORGANIZATION

Chapter 11
What is technology?

11.1	**Large group activity:**	**Stakeholder analysis**
11.2	**Small group activity:**	**Technology rules, does it?**
11.3	**Prepared task:**	**Unobtrusive observation**
11.4	**Review:**	**Who said that?**

11.1 LGA: Stakeholder analysis

Objectives

❑ To develop understanding of the potential impact of technology change in organizations.

❑ To highlight the distinction between material technology and social technology.

Introduction

A *stakeholder* is someone who is likely to be affected by a change in technology, whether they regard the change as beneficial to them or damaging. One way to explore and predict the implications of technology change is through the procedure of *stakeholder analysis*. This exercise demonstrates what a *stakeholder analysis* involves. Such an analysis can also be used to shape the nature and direction of technology change, by anticipating problems and suggesting action to avoid them. A case exercise is provided as a basis for this analysis. Students may, however, like also to consider conducting a *stakeholder analysis* with respect to technology change current in their institution. This can raise the question of 'What counts as technology change?'. Chapter 11 in *ORBIT* discusses the definitional problems in this field and draws a distinction between *material technology* on the one hand and *social technology* on the other. This can also be expressed as a distinction between apparatus and organizational arrangements. In conducting a stakeholder analysis, it is usually necessary to consider not only the technology or apparatus, but also how it will be used in the context of particular organizational arrangements.

Stakeholder analysis is based first on a stakeholder map. Let us assume that somebody has at last developed an effective computer-based learning methodology for teachers and students of organizational behaviour. Much easier to programme and use than previous cumbersome approaches, the technology is still expensive and specialized, but offers the promise of reducing formal lecturing and allowing increased self-instruction by students at their own pace. A stakeholder map would look something like this:

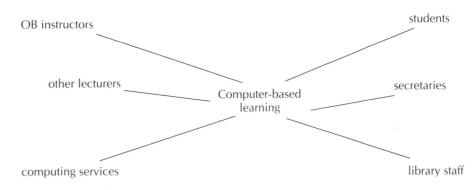

You may like to add other stakeholders to this map for yourself (what about the publishers of conventional textbooks?). It should then be possible to identify for each stakeholder what benefits and disadvantages they might see in the proposed change. From this, we can then anticipate their respective perceptions and behaviours in relation to the proposed changes. Potential problems can then also be anticipated, and action identified to address those problems.

Let us now apply such an analysis to a specific case.

Procedure

Step 1   Read the following *Maintenance planning case*.

Step 2   Produce a stakeholder map.

Step 3   Complete the analysis table that follows the case description, identifying how the different stakeholders can expect to benefit from the change, how they can expect to be disadvantaged by the change, their anticipated behaviour, possible coalitions and action suggested by this analysis.

Step 4   Report findings in accordance with your Instructor's wishes.

The maintenance planning case

Consider yourself part of the management team for a large manufacturing company. You are committed to improving the efficiency of plant maintenance and you have come up with the following proposal.

At present, each of the fourteen separate manufacturing plants on your site have their own maintenance crews, including skilled and unskilled personnel, team supervisors and support equipment. However, a system has been designed which you know will improve efficiency and reduce the costs of maintenance work. It will depend on the manufacturing supervisor responsible for each production plant entering maintenance requests through the computer terminal in his office. These maintenance requests will then be electronically mailed to a central computer which will allocate a priority to each request relative to other requests in the system at that time. Routine tasks, day-to-day workshop jobs and emergency work can also be input to the system and scheduled along with regular maintenance requests. The computer system will also keep a record of all the skills acquired by each individual maintenance engineer.

When considering each maintenance request, the system will use three items of information to calculate the time and staff required to schedule and to complete the work. This includes information about the work requested, the availability of maintenance engineering personnel and the skills possessed by each engineer. This will ensure that the right staff are sent to each maintenance job. When allocating work and determining priorities, the system can also schedule activities to occur during plant shutdowns or at other appropriate periods to reduce interruptions to manufacturing output.

This new system will therefore centralize maintenance management and the issuing of maintenance work instructions in one site engineering department. Records will also be kept of the actual times taken for jobs, so that these can be compared with the time forecasts for the work. The costs of staff and equipment time, consumables and stocks of spares and other items will also be monitored by the system.

Stakeholder analysis

Stakeholder: benefits?   disadvantages?   reactions?

Can you expect any coalitions or partnerships between stakeholders either to support or to challenge the system?

What ideas for action does this analysis suggest? Are there ways of minimizing the implications for the 'losers'? How could 'losers' be turned into 'winners'?

This case is drawn from *The Technical Change Audit: Action for Results*, by David Boddy and David Buchanan, Manpower Services Commission, Sheffield, 1987, 'The diagnostics module', p. 32.

11.2 SGA: Technology rules, does it?

Objectives

❏ To develop understanding of the ways in which management assumptions about people affect the way in which technology is used and the effect it has on work and job satisfaction.

❏ To develop understanding of the ways in which management assumptions about organization structure also affect the way in which technology is used and the effect it has on work and job satisfaction.

❏ To expose the limitations of 'technological determinism' as an approach to predicting 'technological implications'.

Introduction

To what extent does technology shape and determine the character of work, the demands made on people, the challenges and satisfactions experienced? To the extent that technology does have such an impact, we can rely on *technological determinism* to anticipate the outcomes. The job of the airline pilot and the bus driver differ primarily, and obviously, because of the differing nature of the technologies under their respective control. That is not the end of the argument, however. The work experience of airline pilots and bus drivers differs from company to company; the work experience of secretaries, lecturers, bank tellers, retail checkout staff, pizza restaurant waiters and theatre musicians differs from one organization to another irrespective of the technology in use. Whatever the causal link between technology on the one hand and the nature and quality of working life on the other, organizational factors also play a significant causal role.

Procedure

Step 1   Divide into two groups. One half will consider a manufacturing setting. The other half will consider an office setting.

Step 2   Form syndicates of up to five members each. Half will be 'manufacturing' syndicates, and half will be 'office' syndicates. (Clearly if there are only ten people in the class, there will be two syndicates only.)

Step 3   Select either a manufacturing setting (say, biscuit manufacture) or an office setting (say, typing pool) with which at least some members of your syndicate are familiar. Consider the bottom-level jobs in that context, those most likely to come into direct contact with the technology of the organization (dough cutting and baking ovens; word processing and photocopying equipment).

Step 4   Working individually and without discussion, complete the *human behaviour scale* and *organizational structure scale* questionnaires on the following pages.

Step 5   Working now in syndicates, compare your responses to these two questionnaires and try to arrive at a group consensus. Plot your group profile on the seven *behaviour* continua and the eight *structure* continua; use a different colour pen or pencil on your individual questionnaires. Calculate your group score on the two profiles; from 7 to 49 on the *behaviour* scale, and from 8 to 56 on the *structure* scale. This will be useful for comparisons later.

Step 6   Applying these profiles to your chosen work setting, nominate a spokesperson and prepare a syndicate report dealing with the following issues:

- How would you describe the functions of first line supervisors?

- Will your lowest-level employees be highly trained, moderately skilled and knowledgeable, or unskilled?

- Who will be responsible for dealing with day-to-day problems that arise on the shop- or office-floor?

- Who will be responsible for handling the new, particularly awkward, and challenging problems that arise from time to time?

- Who will be responsible for allocating jobs to employees when difficulties arise (emergencies, priorities, staff shortages and so on)?

- To what extent will the layout of facilities (desks, machinery) take account of the desire for employees to talk to each other?

- Will employees be allowed to decide on their own job methods, or will other technically trained staff take these decisions on their behalf?

- How would members of your syndicate group feel about working in the setting that you are considering – and why?

Step 7   Present your syndicate report to the whole class.

Step 8   Instructor's debriefing.

Human behaviour scale

Tick on the scale how you see the general characteristics of the majority of employees:

They	1 2 3 4 5 6 7	They
Work best on simple, routine work that makes few demands of them		Respond well to varied, challenging work requiring knowledge and skill
They are		
Not too concerned about having social contact at work		Regard opportunities for social contact at work as important
They		
Work best if time and quality targets are set by supervision		Are able to set their time and quality targets
Work best if their output and quality standards are clearly monitored by supervision		Could be given complete control over output and quality standards
Like to be told what to do next and how to do it		Can organize the sequence of their work and choose the best method themselves
Do not want to use a great deal of initiative or take decisions		Like, and are competent to use, initiative and take decisions
Work best on jobs with a short task cycle		Able to carry out complex jobs which have a long time span between start and finish

Organizational structure scale

Tick on the scale below what you believe to be the best form of organization structure:

	1 2 3 4 5 6 7	
Jobs should be clearly defined, structured and stable		Jobs should be flexible and permit group problem-solving
There should be a clear hierarchy of authority with the person at the top carrying ultimate responsibility for all aspects of work		There should be a delegation of authority and responsibility to those doing the job regardless of formal title and status
The most important motivators should be financial, e.g. high earnings and cash bonuses.		The most important motivators should be non-financial, e.g. work challenge, opportunity for teamwork
Jobs should be carefully defined by a work-study department, management services or supervision and adhered to		The development of job method should be left to the group and individual doing the job
Targets should be set by supervision and monitored by supervision		Targets should be left to the employee groups to set and monitor
Groups and individuals should be given the specific information they need to do the job but no more		Everyone should have access to all information which they regard as relevant to their work
Decisions on what is to be done and how it is to be done should be left entirely to management		Decisions should be arrived at through discussions involving all employees
There should be close supervision, tight controls and well-maintained discipline		There should be loose supervision, few controls and a reliance on employee self-discipline

This exercise is reflected in style, and in part in substance, in exercise 15.3 PREP which explores management assumptions about organization structure, using McGregor's famous distinction between Theory X and Theory Y. The argument is the same. The nature of the organization structure in relation to the task of the organization is determined largely by management decisions reflecting management assumptions. The nature of work experience in relation to the technology of production (of goods or services) is similarly determined largely by management decisions reflecting management assumptions about people and organizational functioning.

11.3 PREP: Unobtrusive observation

Objectives

❏   To explore the effects of technology on human behaviour.

❏   To gain experience in the use of unobtrusive observation as a research method.

❏   To assess the practical value of the approach used in this exercise as a basis for introducing organizational and technical improvements.

Introduction

We tend not to notice the everyday, the commonplace. To the extent that the familiar affects our behaviour, we may therefore not be fully aware of the nature and implications of that impact. In our society and in our organizations, technology is now commonplace and, therefore, is often taken for granted. Life without whatever technology sits around you as you read this text would be extremely difficult – if not painful or impossible to contemplate. It can therefore be interesting and valuable to question the commonplace, and to examine everyday actions and artefacts as if they were novel. That is what you are invited to do in this exercise. The central questions addressed here concern the ways in which people interact with technology in organizations and the impact that technology has on behaviour in an organizational setting.

Procedure

Step 1   Select a location in your institution, on your campus, or in another appropriate public place *where people use or interact with technology* on a regular basis. Examples would be vending machines, self-service cafeteria counters, photocopying machines, the kitchen in a hall of residence, computerized library catalogues, the checkouts at your supermarket, an automated teller device at a bank . . . The choice is yours. Select a location that, in your judgement, is *interesting* in some way.

Step 2   Arrange to observe people at your location at at least three appropriate times during one week, for up to one hour each time, at different times of the day on each occasion. Draw up your plan, and stick with it.

Step 3   Your task on each occasion is *unobtrusive systematic observation*. Ensure that, where possible, the people visiting your chosen location are not aware that you are observing them. Make whatever notes you feel are relevant on the behaviour that you observe, paying attention to behaviour that may appear mundane as well as to behaviour that may appear strange or surprising. Your observation will probably cover individual behaviours and interactions between people as well as the use of the technology at your chosen location.

Step 4   Write a technical report that:

1.   explains and describes your choice of location;

2.   describes the behaviours that you observed;

3.   makes recommendations for the improved use or operation of the chosen location.

Step 5   Prepare a class presentation of your findings, as guided by your instructor.

11.4 REV: Who said that?

Objectives

❑ To test your memory of key ideas from Chapter 11 in *ORBIT* concerning the definition and understanding of the place of technology in organizational behaviour.

❑ To encourage the habit of remembering accurately the authorship of ideas, as a memory aid and also as good study practice.

Introduction

Whose argument is that? Who defined that concept in that way? What did so-and-so have to say about that issue? Chapter 11 draws on the work of a relatively small number of authors who have been concerned with aspects of technology and behaviour in organizations. It is a matter of common courtesy to be able to attribute ideas and arguments accurately to their originators. In terms of one's learning ability, it is often important to remember what an author said or argued in case you come across that author again and find them building on or perhaps contradicting what they said previously. In terms of personal memory, the idea, concept or argument is often more easily recalled when one can recall also the source – and particularly where recall of the source brings back into conscious awareness related ideas from the same author or the chapter in the book where it appeared.

Procedure

Step 1 Ensure that you are familiar with the material in Chapter 11 in ORBIT. Then put the book aside. You should not refer to it for the purposes of completing this review.

Step 2 Read the following list of statements, definitions, ideas and arguments. Then refer to the author list that follows. Place the relevant author number beside each statement, depending on your understanding and memory of the source. Warning: one author (or pair of authors) may be responsible for more than one item on the ideas list.

Step 3 Score your review according to the wishes of your Instructor, and congratulate or commiserate accordingly.

Ideas list

Author number

1. Technological change entails a process of choice and negotiation.

_____

2. Computer systems have developed through three main phases
    – defence applications, hardware improvements and user relations.

_____

3. Strategic choice is a political process in which constraints and
    opportunities are functions of decision-making power.

_____

4. Most of the evidence now seems to show that new technology
    creates more jobs than redundancies.

_____

5. Developments in technology influence the way in which we think
    and understand the world around us.

_____

6. 'Technology' used to be a term with a very precise meaning
    but is today used to refer to a diverse collection of phenomena.

_____

7. Computing technology is autogenerative in that innovations can be introduced by users as well as original designers.   _____

8. The term 'technology' can refer to apparatus, technique, or to organization.   _____

9. The technology of the organization is the collection of plant, machines, tools and recipes available for the execution of the production task.   _____

10. Technological change generates contradictory imperatives.   _____

11. Material technology is that which can be seen, touched and heard; social technology involves the structure of coordination, control, motivation and reward.   _____

12. An engineering approach to technology potentially ignores relationships between machine and user.   _____

13. There are thirteen levels of mechanization, from manual to anticipatory control.   _____

Author list

1. Langdon Winner
2. Alan Fox
3. James Bright
4. Tom Forester
5. Andrew Friedman and Dominic Cornford
6. Harry Braverman
7. Joan Woodward
8. Ian McLoughlin and Jon Clark
9. John Child
10. Alvin Toffler

Chapter 12
Scientific management

12.1 LGA: Improving library performance

Objective

- ❏ To introduce students to the scientific management approach.

Introduction

This exercise is intended to be used before students have read or been told about Frederick Taylor and scientific management. As such, it can be used as an ice-breaker introduction to the topic.

Procedure

Step 1 Working with the person next to you, imagine that:

> You are a management efficiency expert. You have been called in by the local branch of your public library to help the chief librarian ensure that the performance of its lending department is at the maximum state of efficiency.
>
> As a first step in your study, make a list of the facts and figures that you would wish to collect about (i) work organization, and (ii) the layout of the library, so as to help you make suggestions for efficiency improvements.

You have fifteen minutes for this task.

12.2 SGA: Paper boat builders

Objectives

- ❏ To apply the principles of scientific management to physical tasks.
- ❏ To apply time and motion study to a job.

Introduction

The focus of this activity is on time and motion study. Its purpose is to give you the opportunity to apply scientific management techniques of observing jobs, measuring their duration and using that information to plan and organize production. Each team will seek to identify the 'one-best-way' of production and scientifically select its squad of workers.

Procedure

Step 1   The class will divide into teams of between six and eight students. Each team is identified by a letter (A, B, C, etc.) and has a team leader. At least one member of each team should have a watch with a stopwatch function.

Step 2   Note that:

1. The purpose of the exercise is to apply scientific management techniques to production. The aim of each team will be to study the jobs of its workers, and to make them as efficient as possible. This means ensuring:

    - Maximum output.
    - Minimum waste.
    - Meeting quality control standards.
    - Matching budgeted output with actual output.

2. The same product, a paper boat, will be assembled in all three production runs by all the teams.

3. An acceptable finished product is a completed boat whose mast tip is a point (not a curve) and which projects above its sides.

4. During the production runs, only four students will be workers, while the remainder will be work study experts. However, during the preparation phase, all team members will participate in the decisions about production.

5. There will be THREE production runs:

    Run 1: All teams will use craft system in which each of its four workers will complete all fourteen steps of the boat assembly process.

    Run 2: All teams will use an assembly line system in which the fourteen production steps will be divided between the four workers.

    Run 3: All teams will use an assembly line system, modified in the light of production experience.

6. Before each run, each team will have to specify how many boats it intends to make. It will then be supplied with the appropriate amount of raw material.

Step 3   Review your written instructions for making the paper boat which are located at the end of this exercise. Practise assembling the boat.

Step 4   Prepare for production run 1 (craft – 20 minutes). Team leaders inform the instructor about their projected outputs.

Step 5   Production run 1 (craft – 5 minutes).

Step 6   Teams review actual production and compare with projected production.

Step 7   Teams prepare for run 2 (assembly line – 20 minutes).

1. Teams select the workers for their four-person work squad.
2. Work study experts time each of the fourteen assembly steps.
3. Time and motion experts analyse some of the key motions so as to increase output.
4. Experts decide which steps will be carried out by which squad member in which manner.
5. The team leader informs instructor on projected output.
6. The team leader's decision on all these matters is final.

Step 8   Production run 2 (assembly line – 5 minutes).

Step 9   Teams review actual production and compare with projected production.).

Step 10   Teams prepare for run 3 (assembly line, modified – 10 minutes).

Step 11   Production run 3 (assembly line, modified – 5 minutes).

Step 12   Teams review actual production and compare with projected production.

Building the boat

These are the directions for making a paper boat. For each step there is a diagram showing what to do, and another showing what it should look like then. There are fourteen steps.

1. Hold the sheet of paper so the printing on it is facing up.

YOU

2. Fold AB to CD

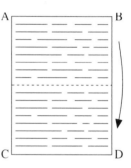

It should look like this:

3. Fold in along JG and JH so that E and F meet at point K.

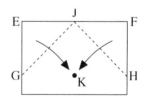

It should look like this:

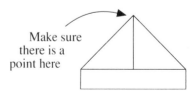

Make sure
there is a
point here

4. Fold one layer (up direction) along LM.

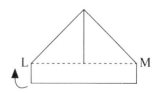

It should look like this:

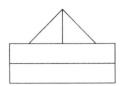

5. Turn the boat over to the other side. It should look like this:

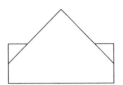

6. Fold (up direction) along NP.

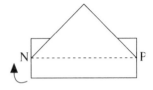

It should look like this:

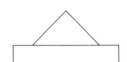

7. Tuck section Q (just the top layer) back around the edge of the boat, so it is between the back of the boat and the back layer of paper.

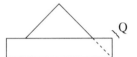

Fold section Q (back piece) towards you over the edge of the boat and press flat.

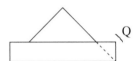

It should look like this:

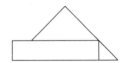

8. Do the same thing to the left end (don't turn it over). It should look like this:

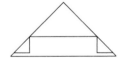

9. Pick up the boat and hold it in your hands with the open side (R) down. Open up R with your fingers and keep pulling it apart until points S and T meet.

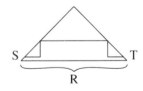

Turn the paper so that S is facing up and T is underneath. It should look like this:

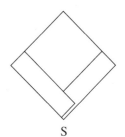

S

10. Fold up S to U.

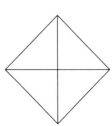

It should look like this:

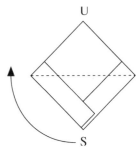

11. Turn over so that T is facing up. Fold up T to U.

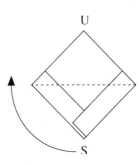

It should look like this:

12. Pick up the boat and hold it in your hands, with the open side, V, down. Open V with your fingers and keep pulling apart so that W is facing up and X is underneath. It should look like this:

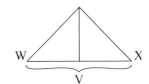

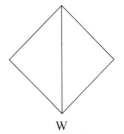

13. Fold W to A and then bring back down again to its original position. There should now be a crease at BC.

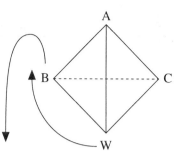

Turn over so that X is facing up. Fold X to A and then bring X down again to its original position. There should now be a crease at DE.

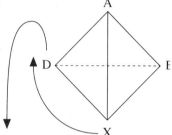

Hold Y (front and back at the top left point) with left hand, and Z (front and back at the top right point) with the right hand, and pull apart as far as it will go.

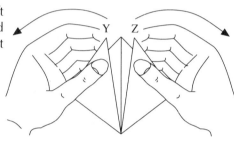

It should look like this:

14. Stand it up. You have finished your boat !

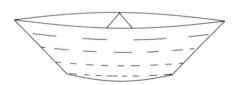

Quality control points for the boat

- The middle point must be a point, not a curve.
- The middle point must be even with, or above, the sides of the boat.
- Only completed boats are accepted.

Assembly times

One-person assembly times:

Fast assembly time (top 10 per cent)	35–45 seconds
Average time	45–55 seconds
Slow assembly time (bottom 10 per cent)	over 55 seconds

12.3 PREP: Brave new management

Objective

❏ To identify the concepts of scientific management and rationalistic learning within the context of a science fiction novel.

Introduction

Published in 1932, Aldous Huxley's book, *Brave New World*, ranks alongside Ray Bradbury's *Fahrenheit 451*, and George Orwell's *1984*, as one of the world's most significant futuristic novels. At the start of his story, Huxley describes a society which is very different from today's. It is a society based on the theories of Frederick Taylor, Henry Ford and Ivan Pavlov. While examining this imaginary society of the future, it is interesting to consider to what extent the practices described are already used (in a modified and less intense form) in the real organizations of today.

Procedure

Step 1 As preparation for a classroom-based discussion read, in your own time, the abridged section of *Brave New World*, before coming to class. Then, referring to Chapters 1, 5 and 12 and 16 of *ORBIT*, make notes in response to the questions set out below:

1. If the World State's motto is 'Community, Identity, Stability', what might be the motto of all organizations? (Hint: see Chapter 1.)

2. Sum up the 'message' that Huxley seeks to convey in the case.

3. Which organizational processes, practices and procedures that are found in all large organizations of today, would broadly serve the purposes of:

    (a) Ecto-genesis (Bokanovsky process);

    (b) Pre-destination;

    (c) Neo-Pavlovian conditioning.

4. What are the main points that the Director wants to impress upon his students?

5. How is social stability achieved and what kind of society is created?

6. How is Henry Ford's deification in the novel linked to Frederick Taylor's scientific management principles?

Brave New World

I

(1) A squat grey building of only thirty-one storeys. Over the main entrance the words, CENTRAL LONDON HATCHERY AND CONDITIONING CENTRE, and, in a shield, the World State's motto, COMMUNITY, IDENTITY, STABILITY.

(2) The enormous room on the ground floor faced towards the north. Cold for all the summer beyond the panes, for all the tropical heat of the room itself, a harsh thin light glared through the windows, hungrily seeking some draped lay figure, some pallid shape of academic goose-flesh, but finding only the glass and nickel and bleakly shining porcelain of a laboratory. The overalls of the workers were white, their hands gloved with a pale corpse-coloured rubber. The light was frozen, dead, a ghost. Only from the yellow barrels of the microscopes did it borrow a certain rich and living substance, lying along the polished tubes like butter, streak after luscious streak in log recession down the work tables.

(3) 'And this,' said the Director opening the door, 'is the Fertilizing Room.'

Bent over their instruments, three hundred Fertilizers were plunged, as the

Director of Hatcheries and Conditioning entered the room, in the scarcely breathing silence, the absentminded, soliloquizing hum or whistle, of absorbed concentration. A troop of newly arrived students, very young, pink and callow, followed nervously, rather abjectly, at the Director's heels. Each of them carried a notebook, in which, whenever the great man spoke, he desperately scribbled. Straight from the horse's mouth. It was a rare privilege. The DHC for Central London always made a point of personally conducting his new students round the various departments.

(4) 'Just to give you a general idea,' he would explain to them. For of course some sort of general idea they must have, if they were to do their work intelligently – though as little of one, if they were to be good and happy members of society, as possible. For particulars, as everyone knows, make for virtue and happiness; generalities are intellectually necessary evils. Not philosophers, but fret-sawyers and stamp collectors compose the backbone of society.

'Tomorrow,' he would add, smiling at them with a slightly menacing geniality, 'you'll be settling down to serious work. You won't have time for generalities. Meanwhile . . .'

Meanwhile, it was a privilege. Straight from the horse's mouth into the notebook. The boys scribbled like mad.

(5) Tall and rather thin but upright, the Director advanced into the room. He had a long chin and big, rather prominent teeth, just covered, when he was not talking, by his full, floridly curved lips. Old, young? 30? 50? 55? It was hard to say. And anyhow the question didn't arise; in this year of stability, A.F. 632, it didn't occur to you to ask it.

(6) 'I shall begin at the beginning,' said the DHC, and the more zealous students recorded his intention in their notebooks: *Begin at the beginning.* 'These,' he waved his hand, 'are the incubators.' And opening an insulated door he showed them racks of numbered test-tubes. 'This week's supply of ova. Kept,' he explained, 'at blood heat; whereas the male gametes,' and here he opened another door, 'have to be kept at thirty-five instead of thirty-seven. Full blood heat sterilizes.' Rams wrapped in thermogene beget no lambs.

(7) Still leaning against the incubators he gave them, while the pencils scurried illegibly across the pages, a brief description of the modern fertilizing process; spoke first, of course, of its surgical introduction – 'the operation undergone voluntarily for the good of Society, not to mention the fact that it carries a bonus amounting to six months' salary'; continued with some account of the technique of preserving the excised ovary alive and actively developing; passed on to a consideration of optimum temperature, salinity, viscosity; referred to the liquor in which the detached and ripened eggs were kept; and leading his charges to the work tables, actually showed them how the liquor was drawn off from the test-tubes; how it was let out drop by drop on to the specially warmed slides of the microscopes; how the eggs which it contained were inspected for abnormalities, counted and transferred to a porous receptacle; how (and he now took them to watch the operation) this receptacle was immersed in a warm bouillon containing free-swimming spermatozoa – at a minimum concentration of 100,000 per cubic centimetre, he insisted; and how, after ten minutes, the container was lifted out of the liquor and its contents re-examined; how, if any of the eggs remained unfertilized, it was again immersed, and, if necessary, yet again; how the fertilized ova went back to the incubators; where the Alphas and the Betas remained until definitely bottled; while the Gammas, Deltas and Epsilons were brought out again, after only thirty-six hours, to undergo Bokanovsky's Process.

(8) 'Bokanovsky's Process,' repeated the Director, and the students underlined the words in their little notebooks.

One egg, one embryo, one adult – normality. But a Bokanovskified egg will bud, will proliferate, will divide. From eight to ninety-six buds, and every bud will grow into a perfectly formed embryo, and every embryo into a full-sized adult. Making ninety-six human beings grow where only one grew before. Progress.

'Essentially,' the DHC concluded, 'Bokanovskification consists of a series of arrests of development. We check the normal growth and, paradoxically enough, the egg responds by budding.'

Responds by budding. The pencils were busy.

He pointed. On a very slowly moving band a rack-full of test-tubes was entering a large metal box, another rack-full was emerging. Machinery faintly purred. It took eight minutes for the tubes to go through, he told them. Eight minutes of hard X-rays being about as much as an egg can stand. A few died; the rest, the least susceptible divided into two; most put out four buds; some eight; all were returned to the incubators, where the buds began to develop; then, after two days, were suddenly chilled, chilled and checked. Two, four, eight, the buds in their turn budded; and having budded were dosed almost to death with alcohol; consequently burgeoned again and having budded – bud out of bud out of bud were thereafter – further arrest being generally fatal – left to develop in peace. By which time the original egg was in a fair way to becoming anything from eight to ninety-six embryos – a prodigious improvement – you will agree on nature. Identical twins – but not in piddling twos and threes as in the old viviparous days, when an egg would sometimes accidentally divide; actually by dozens, by scores at a time.

'Scores,' the Director repeated and flung out his arms, as though he were distributing largesse. 'Scores.'

(9) But one of the students was fool enough to ask where the advantage lay.

'My good boy!' The Director wheeled sharply around on him. 'Can't you *see*? Can't you *see*? ' He raised a hand; his expression was solemn. 'Bokanovsky's Process is one of the major instruments of social stability!'

Major instruments of social stability.

Standard men and women; in uniform batches. The whole of a small factory staffed with the products of a single bokanovskified egg.

'Ninety-six identical twins working ninety-six identical machines!' The voice was almost tremulous with enthusiasm. 'You really know where you are. For the first time in history.' He quoted the planetary motto. 'Community, Identity, Stability.' Grand words. 'If we could bokanovskify indefinitely the whole problem would be solved.'

Solved by standard Gammas, unvarying Deltas, uniform Epsilons. Millions of identical twins. The principle of mass production at last applied to biology.

II

(10) In the Bottling Room all was harmonious bustle and ordered activity. Flaps of fresh sow's peritoneum ready cut to the proper size came shooting up in little lifts from the organ store in the sub-basement. Whizz and then, click! the lift-hatches flew open; the Bottle-Liner had only to reach out a hand, take the flap, insert, smooth-down, and before the lined bottle had to travel out of reach along the endless band, whiz, click! another flap of peritoneum had shot up from the depths, ready to be slipped into yet another bottle, the next of that slow interminable procession on to the band.

Next to the Liners stood the Matriculators. The procession advanced; one by one the eggs were transferred from their test-tubes to the larger containers; deftly the peritoneal lining was slit, the morula dropped into place, the saline solution poured in . . . and already the bottle had passed, and it was the turn of the labellers. Heredity, date of fertilization, membership of Bokanovsky Group – details were transferred from test-tube to bottle. No longer anonymous, but named, identified, the procession marched slowly on; on through an opening in the wall, slowly into the Social Predestination Room.

(11) . . . the sultry darkness into which the students now followed him was visible and crimson, like the darkness of closed eyes on a summer's afternoon. The bulging

flanks of row upon row and tier above tier of bottles glinted with innumerable rubies, and among the rubies moved the dim red spectres of men and women with purple eyes and all the symptoms of lupus. The hum and rattle of machinery faintly stirred the air.

'Give them a few figures, Mr Foster,' said the Director, who was tired of talking.

Mr Foster was only too happy to give them a few figures.

Two hundred and twenty metres long, two hundred wide, ten high. He pointed upwards. Like chickens drinking, the students lifted their eyes towards the distant ceiling.

Three tiers of racks; ground-floor level, first gallery, second gallery.

The spidery steelwork of gallery above gallery faded away in all directions into the dark. Near them, three red ghosts were busily unloading demijohns from a moving staircase.

The escalator from the Social Predestination Room.

Each bottle could be placed on one of fifteen racks, each rack, though you couldn't see it, was a conveyor travelling at the rate of thirty-three and a third centimetres an hour. Two hundred and sixty-seven days at eight metres a day. Two thousand one hundred and thirty-six metres in all. One circuit of the cellar at ground level, one on the first gallery, half on the second, and on the two hundred and sixty-seventh morning, daylight in the Decanting Room. Independent existence – so called.

(12)　'But in the interval,' Mr Foster concluded, 'we've managed to do a lot to them. Oh, a very great deal.' His laugh was knowing and triumphant.

'That's the spirit I like,' said the Director once more. 'Let's walk round. You tell them everything Mr Foster.'

Mr Foster duly told them.

Told them of the growing embryo on its bed of peritoneum. Told them of the tests for sex carried out in the neighbourhood of Metre 200. Explained the system of labelling – a T for the males, a circle for the females and for those who were destined to become freemartins a question mark, black on a white ground.

He rubbed his hands. For of, course, they didn't content themselves with merely hatching embryos; any cow could do that.

'We also predestinate and condition. We decant our babies as socialized human beings, as Alphas or Epsilons, as future sewerage workers or future . . . ' He was going to say future World Controllers, but correcting himself, said 'future Directors of Hatcheries' instead.

The DHC acknowledged the compliment with a smile.

(13)　They were passing Metre 320 on Rack 11. A young Beta-minus mechanic was busy with a screw-driver and spanner on the blood-surrogate pump of a passing bottle. The hum of the electric motor deepened by fractions of a tone as he turned the nuts. Down, down . . . A final twist, a glance at the revolution counter, and he was done. He moved two paces down the line and began the same process on the next pump.

'Reducing the number of revolutions per minute,' Mr Foster explained. 'The surrogate goes round slower; therefore passes through the lung at longer intervals; therefore gives the embryo less oxygen. Nothing like oxygen-shortage for keeping an embryo below par.' Again he rubbed his hands.

'But why do you want to keep the embryo below par?' asked an ingenuous student.

'Ass!' said the Director, breaking a long silence. 'Hasn't it occurred to you that an Epsilon embryo must have an Epsilon environment as well as an Epsilon heredity?'

It evidently hadn't occurred to him. He was covered with confusion.

'The lower the caste,' said Mr Foster, 'the shorter the oxygen.' The first organ affected was the brain. After that the skeleton. At 70 per cent of normal oxygen you got dwarfs. At less than 70, eyeless monsters.

'Who are no use at all,' concluded Mr Foster.'

'. . . in Epsilons,' said Mr Foster very justly, 'we don't need human intelligence.'

Didn't need and didn't get it. But though the Epsilon mind was more mature at 10, the Epsilon body was not fit to work till 18. Long years of superfluous and wasted immaturity. If the physical development could be speeded up till it was as quick, say, as a cow's, what an enormous saving to the Community!

'Enormous!' murmured the students. Mr Foster's enthusiasm was infectious.

(14) Their wanderings through the crimson twilight had brought them to the neighbourhood of Metre 170 on Rack 9. From this point onwards Rack 9 was enclosed and the bottles performed the remainder of their journey in a kind of tunnel, interrupted here and there by openings two or three metres wide.

'Heat conditioning,' said Mr Foster.

Hot tunnels alternated with cool tunnels. Coolness was wedded to discomfort in the form of hard X-rays. By the time they were decanted the embryos had a horror of cold. They were predestined to emigrate to the tropics, to be miners and acetate silk spinners and steel workers. Later on their minds would be made to endorse the judgement of their bodies. 'We condition them to thrive on heat,' concluded Mr Foster. Our colleagues upstairs will teach them to love it.'

'And that,' put in the Director sententiously, 'that is the secret of happiness and virtue – liking what you've *got* to do. All conditioning aims at that: making people like their inescapable social destiny.'

'. . . the Director . . . looked at his watch. 'Ten to three,' he said. 'We must go up to the Nurseries before the children have finished their afternoon sleep.'

III

(15) Mr Foster was left in the Decanting Room. The DHC and his students stepped into the nearest lift and were carried up to the fifth floor.

INFANT NURSERIES. NEO-PAVLOVIAN CONDITIONING ROOMS, announced the notice board.

The Director opened the door. They were in a large bare room, very bright and sunny; for the whole of the southern wall was a single window. Half a dozen nurses, trousered and jacketed in the regulation white viscose-lined uniform, their hair aseptically hidden under their white caps, were engaged in setting out bowls of roses in a long row across the floor. Big bowls, packed tight with blossom. Thousands of petals, ripe-blown and silky smooth, like the cheeks of innumerable little cherubs, but of cherubs, in that bright light, not exclusively pink and Aryan, but also luminously Chinese, also Mexican, also apoplectic with too much blowing of celestial trumpets, also pale as death, pale with the posthumous whiteness of marble.

(16) The nurses stiffened to attention as the DHC came in.

'Set out the books,' he said curtly.

In silence the nurses obeyed his command. Between the rose bowls the books were duly set out – a row of nursery quartos opened invitingly each at some gaily coloured image of a beast or fish or bird.

'Now bring in the children.'

They hurried out of the room and returned in a minute or two, each pushing a kind of dumb waiter laden, on all of its wire-netted shelves, with 8-month-old babies, all exactly alike (a Bokanovsky Group, it was evident) and all (since their caste was Delta) dressed in khaki.

'Put them down on the floor.'

The infants were unloaded.

'Now turn them so they can see the flowers and books.'

(17) Turned, the babies at once fell silent, then began to crawl towards those clusters of sleek colours, those shapes so gay and brilliant on the white pages. As they approached, the sun came out of momentary eclipse behind a cloud. The roses flamed up as though with a sudden passion from within; a new and profound significance seemed to suffuse the shining pages of the books. From the ranks of the

crawling babies came little squeals of excitement, gurgles and twitterings of pleasure.

The Director rubbed his hands. 'Excellent!' he said. 'It might almost have been done on purpose.'

The swiftest crawlers were already at their goal. Small hands reached out uncertainly, touched, grasped, unpetalling the transfigured roses, crumpling the illuminated pages of the books. The Director waited until all were happily busy. Then, 'Watch carefully,' he said. And lifting his hand, he gave the signal.

The Head Nurse, who was standing by a switchboard at the other end of the room, pressed down a little lever.

There was a violent explosion. Shriller and ever shriller, a siren shrieked. Alarm bells maddeningly sounded.

The children started, screamed; their faces were distorted with terror.

'And now,' the Director shouted (for the noise was deafening), 'now we proceed to rub in the lesson with a mild electric shock.'

He waved his hand again, and the Head Nurse pressed a second lever. The screaming of the babies suddenly changed its tone. There was something desperate, almost insane, about the sharp spasmodic yelps to which they now gave utterance. Their little bodies twitched and stiffened; their limbs moved jerkily as if to the tug of unseen wires.

We can electrify that whole strip of floor,' bawled the Director in explanation. 'But that's enough,' he signalled to the nurse.

The explosions ceased, the bells stopped ringing, the shriek of the siren died down from tone to tone into silence. The stiffly twitching bodies relaxed, and what had become the sob and yelp of infant maniacs broadened out once more into a normal howl of terror.

'Offer them the flowers and books again.'

The nurses obeyed; but at the approach of the roses, at the mere sight of those gaily-coloured images of pussy and cock-a-doodle-doo and baa-baa black sheep, the infants shrank away in horror; the volume of their howling suddenly increased.

'Observe,' said the Director triumphantly, 'observe.'

Books and loud noises, flowers and electric shocks – already in the infant mind these couples were compromisingly linked; and after two hundred repetitions of the same or a similar lesson would be wedded indissolubly. What man had joined, nature is powerless to put asunder.

(18)   'They'll grow up with what the psychologists used to call an "instinctive" hatred of books and flowers. Reflexes unalterably conditioned. They'll be safe from books and botany all their lives.' The Director turned to his nurses. 'Take them away.'

One of the students held up his hand; and though he could see quite well why you couldn't have lower-caste people wasting the Community's time over books, and that there was always the risk of their reading something which might undesirably decondition one of their reflexes, yet . . . well, he couldn't understand about the flowers. Why go to the trouble of making it psychologically impossible for Deltas to like flowers?

Patiently the DHC explained. If the children were made to scream at the sight of a rose, that was on the grounds of high economic policy. Not very long ago (a century or thereabouts), Gammas, Deltas, even Epsilons, had been conditioned to like flowers – flowers in particular and wild nature in general. The idea was to make them want to be going out at every opportunity, and so compel them to consume transport.

'And didn't they consume transport?' asked the student.

'Quite a lot,' the DHC replied. 'But nothing else.'

Primroses and landscapes, he pointed out, have one grave defect: they are gratuitous. A love of nature keeps no factories busy. It was decided to abolish the love of nature, at any rate among the lower classes; to abolish the love of nature, but *not* the tendency to consume transport. For of course it was essential that they should keep on going to the country, even though they hated it. The problem was to find an economically sounder reason for consuming transport than a mere affection for primroses and landscapes. It was duly found.

'We condition the masses to hate the country,' concluded the Director. 'But simultaneously we condition them to love all country sports. At the same time, we see to it that all country sports shall entail the use of elaborate apparatus. So that they consume manufactured articles as well as transport. Hence those electric shocks.'

'I see,' said the student, and was silent, lost in admiration.

IV

(19) There was a silence; then, clearing his throat, 'Once upon a time,' the Director began, 'while Our Ford was still on earth, there was a little boy called Reuben Rabinovitch. Reuben was the child of Polish-speaking parents.' The Director interrupted himself. 'You know what Polish is, I suppose?'

'A dead language.'

'Like French and German,' added another student, officiously showing off his learning.

He returned to Little Reuben – to Little Reuben in whose room, one evening, by an oversight, his father and mother . . . happened to leave the radio turned on.

While the child was asleep, a broadcast programme from London suddenly started to come through; and the next morning, to the astonishment of his . . . [parents] . . . , Little Reuben woke up repeating word for word a long lecture by that curious old writer ('one of the very few whose works have been permitted to come down to us'), George Bernard Shaw, who was speaking, according to a well-authenticated tradition, about his own genius.

'The principle of sleep-teaching or hypnopaedia, had been discovered.' The DHC made an impressive pause.

The principle had been discovered; but many, many years were to elapse before the principle was usefully applied.

(20) 'The case of Little Reuben occurred only twenty-three years after Our Ford's first T-model was put on the market.' (Here the Director made a sign of the T on his stomach and all the students reverently followed suit.) Furiously the students scribbled, *Hypnopaedia, first used officially in A.F. 214. Why not before?*

'The early experimenters,' the DHC was saying, 'were on the wrong track. They thought that hypnopaedia could be made an instrument of intellectual education . . . Whereas, if they'd only started on *moral* education,' said the Director, leading the way towards the door. The students followed him, desperately scribbling, as they walked and all the way up in the lift. 'Moral education, which ought never, in any circumstances, to be rational.'

'Silence, silence,' whispered a loud speaker as they stepped out at the fourteenth floor, and 'Silence, silence,' the trumpet mouths indefatigably repeated at intervals down every corridor. The students and even the Director rose automatically to the tips of their toes. They were Alphas, of course; but even Alphas have been well conditioned. 'Silence, silence.' All the air of the fourteenth floor was sibilant with the categorical imperative.

Fifty yards of tiptoeing brought them to a door which the Director cautiously opened. They stepped over the threshold into the twilight of a shuttered dormitory. Eighty cots stood in a row against the wall. There was a sound of light regular breathing and a continuous murmur, as of very faint voices remotely whispering.

A nurse rose as they entered and came to attention before the Director.

'What's the lesson this afternoon?' he asked.

'We had Elementary Sex for the first forty minutes,' she answered. 'But now it's switched over to Elementary Class Consciousness.'

The Director walked slowly down the long line of cots. Rosy and relaxed with sleep, eighty little boys and girls lay softly breathing. There was a whisper under every pillow. The DHC halted and, bending over one of the little beds, listened attentively.

'Elementary Class Consciousness, did you say? Let's have it repeated a little louder by the trumpet.'

At the end of the room a loud speaker projected from the wall. The Director walked up to it and pressed a switch.

'. . . all wear green,' said a soft but very distinct voice, beginning in the middle of a sentence, 'and Delta children wear khaki. Oh no, I don't want to play with Delta children. And Epsilons are still worse. They're too stupid to be able to read or write. Besides, they wear black, which is such a beastly colour. I'm *so* glad I'm a Beta.'

There was a pause and the voice began again.

'Alpha children wear grey. They work much harder than we do, because they're so frightfully clever. I'm really awfully glad I'm Beta, because I don't work so hard. And then we are much better than the Gammas and the Deltas. Gammas are stupid. They all wear green, and Delta children wear khaki. Oh no, I don't want to play with Delta children. And Epsilons are still worse. They're too stupid to be able . . .'

(21) The Director pushed back the switch. The voice was silent. Only its thin ghost continued to mutter from beneath the eighty pillows.

'They'll have that repeated forty or fifty times more before they wake; then again on Thursday, and again on Saturday. A hundred and twenty times three times a week for thirty months. After which they go on to a more advanced lesson.'

Roses and electric shocks, the khaki of Deltas and a whiff of asafoetida – wedded indissolubly before the child can speak. But wordless conditioning is crude and wholesale; cannot bring home the finer distinctions, cannot inculcate the more complex courses of behaviour. For that there must be words, but words without reason. In brief, hypnopaedia.

'The greatest moralizing and socializing force of all time.'

The students took it down in their books. Straight from the horse's mouth.

V

(22) It was a small factory of lighting-sets for helicopters, a branch of the Electrical Equipment Corporation. They were met on the roof itself (for that circular letter of recommendation from the Controller was magical in its effects) by the Chief Technician and the Human Element Manager. They walked downstairs into the factory.

'Each process,' explained the Human Element Manager, 'is carried out, as far as possible, by a single Bokanovsky group.'

(23) And, in effect, eighty-three almost noseless black brachycephalic Deltas were cold-pressing. The fifty-six four-spindle chucking and turning machines were being manipulated by fifty-six aquiline and ginger Gammas. One hundred and seven heat-conditioned Epsilon Senegalese were working in the foundry. Thirty-two Delta females, long-headed, sandy, with narrow pelvises, all within 20 millimetres of 1 metre 69 centimetres tall, were cutting screws. In the assembling room, the dynamos were being put together by two sets of Gamma-Plus dwarfs. The two low work tables faced one another; between them crawled the conveyor with its load of separate parts; forty-seven blond heads were confronted by forty-seven brown ones. Forty-seven snubs by forty-seven hooks; forty-seven receding by forty-seven prognathous. The completed mechanisms were inspected by eighteen identical curly auburn girls in Gamma green, packed in crates by thirty-four short-legged, left-handed male Delta-Minuses, and loaded into the waiting trucks and lorries by sixty-three blue-eyed, flaxen and freckled Epsilon Semi-Morons.

(24) 'O brave new world . . .' By some malice of his memory the Savage found himself repeating Miranda's words. 'O brave new world that has such people in it.'

'And I assure you,' the Human Element Manager concluded, as they left the factory, 'we hardly ever have any trouble with our workers. We always find . . .'

But the Savage had suddenly broken away from his companions and was violently retching behind a clump of laurels, as though the solid earth had been a helicopter in an air pocket.

The case is taken from Aldous Huxley, *Brave New World*, Collins, London, 1932. Abridged from pp. 19–63 and 161–2.

12.4 REV: Question search

Objective

❏ To encourage students to revise the key facts and concepts associated with Chapter 12 scientific management.

Introduction

The purpose of this test is to ensure that students read the chapter thoroughly, and are fully conversant with its content. On this occasion, you are provided with answers, and are required to find the relevent questions.

Procedure

Your instructor will brief you on how the test will be conducted.

Test

Answers	Questions
1. 1.85	
2. 5	
3. 12.5	
4. 18	
5. 20–50	
6. 92	
7. 350	
8. Bethlehem	
9. Billancourt	
10. Bunker	
11. Midvale	

Answers	**Questions**
12. Philadelphia	
13. Watertown	
14. Winslow	
15. 1856	
16. 1898	
17. 1905	
18. 1911	
19. 1914	
20. Best-known-way-at-present	
21. Betterment-of-work	
22. Initiative-and-incentive	
23. Fatigue	
24. Field system	
25. Functional	
26. Mental revolution	
27. One-best-way	
28. Ergonomics	
29. Standardization	
30. Systematic soldiering	
31. Therbligs	

Chapter 13

Technology and work organization

13.1 Large group activity: Who controls the furnace?
13.2 Small group activity: The story of the pig
13.3 Prepared task: Plastic inserts
13.4 Review: That was then, this is now

13.1 LGA: Who controls the furnace?

Objectives

❑   To explore the nature of management and organizational choices with respect to the operation of technology in a work setting.

❑   To expose the limits of 'technological determinist' arguments.

Introduction

It seems obvious to claim that the technology of production shapes the nature of the work activity of those involved directly in its operation. What is perhaps less obvious, however, is the way in which the nature of work activity is also shaped by management decisions concerning specific task allocations and responsibilities across different individuals and different occupational groups. In the exercise that follows, you are invited to consider those management decisions, the constraints imposed by technology and the implications of particular decisions in a given setting.

Procedure

Step 1   Working on your own, read the following case description, *Who controls the furnace?* Make brief notes for yourself in response to the analysis questions that follow the case description.

Step 2   Working in small buzz groups with two or three members, compare your answers to the three analysis questions. Be prepared to feed some of your conclusions back to your instructor.

Step 3   Debriefing and open discussion.

Who controls the furnace?

Consider yourself a member of the management team in a company that manufactures forged components for the oil and aircraft industries. The metallurgical quality of your forgings is critical to your ability to compete in this business. Quality depends on a number of factors, but the key to quality lies in the accurate operation of the heat treatment furnaces.

Components for heat treatment are loaded into the furnaces by plant operators, who have traditionally adjusted the temperature and other controls manually, following the process instructions relevant to the particular components they are making. Your plant operators are experienced, semi-skilled men who are working within their capacity.

However, following the advice of your process engineers, and being aware of what your main competitors are doing, you have acquired a new computer-controlled furnace. Process instructions for this system can now all be entered through a keyboard at a control terminal, without the need for manual intervention. Your suppliers are providing the basic equipment. Your plant engineers still have the task of designing the linkages with the computer system and the furnaces and with other plant operations.

One central question that the plant engineers feel they have resolved is: Will the furnace control task using the new control terminals be carried out by the plant operators, or by plant technicians? Your plant technicians are younger than the plant operators and therefore have less process experience, but they all have formal technical qualifications and are employed on a wide range of analytical and technical work. The plant engineers are recommending that the control terminals should be the responsibility of the technicians because this task now requires more skill than the operators will be able to handle, and because this approach would offer greater management control over the manufacturing operation.

A majority of other managers in the company agree with the solution proposed by the plant engineers, to let the technicians run the new computer control system for the furnaces. Some managers, however, have disagreed. They argue that this would leave the plant operators underutilized, would reduce their motivation and commitment and would limit their understanding of the process thereby restricting their ability to respond effectively to emergencies. These difficulties would be overcome if existing plant operators were trained to use the new control systems.

- Which solution would you support?
- For what reasons would you support that approach?
- Why did you reject the alternative?

This case exercise is based on an illustration used in: David Boddy and David Buchanan, *The Technical Change Audit: Action for Results*, Manpower Services Commission, Sheffield, Module 4, 1987, p. 12.

13.2 SGA: The story of the pig

Objectives

❏ To develop understanding of the socio-technical systems approach to organizational analysis.

❏ To examine the potential of a socio-technical systems analysis for identifying practical organizational changes.

Introduction

There is a well-established research tradition which draws on the concept of the organization as an *open socio-technical system*. This term is a daunting one to many students, and much of the terminology associated with this perspective is similarly awkward. The perspective, however, is a powerful one and has remained influential for half a century, since the approach was first formulated by consultants working with the Tavistock Institute of Human Relations in London in the mid- to late 1940s. This exercise is designed to offer an illustration of the potential of a socio-technical systems analysis. *The story of the pig* is a true one, not fictitious.

Procedure

Step 1 Read *The story of the pig* which follows.

Step 2 Working on your own, make notes in answer to the questions that follow the case description.

Step 3 Working in syndicate groups of three to five members, nominate a spokesperson and prepare a syndicate response to the case analysis questions.

Step 4 Each group presents their answers to the class as a whole, with a few minutes after each presentation for criticisms, questions and suggestions.

The story of the pig

In one of the slaughterhouses of a meat products company, a dispute broke out between a group of slaughtermen and their foreman, during which the slaughtermen threatened to strike unless the foreman was immediately sent home. Management immediately agreed to their demand without an inquiry into the rights and wrongs of the parties' respective claims. The case eventually went to arbitration and, not surprisingly, the arbitrator asked why the foreman had been so summarily treated. The senior management replied, 'well it's the question of the pig'.

Apparently, in response to consumer demand for lean bacon, a particular type of pig had been bred for the company's farms which produced the maximum lean meat for the minimum cost. To produce an appropriate flow of pigs to meet levels and fluctuations in demand, a particular breeding cycle and rearing schedule was followed on the farms, so that the animals reached their optimum condition immediately before their planned despatch to the slaughterhouse. Because calculation of production costs and consumer preference demanded immediate slaughter of the pigs, after a fixed number of weeks' rearing, a complicated despatch system had theoretically eliminated the desirability or necessity of large stock pens at the slaughterhouse, the animals moving, almost on a conveyor belt, from farm to slaughterhouse and ultimately to the consumer.

In theory, this system combined the production of the type of bacon demanded by the customer with an admirably tight control on costs of production and overheads. In practice, however, it gave the slaughtermen the whip hand. For, if they caused a bottleneck in the throughput of pigs from slaughterhouse to customer, its repercussions were felt right back on the farm. Only a certain number of pigs could be kept alive in the stockyard and these would go rapidly past their peak and start putting on undesirable and expensive fat. The same could be said of the carefully scheduled pigs in delivery vans on the roads of Britain, who had no place to go except back to the farms where they could only consume costly fodder, producing valueless fat and utilizing accommodation required by their replacements. At the same time, constraints on stockholding, due to the perishability of the product, afforded management no alternative flexibility in maintaining market supply, if their slaughterhouse was out of operation, while the nature of the market demand and competition meant that sales lost in one period were unlikely to be recovered in another.

A shut-down in the slaughterhouse thus meant irrecoverable losses in the product market, and hence direct implications for profitability. Thus, a product was designed that unintentionally delivered negotiating power straight into the hands of a strategically placed group of workers. But, as management sadly acknowledged, 'who would consider that industrial relations specialists should have been involved in the design of a pig and the successive scheduling arrangements?'

This case exercise is drawn from Karen Legge, *Power, Innovation and Problem Solving in Personnel Management*, McGraw-Hill, London, 1978, p. 43.

The story of the pig: analysis questions

1. Explain how the slaughterhouse can be viewed as an *open socio-technical system*, and in particular explain the use of *the organic analogy* in this respect.

2. What are the main components of the technical system in the slaughterhouse?

3. What are the main components of the social system in the slaughterhouse?

4. Explain how the management problems arise from the relationships between the technical and social sub-systems. How could these problems be addressed?

5. Many commentators argue that technology is not neutral, that it can be used as a political tool. Explain how the story of the pig supports that argument.

13.3 PREP: Plastic inserts

Objectives

❑ To develop understanding of the practical application of the *work organization approach* to job design.

❑ To develop understanding of the strengths and weaknesses in this approach.

Introduction

Some work is boring. Managers often claim that the nature of the task is such that few meaningful changes can be made to reduce boredom levels. It may also be the case that the kinds of changes that would make a difference would be too expensive and raise costs to uncompetitive levels. In this exercise, you are invited to consider the problems of a specific work location, and to apply the Tavistock *work organization approach* in an attempt to find solutions.

Procedure

Step 1 Ensure that you are familiar with Chapter 13 in *ORBIT*, dealing with technology and work organization. The sections on the characteristics of mass production and socio-technical system design are the most relevant.

Step 2 Read the *Plastic inserts* case which follows, and prepare a response for the consultancy assignment.

Step 3 Produce a consulting report according to your instructor's requirements. You may in addition be asked to present your conclusions in a class session.

Plastic inserts

The factory makes plastic 'inserts' for boxes of biscuits and chocolates. The inserts are actually made on vacuum forming machines. There are fifteen such vacuum forming machines in operation, all similar in design and operation, but all capable of being set up to manufacture a range of different types and sizes of inserts. Once set up and running, however, to change a machine over from one product to another takes a maintenance crew about an hour and a half.

A roll of plastic sheet of the correct colour is first loaded onto the back of the vacuum former. The sheet is then pulled over a special metal former, and is heated as it does so. The warm plastic sheet is then drawn into the former by evacuating the air between former and sheet through small holes in the former. The plastic sheet thus takes on the shape of the design of the former. Typically up to a dozen plastic 'inserts' for a box of chocolates or biscuits can be made on one draw in this way, depending on the size of each insert. The sheet is then passed off the machine. Half a dozen sheets are then 'nested' before being passed, by hand, through a guillotine which cuts the individual inserts from their sheets. The individual inserts are then separated from the scrap plastic, from around the edges, and are placed manually in cardboard boxes for despatch to customers.

The machines are set up and loaded with plastic roll by one of the two maintenance crews, each with four members, including a crew leader (who is the most experienced member of the crew). The plastic rolls are manufactured in a separate production area adjacent to the vacuum forming bays. Each vacuum forming machine is operated by three women. One takes the formed sheets from the machine and nests them, and generally observes the operation of the machine in case a problem arises and maintenance have to be called. The second passes the nested sheets through the guillotine and removes the scrap. The third packs the inserts into cardboard boxes.

There are three supervisors, one for each bank of five machines. The supervisors are machine operators who have been promoted and thus understand the work. Their main jobs are to make sure that the machines are properly loaded and staffed, to ensure that production targets are fulfilled and to liaise with maintenance when problems arise. The supervisors allow the machine operators to rotate roles if they become bored with any one particular task.

Counting supervisors, maintenance crews and machine operators, there should be fifty-six people on each of the two shifts. However, there is a very high rate of absenteeism among machine operators in particular, and management actually employ fifty-five machine operators on each shift to make sure that there are enough staff available to run the machines. The supervisors spend a lot of their time early in each shift making sure that enough operators are allocated to each of the machines. There is also some absenteeism among maintenance staff, and this sometimes leads to delays in machine set-up and repair, and this in turn leads to lost production. The past twelve months have in addition seen a steady rise in the volume of scrap material being produced. This is strange, because the insert nests are guillotined in a predetermined manner which machine operators cannot directly influence, and management are puzzled as to the sources and causes of the increased scrap level. Automation of the machine set-up and operation tasks would be difficult and prohibitively expensive. The absenteeism is also expensive, but is much less costly than investment in new automated equipment would be.

The consulting assignment

You have been asked to advise management on what action, if any, they can take to reduce the absenteeism problems with respect to machine operators in particular, and perhaps with respect to maintenance personnel as well.

> How would you diagnose the problems here? Base your diagnosis on the work of Charles Walker and Robert Guest.
>
> How would you address the problems here? Base your recommendations on the *work organization approach* to job design.
>
> Conclude your consulting report with a realistic assessment of the strengths and weaknesses of your proposals.

13.4 REV: That was then, this is now

Objectives

❑ To test understanding of the concept of *mass production characteristics* using a specific illustration.

❑ To test understanding of *socio-technical system design* concepts introduced in Chapter 13 of *ORBIT*.

Introduction

A focus on 'leading edge' practice with respect to technology and work organization has two potential drawbacks. First, we tend to forget how work has been organized in the past and are thus in danger of losing an appreciation of the nature of progress and development in this sphere. Second, we may also forget that many organizations still design jobs and offer work experiences based on traditional, 'outdated' thinking and practice. This *review* therefore begins with a review of the 'traditional' approach to work design and with an appreciation of mass production characteristics. The extent to which these methods are applied in shops and factories today remains an open question. However, this *review* then offers a sharp contrast in inviting an analysis of changed working practice in a modern packaging company.

Procedure

Step 1   Remind yourself of the six characteristics of mass production identified by Charles Walker and Robert Guest and described in Chapter 13 in *ORBIT*. Remind yourself also of the health and behavioural consequences of mass production described by Arthur Kornhauser.

Step 2   Watch the first fifteen minutes of the film, *Modern Times*, made in 1936 and starring Charlie Chaplin.

Step 3   Identify as you watch this section of the film as many illustrations of mass production characteristics as possible. Are any of the six characteristics identified by Walker and Guest *not* evident in this film?

Step 4   Note the behaviours of the main characters in the film: assembly line workers, the relief man, the line supervisor. How can you explain some of their behaviours using Kornhauser's findings?

Step 5   Read the following description of team-based methods at Smith, Kline & French Laboratories. Answer the two questions that follow the case description.

Step 6   Instructor's debriefing.

Smith, Kline & French Laboratories

Kroll (1989) describes the introduction of team-based methods at Smith, Kline & French Laboratories which manufacture 'blister packs' for pharmaceutical products. Due to the convenience and popularity of such packaging, extra manufacturing capacity has been required to meet a steady growth in demand since the mid-1980s. The traditional packaging line required three groups of people. First, supervisors and direct labour, responsible for effective equipment operation, reporting to the Blister Packaging Manager. Second, engineers, responsible for changeovers, equipment settings and fault correction, reporting to the Engineering Group Manager. Third, service operators, responsible for ensuring an adequate supply of materials and for cleaning lines between different runs, reporting to the Packaging Services Manager. The Blister Packaging Manager and Packaging Services Manager reported to the Packaging Manager. Each of the three groups had its own separate responsibilities, but they were interdependent. When operators identified a minor modification to improve line efficiency, they had to get an engineer to implement it. Additional materials could not be acquired without a service operator. Breakdowns similarly could not be dealt with until an engineer was free. This combination of interdependence and separation of responsibility led to tension and frequent arguments. The managers each had their different objectives and priorities too. The organization structure inhibited efficiency gains, and the company started to look at other approaches.

As the company identified these problems in 1987, a new high speed blister packaging line was being introduced. The decision was made to run this with a line team – a small group of highly trained operators with all the skills required to carry out the job. The team, with a leader and four members reporting to the Packaging Manager, became responsible for operating the equipment, carrying out in-process checks, performing equipment changeovers, and for correcting minor faults. The line team was responsible for everything except major breakdowns. The retraining involved a two-month programme which covered machinery, materials, documentation and team development. The team leader was also put through a leadership skills course. The total cost of the training programme was £17,000. The resultant output was 2.6 times better than previously obtained from equivalent lines. Management felt this was due to a high level of motivation and to integrated team effort. The experiment on this one line was subsequently extended throughout the blister packaging department with similar performance improvements.

1. Construct a socio-technical analysis of the traditional packaging line approach. Identify in this analysis the extent to which the *psychological requirements of job content* are met with respect to direct labour on the packaging line.

2. Construct a contrasting socio-technical analysis of the new packaging line approach. Identify in this analysis how the *psychological requirements of job content* are met, again with respect to direct labour.

Chapter 14

Advanced technology and work organization

14.1 Large group activity: The 'pro-caution' debate
14.2 Small group activity: McDonaldization
14.3 Prepared task: The head office automation project
14.4 Review: Join the halves

14.1 LGA: The 'pro-caution' debate

Objectives

❑ To expose the main dimensions of the debate concerning the benefits and the drawbacks of technological innovation in a social and in an organizational context.

❑ To offer an opportunity for students to argue for and support a side of the argument contrary to their current values and beliefs.

Introduction

Some commentators, pointing to lack of economic growth and international competitiveness, argue that social and organizational constraints impede technological progress in ways that are disadvantageous to us individually and collectively. Looking further at the 'pro-technology' lobby, it is easy to point to cases where technological advance has improved both living conditions in general and contributed also in significant ways to improved working conditions and quality of working life. Many other commentators, however, have argued for the existence of a 'cultural lag'; advances in technology occur faster than our ability to assimilate such advances effectively into society. It follows that we can also expect to find 'organizational lag'; our organizations need time to learn how to adapt to new technologies and to use them effectively. Looking further at the 'caution' lobby, it is easy to point to cases where technological advance has led to a deterioration in living conditions, and has contributed in significant ways to the deskilling and dehumanization of work and even to loss of employment opportunities. Our individual, organizational and social responses to advances in technology must therefore be tempered by a consideration of a wide range of factors, and by a broad-ranging reflection on the nature of the potential implications. In this exercise, you are invited to consider those factors in an active and, we hope, entertaining manner. We wish to invite you to take part in a *'pro-caution debate'*, in which half the group argue for the 'pro-technology' perspective, and half argue for a 'caution' perspective. The motions before you are:

The pro-case   Technological advance is both inevitable and desirable, and while we can anticipate teething problems with innovations this is not an argument for impeding or delaying beneficial developments.

The caution case Technological advances generate unpredictable consequences and we must adopt a cautious, analytical approach to implementation, ensuring that we understand the social and organizational implications before proceeding.

Procedure

Step 1 Your instructor will select eight individuals at random. Four of these individuals will form *the pro-team* and will argue and defend the pro-case; the other four will form *the caution-team* and will argue and defend the caution case. In allocating the eight people to the two teams, your instructor will ask individuals to consider joining the team which will present the argument *contrary* to their own current views. Once formed, the pro- and caution-teams proceed to their syndicate rooms to consider and prepare their briefs.

Step 2 Your instructor will select a further four individuals at random. This group forms *the journalist team*. The journalists once selected proceed to their syndicate room to consider and prepare their brief.

Step 3 Your instructor will select a *chairperson* for the debate. The instructor can take this role, but it is more useful and entertaining for a member of the class to hold this responsibility. The chairperson once selected retires to consider and prepare his or her brief.

Step 4 While the debating and journalist teams and chairperson work on their briefs, the debate audience consider, in buzz groups of two to four people, their own briefing.

Step 5 Once all parties are ready, the debate can begin. The manner in which the debate is conducted is determined by the chairperson, and can take several different forms.

Step 6 When the debate has been drawn to a close by the chairperson, the journalist team retires to its syndicate room for a few minutes to consider and prepare a summary report. While they are doing this, the room used for the debate can be tidied back to its usual format, as appropriate.

Step 7 The journalists present their report on the debate, summarizing the arguments, and giving their assessment of the outcome with respect to which case they felt was presented and supported better.

The audience's briefing

You are a member of an audience invited specially to listen to and to participate in a debate on the social and organizational role of technological advance. The motions that you will hear presented and defended are:

The pro-case   Technological advance is both inevitable and desirable, and while we can anticipate teething problems with innovations this is not an argument for impeding or delaying beneficial developments.

The caution case   Technological advances generate unpredictable consequences and we must adopt a cautious, analytical approach to implementation, ensuring that we understand the social and organizational implications before proceeding.

Each side of the debate will be presented and defended by a team of hand-picked experts in the subject. However, this is a topic on which you have your own strong views and convictions, based on wide reading and on personal experience. While the two teams are preparing themselves for the debate, you have an opportunity to consider questions to which you would like answers in this area. Consider the following:

- What questions, problems, issues would you like to raise with the pro-team?
- What questions, problems, issues would you like to raise with the caution-team?
- What general questions or issues would you like the two teams to address?

Generate these questions in the following way:

- Work in buzz groups of two to four members.
- Generate questions that you think are of general, topical interest.
- Generate questions that you think are particularly controversial or provocative.
- Write each question clearly on a separate sheet of paper.

The journalists will collect your questions from you before the debate, and discuss with you how you would like them presented to the two teams.

The pro-team briefing

You are a member of an audience invited specially to debate your perspective on the social and organizational role of technological advance. The motion that your team will present and defend is:

The pro-case   Technological advance is both inevitable and desirable, and while we can anticipate teething problems with innovations this is not an argument for impeding or delaying beneficial developments.

You will meet and discuss with a debating team that will oppose this motion. The debate will be chaired, and a team of journalists has also been invited to attend the debate and to report on it and assess the outcome. In addition to discussing the issue with the opposing team, you may be asked to respond to questions from the audience. This aspect of the debate is under the control of the chairperson.

Your team now has some time, before the debate takes place, to decide on the main elements in your case, how you wish to present the case and also how the four members of the team are going to present it and deal with the subsequent discussion.

The debate will take place before a specially invited audience, chosen for their knowledge and strong views on this subject. Your team may be invited to respond to questions from the audience, directly or through the chairperson. Some questions may be directed at your team in particular, some questions may be directed at the two teams in general.

In deciding how to present your case, consider the following issues:

- Make the case as convincing, as powerful, as compelling as possible.
- Use where possible current examples, illustrations and evidence in support of your case.
- Be entertaining where possible and appropriate (you need to keep the audience awake).
- Be as provocative and controversial as you feel appropriate in the circumstances (you need to keep the chairperson on his or her toes).

The conduct of the debate will be managed by a chairperson, who will speak to you beforehand, and give you any special instructions about how the debate will proceed.

The caution-team briefing

You are a member of a team invited specially to debate your perspective on the social and organizational role of technological advance. The motion that your team will present and defend is:

The caution case Technological advances generate unpredictable consequences and we must adopt a cautious, analytical approach to implementation, ensuring that we understand the social and organizational implications before proceeding.

You will meet and discuss with a debating team that will oppose this motion. The debate will be chaired, and a team of journalists has also been invited to attend the debate and to report on it and assess the outcome. In addition to discussing the issue with the opposing team, you may be asked to respond to questions from the audience. This aspect of the debate is under the control of the chairperson.

Your team now has some time, before the debate takes place, to decide on the main elements in your case, how you wish to present the case and also how the four members of the team are going to present it and deal with the subsequent discussion.

The debate will take place before a specially invited audience, chosen for their knowledge and strong views on this subject. Your team may be invited to respond to questions from the audience, directly or through the chairperson. Some questions may be directed at your team in particular, some questions may be directed at the two teams in general.

In deciding how to present your case, consider the following issues:

- Make the case as convincing, as powerful, as compelling as possible.

- Use where possible current examples, illustrations and evidence in support of your case.

- Be entertaining where possible and appropriate (you need to keep the audience awake).

- Be as provocative and controversial as you feel appropriate in the circumstances (you need to keep the chairperson on his or her toes).

The conduct of the debate will be managed by a chairperson, who will speak to you beforehand, and give you any special instructions about how the debate will proceed.

The journalists' briefing

You are a well-known freelance journalist, one of four invited to join and to report on an expert debate on the social and organizational role of technological advance. The motions to be discussed are:

The pro-case   Technological advance is both inevitable and desirable, and while we can anticipate teething problems with innovations this is not an argument for impeding or delaying beneficial developments.

The caution case Technological advances generate unpredictable consequences and we must adopt a cautious, analytical approach to implementation, ensuring that we understand the social and organizational implications before proceeding.

Each side of the debate will be presented and defended by a team of hand-picked experts in the subject. The debate will be managed by a chairperson. Your responsibilities in this debate are as follows:

- To help the chairperson to set up the forum for the debate, arranging the seating to the extent that your facilities allow.

- To help ensure that the briefing period is completed on time to begin the debate at the agreed time.

- To help the chairperson decide how to manage the debate – how the two teams will be invited to present, how questions from the audience will be handled.

- To collect questions from the audience in advance of the debate and to help the chairperson determine how these will be used to drive the discussion.

- To help the chairperson brief the audience on how they are expected to contribute and participate.

- During the debate to take individual notes on the arguments used by the two teams, and by the audience.

- Following the debate to meet as a reporting team, to share and compare notes, and to prepare a summary report which outlines the case presented by each side and offers a concluding assessment of the relative strengths of the two positions represented (or in other terms, to indicate in your view which team won the debate).

- Following the debate to present your summary and assessment to the class as a whole.

The chairperson's briefing

Because of your background, wide experience, published views and colourful personality, you have been invited to chair an expert debate on the social and organizational role of technological advance. The motions to be discussed are:

The pro-case   Technological advance is both inevitable and desirable, and while we can anticipate teething problems with innovations this is not an argument for impeding or delaying beneficial developments.

The caution case   Technological advances generate unpredictable consequences and we must adopt a cautious, analytical approach to implementation, ensuring that we understand the social and organizational implications before proceeding.

Each side of the debate will be presented and defended by a team of hand-picked experts in the subject. Four well-known journalists have been invited to cover the debate, and to produce a summary and assessment report afterwards. It is your task to manage the debate. Your responsibilities are as follows:

- Above all to ensure a lively, controversial, entertaining and informative debate.

- To decide, perhaps in consultation with the teams, how you want each team to present their respective cases.

- To brief the teams on your debate management strategy.

- To liaise with the journalists over the room layout, to the extent that this is flexible.

- To liaise with the journalists in the collection and handling of audience questions, and to decide how to use those questions (read them yourself, call on the member of the audience . . .).

- To open the debate, manage the presentations and discussion, to offer a final closing summary, and to ensure that the debate concludes at the agreed time.

14.2 SGA: McDonaldization

Objectives

❏ To consider the implications of one particular trend in the development of a particular configuration of material and social technology.

❏ To develop understanding of how social and technological trends of this kind can be subverted.

Introduction

In his book, *The McDonaldization of Society* (1993), George Ritzer argues that the process of 'McDonaldization' is affecting many areas of our social and organizational lives, and that this trend is undesirable. He has no particular complaint against McDonalds hamburger restaurants; he merely uses this fast food chain as an illustration of the wider process which is the real focus of his attention. His argument is that the process of McDonaldization is spreading and that, while it yields a number of benefits, the costs and risks are in Ritzer's view considerable. In this exercise, you are introduced to the four central dimensions of McDonaldization that Ritzer identifies. You are then invited to consider the benefits of this trend, the costs and risks attached to it, and finally (using some of Ritzer's ideas as a basis) to consider whether and how such a social trend can be subverted by individual action.

Procedure

Step 1 Working on your own, read the following brief on *McDonaldization* and make preliminary notes in response to the five questions posed.

Step 2 Working in syndicates of three to five members, share and compare individual responses, nominate a spokesperson and prepare a group consensus report in response to the five discussion questions.

Step 3 With the whole group back together, present your syndicate findings for comparison with the findings of the other syndicates.

Step 4 Following this session, you may find it interesting to track down for yourself and read a copy of George Ritzer's book.

McDonaldization

Everybody knows McDonald's. They are all over America. They are all over Britain. There is a McDonald's on the Champs Elysée in Paris. There is a McDonald's in Lisbon in Portugal and in Gothenburg in Sweden. There is a McDonald's in Moscow. The company has come to symbolize many aspects of popular modern culture. The McDonald's large yellow 'M' logo is one of the most widely recognized company symbols in the world (along with Holiday Inn and Coca Cola). In his book *The McDonaldization of Society*, George Ritzer argues that the McDonald's approach has four central dimensions:

1. *Efficiency:* with respect to the speed with which you are transformed from being hungry to being fed, including the drive-through option.

2. *Calculability:* with respect to high value meals for discounted prices – quarter pounders, Big Macs, large fries, all ordered, delivered and consumed with a minimum waste of time.

3. *Predictability:* The Big Mac in New York is the same as the Big Mac in Paris is the same as the Big Mac in Birmingham – no surprises, but nothing special either.

4. *Control:* The staff who work in McDonalds are trained to perform a limited range of tasks in a precisely detailed way, and customers are similarly constrained by queues, limited menu options and by the expectation that they eat and leave.

In addition to the simplified jobs that McDonalds' employees perform, their work is also limited by the sophisticated technology of fast food preparation which gives them little or no discretion in how they prepare and deliver food to customers. Hamburger grilling instructions are precise and detailed, covering the exact positioning of burgers on the grill, cooking times and the sequence in which burgers are to be turned. Drinks dispensers, French-fry machines, programmed cash registers – all limit the time required to carry out a task and leave little or no room for discretion, creativity or innovation on the part of the employee. Such discretion and creativity would of course subvert the aims of efficiency, calculability, predictability and control.

Analysis questions

1. What are the benefits of this approach – to the company, to the customer, to society as a whole?

2. What are the disadvantages of this approach?

3. What examples of McDonaldization can you identify in sectors other than fast foods (for example, to what extent is further and higher education susceptible to McDonaldization)?

4. George Ritzer offers a number of suggestions for coping with McDonaldization. These include the avoidance of daily routine, self-help rather than the use of 'instant repair' chains, using small, local, independent traders and services rather

than large companies, returning all 'junk mail', trying to establish meaningful communications with fast food counter staff, avoiding classes which are assessed using short answer examinations and computer-graded tests and so on. Identify five other subversion strategies for yourself.

5. What is your realistic assessment of the impact of these subversion strategies? Can we really make a difference, individually and/or collectively? Is it worth the effort?

This exercise is based on George Ritzer, *The McDonaldization of Society: An Investigation Into the Changing Character of Contemporary Social Life*, Pine Forge Press, Thousand Oaks, 1993.

14.3 PREP: The head office automation project

Objectives

❑ To identify the scope of organizational choice or 'design space' that accompanies significant technological change.

❑ To explore the organizational 'ripple effects' that accompany significant technological change.

❑ To develop understanding of the nature of the management decision-making process that influences the outcome of technological and organizational change.

Introduction

Technological change is generally accompanied by organizational change. However, as Chapter 14 in *ORBIT* argues, the consequences of technological change are dependent on more than the capabilities and characteristics of the new equipment or apparatus. The consequences are typically a product of a management decision process that concerns what technology is to be deployed, why it is to be used and how it is to be used.

Management objectives and assumptions about work and organizational design thus shape the impact that any new technology may have on an organization. This argument does not imply that the consequences are wholly independent of technological capabilities, only that other factors – in some cases significantly more influential factors – need to be considered too. In this case exercise, based on a real example, you are invited to consider the advice you would offer an information technology manager introducing a new office automation (OA) system at the same time that the company moves to a new office building. The new building is creating a 'climate for change' in the organization; what organizational changes should accompany the introduction of the new technology? As in most organizations today, the technology in this case is not 'new' as staff are already accustomed to working with computer-based systems. The 'new' technology is a more up-to-date, more sophisticated and more powerful version of what is already in use.

Procedure

Step 1 Familiarize yourself with the argument in the *Assessment* section of Chapter 14 in *ORBIT*, beginning on page 356, and summarized in Figure 14.1 on page 357.

Step 2 Read *The head office automation project* case description which follows, and prepare answers to the analysis questions.

Step 3 According to your instructor's guidelines, write a report explaining your answers to the analysis questions, and/or prepare to present and justify your advice in a class meeting.

The head office automation project

It is mid-1992. The information technology manager of a multinational manufacturing and distribution company is planning the design and implementation of a new office automation system. This will be installed early the following year in a new head office which is being built nearby. All the current head office functions are moving to this new building. The present building uses several computing systems, including word processing and many personal computers, much of the equipment is dated and incapable of further development. The Board has agreed that a 'new start' should be made and that a completely new office automation facility be provided in the new building.

Head office contains functions such as the share register, pensions administration and financial accounting. The latter function prepares monthly and quarterly analysis for company managers and for the Board. Four of the company's divisions are also managed from head office, while the others are managed from a London office. The divisions are managed in a way that reflects the group's policy of giving considerable autonomy to local managers who operate in plants and in product markets throughout the world.

Much use is made of telephone and facsimile transmission (FAX) facilities which are handled by two switchboard operators who report to a communications manager. The fax has only recently replaced the old telex facility and is attracting increasing usage.

Much of the information about performance in the divisions' plants comes in written form, and is then re-keyed for further head office processing and analysis. This is widely recognized as wasteful, and half of the subsidiaries now have their own personal computers from which they can pass financial information to head office on diskette directly to the head office main computer system.

Produced by several means, a great deal of data are available in head office. However, that information is not easy to access and use. One senior manager said:

> There's not a great deal of high-powered computation in our job. What is required is a lot of data. And that's what's cumbersome at the moment. I don't think we're holding as much data at the moment as we probably should, and what we have is too difficult to get at, so we don't do the analyses we should. Information about performance – we often have it, but we can't get at it.

In the old building, part of the typing service is provided by a small typing pool. There are five typists here, with a supervisor, each with a terminal linked to a central word processing system. In addition each section in the office has a 'puddle' of two or three secretaries who work for the directors and managers in that particular section. The typists in the puddles also have terminals linked to the same central computerized word processing system.

The typing pool works mainly for the technical and professional staff and also handles any overflow of work from the puddles. Typists in the pool are seen as 'basic grade' in the organization and their only move out is through promotion to a secretarial job. All the directors have their own personal secretaries, while two or three managers share one secretary between them. All the secretaries can use shorthand; only one of the typists in the pool has that skill.

The information technology manager explains the focus of the new office automation system for the new building in the following terms:

> We took the decision fairly early on that our office automation must be based on word processing rather than on data processing. We already had word processing – and would have it in the new building – that would be the basis for our move to OA, and then we would make sure that anything we did on the data processing side would be able to interface with that.

In planning the change, one option being considered is whether to disband the typing pool and to put some or all of the typists into the department puddles. The information technology manager explains this as follows:

> We're considering breaking up typing services and putting them into the groups on each floor. The new building has opened up the options. It has created a climate of change.

Another option being considered is whether to install a system whereby subsidiary companies can send current financial data from their computer systems directly to head office, perhaps more frequently than with the current methods.

There is no overall management view of the benefits of the new office automation system. One manager has said that:

> each individual has very different hopes and aspirations, ranging from 'I hope the system works' to 'won't it be great to access all the financial information, the stock information, from my desk'.

It is also being stressed that, apart from the word processing element, there is a high degree of experimentation involved in the new system. It is based on the need to replace the outdated word processing technology, but has been chosen to give the company the opportunity to experiment with other and more novel applications. This 'experimental' aspect is accepted by the Board, and no attempt has been made to cost-justify the investment in the system in a traditional accounting manner.

Analysis questions

What advice would you give to the information technology manager on the following issues – and why?

1. How should the organization of secretarial and typing services be changed, if at all?

2. How should the flow of performance information from subsidiaries to head office be improved?

3. What should he do about integrating the management of the communications and information technology functions?

14.4 REV: Join the halves

Objectives

❑ To assess understanding of the concepts introduced in Chapter 14 of *ORBIT*.
❑ To assess understanding of the arguments introduced in Chapter 14 of *ORBIT*.

Introduction

How closely did you read Chapter 14? How much of that chapter do you now recall? The following review may appear to imply that you need to recall the material word for word. That is not necessarily so. If you *understood* the concepts and arguments in the chapter, you will find the following review easy. Remember the last piece of fiction you read? You can probably describe the plot of the story, the main characters, what happened and how the story ended (in at least enough detail to spoil the surprise ending for someone who has not read it yet) without any memory whatsoever of any of the lines and sentences written by the author. Simple recall helps. Understanding, however, is more useful and makes fewer demands on memory.

Procedure

Step 1 Read through the two sets of incomplete sentences.

Step 2 Decide which items in Set B complete those in Set A.

Step 3 Score your answers as your instructor requires.

Step 4 Congratulate yourself if you got 15 or more correct; read the chapter again if you scored less than 10.

Sentence completion: Set A

A1   The real lesson of the Vincennes is that electronic systems can

A2   Tom Forester cites an American report commissioned by the National Academy of Science which concluded that

A3   Case study research on the reasons why new computing and information technologies have been introduced reveals that

A4   Technology thus has a limited impact on people and performance

A5   Psychologists concerned with employee attitudes and the quality of working life have argued that process automation

A6   Harold Leavitt and T. L. Whisler argued in 1958 that

A7   The thinking this operator refers to is of a different quality from the thinking that attended the display of action-centred skills. It combines abstraction, explicit inference, and procedural reasoning. Taken together, these elements

A8   The technology of word processing has powerful information management capabilities, but

A9   However, recent research has confirmed that the view expressed by Davis and Taylor over fifteen years ago –

A10   Activities, events and objects are translated into and made visible by information

A11   Noble, for example, described how precision machining in engineering, even with computer numerically controlled machine tools,

A12   They conclude that these four *distancing* features are typical of many jobs

A13   The main health problems associated with computer terminals in offices are

A14   Despite some enthusiastic individuals and some limited achievements, Chris Martin concludes that

A15   The best general statement that we can make about the impact of new technology is perhaps

A16   Trevor Williams concludes that repetitive strain injury is caused by a combination of new technology and

A17   Many senior management decisions are based at least in part on judgement and past experience,

A18   The *control* objectives to which McLoughlin and Clark refer concern

A19   Sociologists have been concerned with the effects of technology on social structure, conflict and industrial relations. These studies depict process operators as

A20   *Human-centred manufacturing* is an attempt to design technology and manufacturing systems that

Sentence completion: Set B

B1   in 'nearly automated' production system, where the operator develops neither the ability nor the motivation to carry out residual functions effectively.

B2   the work experience of many middle managers in the mid-1980s was going to become more programmes, routine and structured, requiring less experience, judgement and creativity, and receiving less status and reward in return.

B3   when a technology *informates* as well as *automates.*

B4   the desires of managers to reduce human intervention, to replace people with machines, to reduce dependence on human control of equipment and processes, to reduce uncertainty, increase reliability, predictability, consistency and order in production operations, and finally to increase the amount of performance information and the speed at which it is generated.

B5   captured by Melvin Kranzberg's First Law which says that, 'Technology is neither good nor bad, nor is it neutral'.

B6   reproductive disorders, repetitive strain injury, and stress.

B7   complement human skills and abilities, and not replace them.

B8   make possible a new set of competences that I call *intellective skills.*

B9   and are not wholly dependent on data and analyses from an information system, manual or computerized.

B10   requires 'close attention to the details of the operation and frequent manual intervention'.

B11   independent of the purposes of those who would use it and the responses of those who operate it.

B12   the meaningless repetition of many traditional office jobs, so improving the design of equipment and furniture will only have a small effect.

B13   produce far too much data for human beings to digest in the heat and strain of battle.

B14   that technical change opens up new opportunities for work organization and can increase the demands made on cognitive and social skills.

B15   information technology ultimately creates more jobs than it destroys through increased productivity and the creation of wealth.

B16   decisions are the outcomes of processes of strategic choice within organizations and that a variety of objectives may be involved.

B17   eliminates dirt and danger, and can create a motivating work environment in which the operator has autonomy, task variety, meaning and opportunities for learning.

B18   the findings of this research suggest that the video typist can only fully exploit these capabilities in an appropriate form of work organization.

B19   computer-based information systems have little to offer senior executives.

B20   victims of managers' use of technology to create work that is unskilled, boring, lonely, repetitive, controlled and lacking in meaning.

PART IV
STRUCTURAL INFLUENCES ON BEHAVIOUR

Chapter 15
Organizational structure

15.1 Large group activity:	Windworth University Business School
15.2 Small group activity:	Words-in-sentences
15.3 Prepared task:	Managerial assumptions about organizational structure
15.4 Review:	Function- or product-based structure?

15.1 LGA: Windworth University Business School

Objectives

- ❑ To introduce the dilemmas in designing an organization.
- ❑ To evaluate the costs and benefits of different organizatinal structures.
- ❑ To apply the theory of organizational design to a specific case.

Introduction

Most people fit into an existing organization structure. Indeed, they are unaware of it until external or internal factors trigger a redesign. Yet the arrangement of levels, responsibilities, job descriptions and reporting relationships is the scaffold that links organizational goals to human performance. An effective structure meets both employee and customer needs within the context of organizational goals. The exercise gives you an opportunity to address the issue of organizational structuring for the first time within a familiar context.

Procedure

Step 1 Individually. Read the case. Respond to the instructor's question.

Step 2 Working with the person next to you, imagine that you are Helen Bond. Decide on TWO different ways of organizing the staff at the business school. You are free to make any assignments that you feel are appropriate, as long as you do not change the assumptions of the case. Prepare an organizational chart showing your dispositions.

   What principles support your decision? What are the strengths and weaknesses of each of your two chosen structures?

Step 3 Compare your two organizational structures with those presented by the instructor.

Windworth University Business School

Windworth University is a large institution attracting students from all parts of the UK as well as from abroad. It was formed in the early 1990s by the renaming of a polytechnic and the amalgamation of a number of smaller educational establishments. It has six faculties, including a business school which was formed by the merging of the polytechnic's departments of management, law, accounting and business studies; a semi-autonomous research institute; and a residential short course centre which came as a dowry when the college of commerce was incorporated into the newly formed university.

   The main campus is on the western edge of the city; the research institute has premises in the city centre, and the residential centre is located some 18 miles east of the city on the road to the coast. The business school offers programmes leading to certificates, diplomas and bachelor's degrees in management. It teaches two Master of Business Administration degrees. One is a 12-month full-time programme for students from around the world. The second is a 2-year part-time programme for managers from local companies who study while continuing to work. WUBS supervises doctoral research, and has a research grant from a Research Council. It offers in-company consultancy, and also runs courses for managers from different firms at its residential centre.

Helen Bond, the newly appointed director of the business school, was thinking about the best way to organize the one hundred or so staff in the school. With the recent higher education reorganization, and the need to increase rapidly the productivity and quality of the services it offered, deciding on the appropriate organizational structure and implementing it swiftly was a priority for her. Otherwise, the opportunity to integrate the diverse staff from different backgrounds into an effective unit would be lost and morale would plummet. However, she also knew that if she chose the wrong structure, the effect would be divisive, and her job would be made more difficult.

She remembered her tasks when she was a lecturer. She was encouraged to apply for research grants, and when awarded, she and a senior colleague had to recruit their research team. She remembered how much time grant application had taken up. Even trickier had been the process of interviewing the short-listed candidates. One appointee had turned out to be so awful that they had had to sack him. It was a long time before she developed her interviewing skills. Doing the actual research was relatively straightforward. The problem came towards the end of the contract when the researchers began looking for new jobs before their grants ran out. This rarely stopped the research itself being finished, but it did mean a delay in publications as absent staff were entreated to complete research papers and articles. It was rare that a book of the research ever got written. It seemed a waste of time doing the research if no one was going to read the results. This problem of lack of output was particularly serious now as both the amount of research grant obtained, and the publication record of the school's staff were being scrutinized much more closely.

Reflecting on the process, Helen remembered what difficulties her research staff had in communicating their research results to students. In the end, the research seminars had to be abandoned because of complaints from undergraduates. The research staff, they grumbled, seemed unable to explain their ideas succinctly to them. Helen had often wondered whether a good researcher could also be a good teacher, or whether an academic was drawn to one area rather than the other. Anyway, she was sure that the business school needed good teachers.

Good teaching attracted students, and students meant income for the business school. The new view of students as customers, certainly put a premium on staff who were high quality performers. The boom in business education meant that there was a great demand for competent lecturers. Beyond the undergraduate level, staff had to teach course members who were managers with years of management experience, and these groups were often highly critical of both the material presented and of the lecturer. You had to be a certain kind of person to deal with a crowd like that. Those that succeeded ('showmen' as her previous boss had called them) did not score well on research and publications at the annual staff appraisal, often saying that they 'weren't really into that sort of thing'.

One of the greatest frustrations that Helen had experienced as a researcher and teacher, was the lack of time to adapt her research findings into material suitable for teaching. Research formed the basis of up-to-date presentations to be communicated to students. She and her colleagues needed time to translate the findings into teaching materials such as case studies, exercises and role-play activities. Not least, new overhead transparencies and 35mm slides had to be prepared. In many cases, a short video film would help students understand the main ideas. Regrettably neither she nor her colleagues had the time or expertise to prepare one. In recent years, knowledge had become a commodity. It was no longer enough to discover it and teach it, you also had to sell it. That's what the vice-chancellor said at the last graduation ceremony. She had been thinking of establishing a business consultancy centre at the residential management centre to market the research expertise of the business school. The centre, specializing in short, non-graduating courses for experienced managers, was the part of the business school that was closest to the business frontline. However, Helen's predecessor had warned her that the teachers at the centre, mainly ex-managers who had switched to teaching as a second career, were not temperamentally suited to going around local businesses selling courses and explaining the consultancy services on offer. For this, he felt, you needed younger, more entrepreneurial individuals, who saw themselves primarily as marketing people.

At the end of the last week, Helen had spoken to one of the top final year students who had accepted a place to do postgraduate work at another university. Asked why he had not stayed at WUBS, he said that although many of her staff were good teachers, few of them had any research reputation or a publications record. Earlier in the day, Helen had had a talk with Susan, a newly appointed member of staff. Although responsible for the undergraduate Bachelor of Accountancy programme, Susan had expressed the desire to contribute to the postgraduate Master of Business Administration programme. She also hoped that Helen would ensure that she was given enough time to conduct her research. Without publications, Susan reminded her, the chances of promotion were limited. Helen thought what kind of organizational structure she could design which would meet all these competing demands.

15.2 SGA: Words-in-sentences

Objectives

❏ To experiment with designing and running an organization.

❏ To compare production and quality outputs under different organizational structures and leadership styles.

Introduction

In this exercise you will have the experience of structuring and managing a production company. Each student group will form a 'mini-company' which will be in competition with several others in their industry. You will therefore have the opportunity to think about and experiment with the best design for your organization before and between the actual production periods. The success of each company will depend on its structure, objectives, planning, quality control and its leadership.

Procedure

Step 1 Read pages 158–9 in your workbook to familiarize yourself with the rules and activities of the exercise. These are specified in the section headed *Directions*.

Step 2 Your instructor will divide you into small groups and will assign you to your workplaces. Each group should consider themselves a company. The instructor may designate a company manager.

Step 3 Follow the statement of instructions and ask any questions for clarification. Each team will need to provide the instructor with a one-word company name and the name of its quality control representative.

Step 4 Your team should prepare for production run 1 first, by designing its organization using as many of its members as it sees fit to produce its 'words-in-sentences'. There are many potential ways of organizing. Some are more efficient than others. Each company may want to consider the following questions:

1. What is its objective?

2. How will that objective be achieved? How should the work be planned given the time allowed?

3. What division of labour, authority and responsibility is most appropriate, given the chosen objective, task and technology?

4. Are certain group members more qualified than others to perform certain tasks?

Second, it should do a 'practice run' using a test word or phrase to identify the possible production problems.

Step 5   Production run 1 (10 minutes)

Once the raw material word/phrase is announced, each company is to manufacture as many words as possible and package them into sentences for delivery to the quality control board.

Step 6   The designated representatives from the various companies form the QC Board. They review the output from each company, ensuring that it meets the standards specified in the rules.

While this is going on, the other company members review their performance and decide on any changes that they would like to make to their work methods or organization for the next run. Companies may reorganize for run 2.

Step 7   Production run 2 (10 minutes).

Step 8   The QC Board again reviews each company's output for run 2.

While the Board is finalizing their figures, the other company team members discuss the following questions:

1. How well did your company perform in the light of the scores of competitors? (Excellent, good, medium, bad)

2. What factors contributed to its success (+) and to failure (−)?

3. Which of Woodward's nine technological types did your company most resemble (*ORBIT*, Chapter 18)?

4. Did you have a formal leader? What was their leadership style (*ORBIT*, Chapters 8 and 19)? What effect did it have on employee motivation and on production?

Directions

You are a small company that manufactures words and then packages them into meaningful (English language) sentences. Market research has established that sentences of at least three words, but no more than six words are in demand. Therefore, packaging, distribution and sales should be set up for three-to-six-word sentences.

The words-in-sentences (WINS) industry is highly competitive. Several new firms have recently entered an expanding market. Since raw materials, technology and pricing are all standard for the industry, your ability to compete depends on two factors, production volume and quality.

Task

Your group must design and operate a WINS company. You should design your organization to be as efficient as possible during each 10-minute production run. After the first production run, you will have the opportunity to reorganize your company if you want to.

Raw materials

For each production run, you will be given a raw material word or phrase. The letters contained in the word or phrase serve as the raw materials available to you to produce new words for your sentences. For example, if the raw material word was organization, you could produce the following words that would form the following sentence, 'Nat ran to a zoo'.

Production standards

There are several rules that have to be followed in producing 'words-in-sentences'. If these rules are not adhered to, your sentences will not meet production specifications, will not pass the quality control specification, and will not count towards your output figure.

1. The same letter may appear only as often in a manufactured word as it appears in the raw material word or phrase. For example, *organization* has two os. Thus the word 'zoo' is acceptable, but 'zoology' is not because it has three os.

2. Once a new word has been manufactured from the raw material letters, those letters become available immediately for the next new word. That is, raw material letters can be used again in different manufactured words.

3. A manufactured word may be used only once in a sentence, and only in one sentence during a production run. For example, if the word *ran* is used once in a sentence, it becomes out of stock.

4. A new word may not be made by adding an *s* to form the plural of an already used manufactured word.

5. A word is defined by its spelling and not its meaning. For example, only one *land* is permissible, irrespective of whether it refers to what an aeroplane does, or where one grows wheat.

6. Nonsense words or nonsense sentences are unacceptable.

7. All words must be in the English language.

8. Names and places are acceptable.

9. Slang is not acceptable.

10. English sentences contain a subject, verb and object ('Man bites dog').

Measuring performance

The output of your WINS company is measured by the total number of acceptable words that are packaged in sentences. The sentences must be legible, listed on one sheet of paper, and must be handed in to the Quality Control Board at the completion of each production run.

Delivery

Delivery must be made to the Quality Control Board within thirty seconds of the instructor signalling the end of each production run.

Quality control

The Quality Control Board (composed of one member from each WINS company) is the final arbiter of sentence acceptability. If *any* word in a sentence does not meet the standards set out above, then *all* the remaining words in that sentence will be rejected. In the event of a tie vote in the Review Board, a coin toss will determine the outcome.

This activity is taken from R. J. Lewicki, D. D. Bowen, D. T. Hall and F. S. Hall, *Experiences in Management and Organizational Behaviour*, Wiley, Chichester, 1988, pp. 219–33. Used with permission.

15.3 PREP: Managerial assumptions about organizational structure

Objective

❑ To demonstrate how managers' assumptions about human behaviour become formalized into an organization's basic structure and operating systems.

Introduction

This activity provides you with an opportunity to consider individual management assumptions with the design of organizational structures. It is based on the belief that structures reflect managerial assumptions about people. This exercise comes in three parts. In the first part, you will be introduced to Douglas McGregor's work, and will receive a briefing on the preparatory task. In the second part, you will carry out the task in your own time. In the third part, you and your fellow students will discuss your findings back in syndicate groups.

Procedure

Step 1   Before the session, complete the *Assumptions about people* instrument in the workbook.

Step 2   Based on your understanding of McGregor's ideas, predict your personal balance between X and Y assumptions (50–50; 70–30; 25–75?).

Step 3   Score your instrument, using the scoring key provided by your instructor.

Step 4   Individuals' assumptions about other people and human nature become translated into an organization's basic structure and operating systems.

For the next session, select one organization with which you are familiar. This may be a past or present company that you have worked for – a shop, school, university, club or some other institution. Using the summaries of McGregor's Theory X and Theory Y assumptions, identify aspects of your chosen organization such as job design, reward systems, procedures, practices, authority and responsibility allocation, division of labour, departmentalization, span of management, administration hierarchy, centralization/decentralization and formalization (rules), and decide if these reflect Theory X or Y assumptions. A single firm may have a predominance of one or a mixture of both, e.g. the procedure of clocking on and off work may be an example of the company's assumption that, 'people are naturally lazy and prefer to do nothing'.

Step 5   *At the class*, in syndicates, and using the following ten dimensions as a discussion framework, syndicate members should supply examples of structural elements which reflect either Theory X or Theory Y assumptions.

Assumptions about people instrument

This instrument is designed to help you to understand the assumptions that you make about people and human nature. There are ten pairs of statements. Assign 10 points across each pair of statements to indicate your relative belief in them (e.g. 10–0; 9–1; 5–5; 2–8, etc.). Remember the points in each pair must total ten. Be honest with yourself, and resist the natural tendency to respond 'like you think you should'. This is not a test, there are no right or wrong answers. The instrument is designed to be a stimulus for personal reflection and discussion.

1. (a) It's only human nature for people to do as little work as they can get away with.
   (b) When people avoid work, it's usually because their work has been deprived of its meaning.

2. (c) If employees have access to any information they want, they tend to have better attitudes and behave more responsibly.
   (d) If employees have access to more information than they need to do their immediate tasks, they will usually misuse it.

3. (e) One problem in asking for ideas of employees is that their perspective is too limited for their suggestions to be of much practical value.
   (f) Asking employees for their ideas broadens their perspective and results in the development of useful suggestions.

4. (g) If people don't use much imagination and ingenuity on the job, it's probably because relatively few people have much of either.

(h) Most people are imaginative and creative but may not show it because of limitations imposed by supervision and the job.

5. (i) People tend to raise their standards if they are accountable for their own behaviour and for correcting their own mistakes.

(j) People tend to lower their standards if they are not punished for their misbehaviour and mistakes.

6. (k) It's better to give people both good and bad news because employees want the whole story, no matter how painful.

(l) It's better to withhold unfavourable news about business because most employees really only want to hear the good news.

7. (m) Because a supervisor is entitled to more respect than those below him/her in the organization, it weakens their prestige to admit that a subordinate was right and that they were wrong.

(n) Because people at all levels are entitled to equal respect, a supervisor's prestige is increased when he or she supports this principle by admitting that a subordinate was right and that they were wrong.

8. (o) If you give people enough money, they are less likely to be concerned with such intangibles as being given responsibility or recognition for the job.

(p) If you give people interesting and challenging work, they are less likely to complain about such things as pay and supplementary benefits.

9. (q) If people are allowed to set their own goals and standards of performance, they tend to set them higher than the boss would.

(r) If people are allowed to set their own goals and standards of performance, they tend to set them lower than the boss would.

10. (s) The more knowledge and freedom a person has regarding his job, the more controls are needed to keep him in line.

(t) The more knowledge and freedom a person has regarding his job, the fewer controls are needed to ensure satisfactory job performance.

1. (a) ____	6. (k) ____
(b) ____	(l) ____
10	10
2. (c) ____	7. (m) ____
(d) ____	(n) ____
10	10
3. (e) ____	8. (o) ____
(f) ____	(p) ____
10	10
4. (g) ____	9. (q) ____
(h) ____	(r) ____
10	10
5. (i) ____	10. (s) ____
(j) ____	(t) ____
10	10

Theory X assumptions	*Theory Y assumptions*
1. People are naturally lazy; they prefer to do nothing.	People are naturally active; they set goals and enjoy striving.
2. People work mostly for money and status rewards.	People seek many satisfactions in work: pride in achievement; enjoyment of process; sense of contribution; pleasure in association; stimulation of new challenges.
3. The main force keeping people productive in their work is fear of being demoted or fired.	The main force keeping people in their work is desire to achieve their personal and social goals.
4. People remain children grown larger; they are naturally dependent on leaders.	People normally mature beyond childhood; they aspire to independence, self-fulfilment, responsibility.
5. People expect and depend on direction from above; they do not want to think for themselves.	People close to the situation see and feel what is needed and are capable of self-direction.
6. People need to be told, shown and trained in proper methods of work.	People who understand and care about what they are doing can devise and improve their own methods of doing work.
7. People need supervisors who will watch them closely enough to be able to praise good work and reprimand errors.	People need a sense that they are respected as capable of assuming responsibility and self-correction.
8. People have little concern beyond their immediate, material concerns.	People seek to give meaning to their lives by identifying with nations, communities, churches, unions, companies, causes.
9. People need specific instructions about what to do and how to do it; larger policy issues are none of their business.	People need ever-increasing understanding; they need to grasp the meaning of the activities in which they are engaged; they have cognitive hunger as extensive as the universe.
10. People appreciate being treated with courtesy.	People crave the genuine respect of their fellows.
11. People are naturally compartmentalized; work demands are entirely different from leisure activities.	People are naturally integrated; when work and play are too sharply separated both deteriorate; 'The only reason a wise man can give for preferring leisure to work is the better quality of the work he can do during leisure'.
12. People naturally resist change; they prefer to stay in the old ruts.	People naturally tire of monotonous routine and enjoy new experiences; to some degree, everyone is creative.
13. Jobs are primary and must be done; people are selected, trained and fitted to pre-defined jobs.	People are primarily seeking self-realization; jobs must be designed, modified and fitted to people.
14. People are formed by heredity, childhood and youth; as adults they remain static; old dogs don't learn new tricks.	People constantly grow; it is never too late to learn; they enjoy learning and increasing their understanding and capability.
15. People need to be 'inspired' (pep talked) or pushed or driven.	People need to be released and encouraged and assisted.

15.4 REV: Function or product-based structure?

Objective

❑ To compare the effects of a chosen organization structure on related aspects of company functioning.

Introduction

A basic decision confronting every enterprise is how to organize. Which structure is most appropriate for it? There are a range of available structural forms (based on division by function, production, geography, client). Each have both advantages and disadvantages. Moreover, a choice of an organizational structure can have consequences that are not always immediately evident. In this example, function-based and product-based structures will be compared.

Procedure

Assume a firm makes a biro whose manufacture involves three primary operations. These are making the plastic tube (operation T), the plastic cap (operation C), and the inkholder (operation I). Each biro requires a tube, cap and inkholder. The firm consists of a plant manager, three supervisors and nine operatives. Under these circumstances, the enterprise could be departmentalized either by function or product.

Function-based structure

Following a functional structure, the firm could be organized as three functional departments. In department 1, all the plastic tubes (T) would be made. In department 2, all the plastic caps (C) would be manufactured. Finally, department 3 would make the ink-tubes (I). Each department would make three units of their product per day. One supervisor (S) would be in charge of each department, and these would report to the plant manager as shown in the organizational chart below.

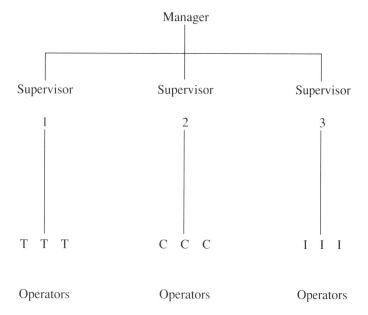

Product-based structure

Using a product-based structure, the firm could be organized into three separate product departments with each operation (tube, cap and ink production) being represented in each department. For example, as shown in the organizational chart below.

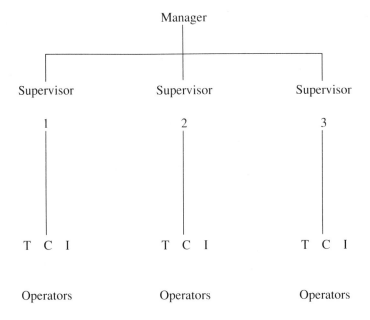

Questions

1. In which structure is the job of the supervisor likely to be more difficult? Why?

2. In which structure will supervisors be most qualified to be promoted to plant manager-level?

3. Which structure produces a greater division of labour for operators?

4. In which structure is conflict between departments most likely to occur?

5. Which structure allows a better assessment of each supervisor's performance?

6. Which structure produces the most experienced candidates for promotion to first line supervisor?

7. In which structure will the firm be most affected if one department shuts down through equipment failure or a strike?

Note

This exercise is based on one developed by Arthur Bedein, *Management*, CBS Publishing, Hinsdale, Ill., p. 269. Used with permission.

Chapter 16
Bureaucracy and roles

16.1 **Large group activity:**   **Organizational characteristics**
16.2 **Small group activity:**   **Organizational culture and socialization**
16.3 **Prepared task:**   **Role-set analysis and role conflict**
16.4 **Review:**   **Crossword**

16.1 LGA: Organizational characteristics

Objectives

❏ To allow you to assess the level of bureaucratization in an organization of your choice.
❏ To familiarize you with the characteristics of Max Weber's ideal type bureaucracy.

Introduction

While the concept of bureaucracy is easily understood by many students, its concrete manifestation in organizational structure is less readily appreciated. The purpose of this exercise is to help you assess the degree to which a given organization possesses bureaucratic characteristics.

Questionnaire

Step 1   This questionnaire measures the degree to which five characteristics are optimally present in a particular organization's structure. Think of an organization with which you are familiar. This may be the university that you are studying at, your present or past firm, your church, social or sports club or trade union. Write in your focus organization in the space below:

Organization: _____

Step 2   The ten questions that follow ask you about certain conditions in the above-named organization. Indicate with a tick, which of the five responses most accurately describes the conditions in it. There are no right or wrong answers as you are only trying to be accurately descriptive of existing organizational conditions and characteristics.

(√)	completely	mostly	partly	slightly	not at all
1. Work roles in this organization are highly specialized; each person has clear cut authority and responsibility.	___	___	___	___	___
2. The formal hierarchy in this organization is formal to the point of being rigid and inflexible.	___	___	___	___	___
3. In this organization people are selected and promoted on the basis of their demonstrated technical competence.	___	___	___	___	___

4. It often seems that people in this organization are so concerned with conforming to rules and procedures that this interferes with their psychological well-being.   ____   ____ ____ ____ ____

5. Everyone in this organization expects to be subject to the same set of rules and controls; there are no favourites.   ____   ____ ____ ____ ____

6. People in this organization are often so wrapped up in their own narrow specialities, that they can't see that we all have common interests. This causes unnecessary conflicts.   ____   ____ ____ ____ ____

7. The job titles and positions in this organization are arranged in a clear and logical hierarchy.   ____   ____ ____ ____ ____

8. Overall, this organization is composed of a managerial elite who got where they are through political wheeling-and-dealing.   ____   ____ ____ ____ ____

9. Managers in this organization see themselves on a clear career ladder and expect to make regular progress in their careers.   ____   ____ ____ ____ ____

10. Many of the rules in this organization have either become ends in themselves, with no logical function, or else have come to specify the minimum tolerable performance levels.   ____   ____ ____ ____ ____

Step 3 Insert the question numbers as supplied by your instructor. Then score your answers using this key:

For question numbers:	*completely*	*mostly*	*partly*	*slightly*	*not at all*		
_____	5 pts	4 pts	3 pts	2pts	1pt	=	_____
For question numbers:							
_____	1 pt	2 pts	3 pts	4 pts	5 pts	=	_____
						Total:	_____

Step 4 Add up the points for all ten questions to get your score. The higher the score, the more your focus organization manifests the characteristics of a true bureaucracy (see *ORBIT*, Chapter 16). Similarly, a low score indicates an absence of bureaucratic features. For example:

Below 18 Serious problems – either overbureaucratic rigidity or underbureaucratic chaos

18–24 Low bureaucracy, indicating a cause for concern

25–35 Average bureaucracy

Over 35 Indicates a 'strong' bureaucratic structure

The overall score above is composed of an analysis of five important characteristics of bureaucracy, each of which was measured by two questions:

Questions 1 and 6 Each office has a clearly defined sphere of competence resulting in work being specialized and each office-holder having a specified amount of authority and responsibility.

Questions 2 and 7   There is a clear and logical hierarchy of authority and responsibility that everyone knows. Through a firmly ordered system of super- and subordination, the supervision of lower offices is carried out by higher ones.

Questions 3 and 8   Candidates are selected on the basis of their technical qualifications, and promoted on their demonstrated competence and performance.

Questions 4 and 9   People see their job as constituting their career, with all managers and professionals having a regular, fixed salary.

Questions 5 and 10   The management of the office follow rules and regulations which are more or less stable, more or less exhaustive, sensible, can be learned, and which are applied in the same way to everyone.

You can add up the scores for the five-item pairs above in order to examine specific bureaucratic characteristics. The scores for each will range from 2 to 10 with:

> Under 5   Suggests specific problems exist with respect to that characteristic
>
> 5–7   Average
>
> Above 7   Effective bureaucratic characteristic

16.2 SGA: Organizational culture and socialization

Objectives

❑ To introduce students to the concept of corporate (or organizational) culture and how it is communicated to new employees through the process of organizational socialization.

❑ To identify specific organizational socialization strategies, describe their purpose and suggest their probable consequences.

❑ To sensitize students to the subtle messages given and received during initial organizational and role experiences.

Introduction

If the organization is to accomplish the controlled performance of collective goals, then the behaviour of its employees has, in some way, to be made predictable and in line with those goals. One way of doing this is to define people's jobs, limit their authority, establish reporting relationships and specify rules. That, in essence, is what organizational structure attempts to do. Such external and highly visible controls may be perceived as oppressive and a burden by employees. For this reason, corporations attempt to instil their culture (values, beliefs and attitudes) which they want their employees to possess. These types of controls, because they are internal, less visible and operated by the staff members themselves, are often more effective. The process by which corporate culture is internalized by new employees is called *organizational socialization*.

Organizational socialization is defined as the manner in which the experiences of people learning the ropes in a new organizational position, status or role are structured for them by others within the organization. Such structuring seeks to communicate the corporation's values, beliefs and attitudes to new recruits. Once instilled, this *corporate culture* helps them to interpret their company world in a standardized and predictable way, and publicly accept it despite any reservations. During the socialization process, the individual goes through what anthropologists call a rite of passage as he or she moves from 'outsider', to 'new body', to 'low man' (in the training group) before finally emerging as a 'fully fledged member'. These transitions are achieved by the processes of anticipation, initiation and assimilation.

Procedure

Read the abridged section from Michael Lewis's book, *Liar's Poker*, and prepare individual answers to the questions. These should be supported by evidence cited from the numbered paragraphs.

I

(1)   The 127 unlikely members of the class of 1985 were one of a series of human waves to wash over what was then the world's most profitable floor. At the time, we were the largest training class in Salomon's history, and the class after us was nearly twice as large again . . .

(2)   We were a paradox. We had been hired to deal in a market, to be more shrewd than the next guy, to be, in short, traders. Ask any astute trader and he'll tell you that his best work cuts against the conventional wisdom. Good traders tend to do the unexpected. We, as a group, were painfully predictable. By coming to Salomon Brothers, we were doing what every sane money-hungry person would do. If we were unable to buck convention in our lives, would we be likely to buck convention in the market? After all, the job market is a *market.*

(3)   We were as civil to the big man addressing the class as we had been to anyone, which wasn't saying much. He was the speaker for the entire afternoon. That meant he was trapped for three hours in the 10-yard trench in front of the room with a long table, a podium and a blackboard. The man paced back and forth in the channel like a coach on the sidelines, sometimes staring at the floor, other times menacingly at us. We sat in rows of interconnected school chairs – twenty-two rows of white male trainees, in white shirts, punctuated by the occasional female in a blue blazer, two blacks, and a cluster of Japanese. The dull New England clam-chowder colour of the training room walls and floor set the mood of the room. One wall had long narrow slits for windows with a sweeping view of New York Harbour and the Statue of Liberty, but you had to be sitting right beside them to be able to see anything, and even then you were not supposed to soak in the view.

(4)   It was, all in all, more like a prison than an office. The room was hot and stuffy. The seat cushions were in an unpleasant AstroTurf green; the seat of your trousers stuck both to it and to you as you rose at the end of each day. Having swallowed a large and greasy cheeseburger at lunch, and having only a mild sociological interest in the speaker, I was overcome with drowsiness. We were only one week into our five-month training programme, and I was already exhausted. I sank into my chair.

(5)   The speaker was a leading bond salesman at Salomon. On the table in the front of the room was a telephone which rang whenever the bond market went berserk. As the big man walked, he held his arms tight to his body to hide the half-moons of sweat growing under his armpits. Effort or nerves? Probably nerves. You couldn't blame him. He was airing his heartfelt beliefs, and in so doing, making himself more vulnerable than any speaker yet. I was in the minority in finding him a bit tedious. He was doing well with the crowd. People in the back row listened. All around the room, trainees put down their *New York Times* crossword puzzles. The man was telling us how to survive. 'You've got to think of Salomon Brothers as like a jungle,' he said. Except it didn't come out that way. It came out: 'Ya gotta tink of Salomon Bruddahs as like a jungle'.

(6)   'The trading floor is a jungle,' he went on, 'and the guy you end up working for is your jungle leader. Whether you succeed here or not depends on knowing how to survive in the jungle. You've got to learn from your boss. He's key. Imagine if I take two people and put them in the middle of the jungle and I give one person a jungle guide and the other person nothing. Inside the jungle there's a lot of bad shit going down. Outside of the jungle there's a TV that's got the NCAA finals on and a huge fridge full of Bud . . .'

(7) The speaker had found the secret of managing the Salomon Brothers' class of 1985: win the hearts and minds of the back row. The back row, from about the third day of the classes on, teetered on the brink of chaos. Even when they felt merely ambivalent about a speaker, back-row people slept or chucked paper wads at the wimps in the front row. But if the back-row people for some reason didn't care for a speaker, all hell broke loose. Not now. Primitive revelation swept through the back row of the classroom at the sound of the jungle drums; it was as if a hunting party of Cro-Magnon men had stumbled upon a new tool. The guys in the back row were leaning forward in their seats for the first time all day. Oooooooo! Aaaahhhhh!

(8) With the back row neutralized, the speaker effectively controlled the entire audience, for the people sitting in the front row were on automatic pilot. They were the same as front row people all over the world, only more so. Most graduates of Harvard Business School sat in the front row. One of them greeted each new speaker by drawing an organization chart. The chart resembled a Christmas tree, with John Gutfreund on the top and us at the bottom. In between were lots of little boxes like ornaments. His way of controlling the situation was to identify the rank of the speaker, visualize his position in the hierarchy, and confine him to his proper box.

(9) They were odd, these charts, and more like black magic than business. Rank wasn't terribly important on the trading floor. Organizational structure at Salomon Brothers was something of a joke. Making money was mostly what mattered. But the front row was less confident than the back that the firm was a meritocracy of money lenders. They were hedging their bets – just in case Salomon Brothers after all bore some relation to the businesses they had learned about at school.

(10) '. . . a huge fridge of Bud,' said the speaker a second time. 'And chances are good that the guy with the jungle guide is gonna be the first one through the jungle to the TV and the beer. Not to say that the other guy won't eventually get there too. But (here he stopped pacing and even gave the audience a little sly look), he'll be *reeeaaal* thirsty and there's not going to be any beer left when he arrives.'

(11) This was the punch-line. Beer. The guys in the back row liked it. They fell all over each other slapping palms, and looked as silly as white men in suits when they pretend to be black soul brothers. They were relieved as much as excited. When not listening to this sort of speech, we faced a much smaller man with a row of Bic fine points in a plastic case in his breast pocket – otherwise known as a nerd pack – explaining to us how to convert a semi-annual bond yield to an annual bond yield. The guys in the back row didn't like that. 'Fuck the fuckin' bond maths, man,' they said. 'Tell us about the jungle.'

(12) That the back row was more like the post-game shower room than a repository for the future leadership of Wall Street's most profitable investment bank troubled and puzzled the more thoughtful executives who appeared before the training class. As much time and effort had gone into recruiting the back row as the front, and the class, in theory, should have been uniformly attentive and well behaved, like an army. The curious feature about the breakdown in discipline was that it was random, uncorrelated with anything outside itself and therefore uncontrollable. Although most of the graduates from Harvard Business School sat in the front, a few sat in the back. And right beside them were graduates from Yale, Stanford and Pennsylvania. The back had its share of expensively educated people. It had at least its fair share of brains. So why were these people behaving like this?

(13) And why Salomon let it happen, I still don't understand. The firm's management created the training programme, filled it to the brim, then walked away. In the ensuing anarchy, the bad drove out the good, the big drove out the small, and the brawn drove out the brains. There was a single trait common to denizens of the back row, though I doubt it ever occurred to anyone: they sensed that they needed to shed whatever refinements of personality and intellect they had brought with them to Salomon Brothers. This wasn't a conscious act, more a reflex. They were the victims of the myth, especially popular at Salomon Brothers, that the trader is a

savage, and a great trader a great savage. This wasn't exactly correct. The trading floor held evidence to that effect. But it also held evidence to the contrary. People believed whatever they wanted to.

(14) There was another cause of hooliganism. Life as a Salomon trainee was like being beaten up every day by the neighbourhood bully. Eventually you grew mean and surly. The odds of making it into the Salomon training programme, in spite of my fluky good luck, had been six to one against. You beat the odds and you felt you deserved some relief. There wasn't any. The firm never took you aside and rubbed you on the back to let you know that everything was going to be fine. Just the opposite: the firm built a system around the belief that trainees should wriggle and squirm. The winners of the Salomon Brothers interviewing process were pitted against one another in the classroom. In short, the baddest of the bad were competing for jobs.

(15) Jobs were doled out at the end of the programme on a blackboard beside the trading floor. Contrary to what we had expected when we arrived, we were not assured of employment. 'Look to your left and look to your right,' more than one speaker said, 'In a year, one of those people will be out on the street.' Across the top of the job-placement blackboard appeared the name of each department on the trading floor: municipal bonds, corporate bonds, government bonds, etc. Along the side of the board was each office in the firm: Atlanta, Dallas, New York, etc. The thought that he might land somewhere awful in the matrix – or nowhere at all – drove the trainee to despair. He lost all perspective on the relative merits of the jobs. He did not count himself lucky just to be at Salomon Brothers, anyone who thought that way would not have got in in the first place. The Salomon trainee saw only the extremes of failure and success. Selling municipal bonds in Atlanta was unthinkably wretched; trading mortgages in New York was mouth-wateringly good.

(16) I considered myself an exception of course. I was accused by some of being a front-row person because I liked to sit next to the man from the Harvard Business School and watch him draw the organization charts. I wondered if he would succeed (he didn't). Also, I asked too many questions. It was assumed that I did this to ingratiate myself with the speakers, like a front-row person. This was untrue. But try telling that to the back row. I lamely compensated for my curiosity by hurling a few paper wads at important traders. And my stock rose dramatically in the back row when I was thrown out of class for reading the newspaper while a trader spoke. But I was never an intimate of those in the back row.

(17) Of all exceptions, the Japanese were the greatest. The Japanese undermined any analysis of the classroom culture. All six of them sat in the front row and slept. Their heads rocked back and forth, and on occasion fell over to one side, so that their cheeks ran parallel to the floor. So it was hard to argue that they were listening with their eyes shut, as Japanese businessmen are inclined to do. The most charitable explanation for their apathy was that they could not understand English. They kept to themselves, however, and you could never be sure of either their language skills or their motives. Their leader was a man called Yoshi. Each morning and afternoon, the back-row boys made bets on how many minutes it would take Yoshi to fall asleep. They liked to think that Yoshi was a calculating troublemaker. Yoshi was their hero. A small cheer would go up in the back row when Yoshi crashed, partly because someone had just won a pile of money, but also in appreciation of any man with the balls to fall asleep in the front row.

(18) Still, in the end, the Japanese were reduced to nothing more than a bizarre distraction. The back row set the tone of the class because it acted throughout as one, indivisible, incredibly noisy unit. The back-row people moved in herds, for safety and for comfort, from the training class in the morning and early afternoon, to the trading floor at the end of the day, to the Surf Club at night, and back to the training programme the next morning. They were united by their likes as well as their dislikes. They rewarded the speakers of whom they approved by standing and doing The Wave across the back of the class.

(19) And they approved wholeheartedly of the man at the front of the room now. The speaker paused, as if lost in thought, which was unlikely. 'You know,' he finally said, 'you think you're hot shit, but when you start out on the trading floor, you're going to be at the bottom.' Was it really necessary? He was playing so well by telling the hooligans what they liked to hear; being a winner at Salomon meant being a He-man in a jungle. Now he risked retaliation by telling the hooligans what they didn't like to hear: in the jungle, their native talents didn't mean a thing. I checked around for spitballs and paper wads. Nothing. The speaker had built sufficient momentum to survive his mistake. Heads in the back row nodded right along. It is possible that they assumed the speaker intended the remark for the front row.

(20) In any case, on this point, the speaker was surely wrong. A trainee didn't have to stay on the bottom for more than a couple of months. Bond traders and salesmen age like dogs. Each year on the trading floor counts for seven in any other corporation. At the end of his first year, a trader or salesman had stature. Who cared for tenure? The whole beauty of the trading floor was its complete disregard for tenure.

(21) A new employee, once he reached the trading floor, was handed a pair of telephones. He went on line almost immediately. If he could make millions of dollars come out of those phones, he became the most revered of all species: a Big Swinging Dick. After the sale of a big block of bonds and the deposit of a few hundred thousand dollars into the Salomon till, a managing director called whoever was responsible to confirm his identity: 'Hey, you Big Swinging Dick way to be.' To this day, the phrase brings to my mind the image of the elephant's trunk swaying from side to side. Swish. Swash. Nothing in the jungle got in the way of the Big Swinging Dick.

(22) That was the prize we coveted. Perhaps the phrase didn't stick in everyone's mind the way it did in mine; the name was less important than the ambition, which was common to us all. And, of course, no one actually said, 'When I get out on to the trading floor I'm gonna be a Big Swinging Dick'. It was more of a private thing. But everyone wanted to be a Big Swinging Dick, even the women, Big Swinging Dickettes. Christ, even the front row people hoped to be Big Swinging Dicks, once they had learned what it meant. Their problem, as far as the back row was concerned, was that they didn't know how to act the part. Big Swinging Dicks showed more grace under pressure than the front-row people did.

(23) A hand shot up (typically) in the front row. It belonged to a woman. She sat high in her regular seat, right in front of the speaker. The speaker had momentum. The back row was coming out of their chairs to honour him with The Wave. The speaker didn't want to stop now, especially for a front row person. He looked pained, but he could hardly ignore a hand in his face. He called her name, Sally Findlay. 'I was just wondering,' said Findlay, 'if you could tell us what you think has been the key to your success.' This was too much. Had she asked a dry technical question, she might have pulled it off. But even the speaker started to smile . . . he knew he could abuse the front row as much as he wanted. His grin spoke volumes to the back row. It said, 'Hey, I remember what these brown-nosers were like when I went through the training programme, and I remember how much I despised the speakers who let them kiss butt, so I'm going to let this woman hang out and dry for a minute, heh, heh, heh'. The back row broke out in its loudest laughter yet. Someone cruelly mimicked Findlay in a high pitched voice, 'Yes, *do* tell us why you're *sooooo* successful.' Someone else shouted, 'Down Boy' as if scolding an overheated poodle. A third man cupped his hands together around his mouth and hollered, '*Equities in Dallas*'.

(24) Poor Sally. There were many bad places your name could land on the job-placement board in 1985, but the absolute worst was in the slot marked Equities in Dallas. We could not imagine anything less successful in our small world than an equity salesman in Dallas; the equity department was powerless in our firm, and

Dallas was, well, a long way from New York. Thus, Equities in Dallas, became training programme shorthand for 'just bury the lowest form of human scum where it will never be seen again'. Bury Sally, they shouted from the back row. The speaker didn't bother with an answer. He raced to a close before the mob he had incited became uncontrollable. 'You spend a lot of time asking yourself questions: "Are munis right for me? Are goveys right for me? Are corporates right for me?" You spend a lot of time thinking about that. And you should. But think about this. *It might be more important to choose a jungle guide than to choose your product.* Thank you.'

II

(25) The powers of Salomon Brothers relied on the training programme to make us more like them. What did it mean to be more like them? For most of its life, Salomon had been a scrappy, bond-trading house, distinguished mainly by its ability and willingness to take big risks. Salomon had to accept risk to make money because it had no list of fee-paying corporate clients unlike, say, the genteel Gentiles of Morgan Stanley. The image Salomon had projected to the public was of a firm of clannish Jews, social nonentities, shrewd but honest, sinking its nose more deeply into the bond markets than any other firm cared to. This was a caricature of course, but it roughly captured the flavour of the place as it once was. Now, Salomon wanted to change.

(26) Despite the nouveau fluctuation in our corporate identity, the corporate training programme was, without a doubt, the finest start to a career on Wall Street. Upon completion, a trainee could take his experience, and cash it in for twice the salary on any other Wall Street trading floor. He had achieved, by the standards of Wall Street, technical mastery of his subject. It was an education in itself to see how quickly one became an 'expert' on Wall Street.

(27) But the materials were the least significant aspect of our training. The relevant bits, the ones I would recall two years later, were the war stories, the passing on of the oral tradition of Salomon Brothers. Over three months, leading salesmen, traders and financiers shared their experiences with the class. They trafficked in unrefined street wisdom – how money travels around the world (any way it wants); how a trader feels and behaves (any way he wants); and how to smooze a customer. After three months in the class, trainees circulated wearily around the trading floor for two months more. Then they went to work. All the while there was a hidden agenda: to Salomonize the trainee. The trainee was made to understand, first, that inside Salomon Brothers he was, as a trader once described us, lower than whale shit on the bottom of the ocean floor and second, that lying under the whale shit at Salomon Brothers was like rolling in clover compared to not being at Salomon at all.

(28) In the short term, the brainwashing nearly worked. (In the long term it didn't. For people to accept the yoke, they must believe they have no choice. As we shall see, we newcomers had both an exalted sense of our market value, and no permanent loyalties.) A few investment banks had training programmes, but with the possible exception of Goldman Sachs, none was so replete with firm propaganda. A woman from the *New York Times* who interviewed us three months into our programme was so impressed by the universality in attitudes towards the firm, that she called her subsequent article, 'The boot camp for top MBAs'.

III

(29) Each day after class, around three or four or five o'clock, we were pressured to move from the training class on the 23rd floor, to the trading floor on the 41st. You could get away with not going for a few days, but if not seen on the floor occasionally, you were forgotten. Forgotten at Salomon meant unemployed.

Getting hired was a positive act. A manager had to request you for his unit . . . you cruised the trading floor to find a manager who would take you under his wing, a mentor, commonly referred to as a rabbi. You also went to the trading floor to learn. Your first impulse was to step into the fray, select a likely teacher, and present yourself for instruction. Unfortunately this wasn't so easy. First, a trainee by definition, had nothing of merit to say. And second, the trading floor was a minefield of large men on short fuses just waiting to explode, if you so much as breathed in their direction. You didn't just walk up and say hello. Actually, that's not fair. Many, many traders are instinctively polite, and if you said hello, they'd just ignore you. But if you happened to step on a mine, then the conversation went something like this:

(30) *Me:* Hello

Trader: What fucking rock did you crawl out from under? Hey Joe, hey Bob, check out this guy's suspenders.

Me (reddening)*:* I just wanted to ask you a couple of questions.

Joe: Who the fuck does he think he is?

Trader: Joe, let's give this guy a little test! When interest rates go up, which way do bond prices go?

Me: Down.

Trader: Terrific. You get an A. Now I gotta work.

Me: When would you have some time . . .

Trader: What the fuck do you think this is, a charity? I'm busy.

Me: Can I help in any way?

Trader: Get me a burger. With ketchup.

(31) So I watched my step. There were a million little rules to obey. I knew none of them. Salesmen, traders and managers swarmed over the floor, and at first I couldn't tell them apart. Sure, I knew the basic differences. Salesmen talked to investors, traders made bets, and managers smoked cigars. But other than that I was lost. Most of the men were at two phones at once. Most of the men stared at small green screens full of numbers. They'd shout into one phone, then into the other, then at someone across the row of trading desks, then back into the phones and scream '*Fuck!*'.Thirty seconds was considered a long attention span. As a trainee, a pleb, a young man lying under all that whale shit, I did what every trainee did: sidled up to some busy person without saying a word and became the Invisible Man.

(32) That it was perfectly humiliating, was of course, precisely the point. Sometimes I'd wait for an hour before my existence was formally acknowledged, other times a few minutes. Even that seemed like for ever. Who is watching me in my current debased condition, I'd wonder. Will I ever recover from such total neglect? Will someone please notice that the Invisible Man has arrived. The contrast between me standing motionless, and the traders' frenetic movements made the scene particularly unbearable. It underlined my uselessness. But once I'd sidled up, it was difficult to leave without being officially recognized. To leave was to admit defeat in this particular ritual of making myself known.

(33) Anyway, there wasn't really any place else to go. The trading room was about a third the length of a football field and was lined with connected desks. Traders sitting elbow to elbow formed a human chain. Between the rows of desks there was not enough space for two people to pass each other, without first turning sideways. Even if you shed your red suspenders and adopted protective colouration, you were easily identifiable as a trainee. Trainees were impossibly out of step with the rhythm of the place. The movements of the trading floor respond to the movements of the markets as if roped together. The entire Salomon Brothers trading floor might be poised for a number at 8.30 a.m., gripped by suspense and a great deal of hope, ready to leap and shout, to buy or sell billions of dollars-worth of bonds, to make

or lose millions of dollars for the firm, when a trainee arrives, suspecting nothing and says, 'Excuse me, I'm going to the cafeteria, does anybody want anything?' Trainees, in short, were idiots.

(34) To avoid being squashed on my visits to the floor, I tried to keep still, preferably in some corner. Except for Gutfreund, whom I knew from magazine pictures, and thought of more as a celebrity than a businessman, the faces were foreign to me. That made it hard to know whom to avoid. Many of them looked the same, in that most were white, most were male, and all wore the same all-cotton buttoned-down shirts (one of our Japanese once told me he couldn't for the life of him tell them apart). The 41st floor of Salomon New York was Power Central, holding not just the current senior management of the firm, but its future management as well. You had to go by their strut to distinguish between who should be approached and who avoided.

(35) Did I grow more comfortable on the trading floor over time? I suppose. But even when I established myself with the firm, I got the creepy crawlies each time I walked out on to 41. I could see certain developments in myself however. One day, I was playing out the Invisible Man, feeling the warmth of the whale shit and thinking that no one in life was lower than I. On to the floor rushed a member of the corporate finance department wearing his jacket like a badge of dishonour. Nobody wore a jacket on the floor. It must have been his first trip down from his glass-box office, and he looked one way and then the other in the midst of the bedlam. Somebody bumped into him and sharply told him to watch his step. Watch his step? But he was just standing there. You could see him thinking that the gaze of the whole world was on him. And he started to panic, like an actor who has forgotten his lines. He probably forgot why he'd come in the first place. And he left. Then I thought a nasty thought. But it showed I was coming along. What a wimp I thought. He doesn't have a fucking clue.

IV

(36) Four weeks had passed. The class had acquired a sense of its rights. The first inalienable right of a trainee was to dawdle and amuse himself before he settled into his chair for the morning. Cafeteria bagels and coffee were munched and swallowed throughout the room. People read the *New York Post* and laid bets on whatever game was to be played that evening. The *New York Times* crossword puzzle had been Xeroxed 127 times and distributed. Someone had telephoned one of New York's sleazy porno recordings and linked the receiver to a loudspeaker on the table in front of the classroom. Sex talk filled the air. I was, as was my habit at this hour, biting into a knish.

(37) Susan James walked in to interrupt *The Revenge of the Nerds II*. James played a strange role. She was something between a babysitter, and an organizer of the programme. 'Quit fooling around you guys,' she pleaded, like a camp counsellor before parents' day. 'Jim Massey is going to be here in a minute.' Massey, we all thought, was John Gutfreund's hatchet man. He had what some people might consider an image problem: he never smiled. Ostensibly, Massey had come to answer questions we might have about the firm. Thus the bugle was sounded before the chairman's keeper of the corporate culture arrived to answer our questions. He had a short jaw-line, lean and sharp enough to cut cake, and short cropped hair. He wore a grey suit with, unlike other board members, no pocket hankie. He had an economy of style and, like a gifted athlete, an economy of movement, as if he were conserving his energy for a meaningful explosion.

(38) He gave a short talk, the point of which was to stress how singular and laudable was the culture of Salomon Brothers. Yes, we knew it was the best trading firm in the world. Yes, we also knew Salomon stressed teamwork (who doesn't?). Yes, we realized that the quickest way to be fired was to appear in the press boasting about how much money we made (Salomon was modest and discreet). Perhaps we had

heard the fate of the Salomon man in Los Angeles who appeared in Newsweek, lounging beside a swimming-pool and boasting about his good fortune? Yes, he had been sacked. Yes, we knew Salomon's $3 billion in capital made it the most powerful force in the financial markets. Yes, we knew that no matter what we had achieved in our small lives, we weren't fit to get a cup of coffee for the men on the trading floor. Yes, we knew not to concern ourselves too much but rather let the firm decide where on the trading floor we would be placed at the end of the training programme.

V

(39) As the training neared its conclusion, the back-room game of Liar's Poker grew. Bond trading had captured the imaginations of more than half the men in the class. Instead of saying buy and sell like normal human beings, they said 'bid' and 'offer'. Bonds, bonds and more bonds. Anyone who did not want to trade them for a living wanted to sell them. This group now included several women who had initially hoped to trade. At Salomon Brothers, men traded. Women sold. No one ever questioned the Salomon ordering of the sexes. But the immediate prohibition of women in trading was clear to all; it kept women further from power.

(40) More different types of people succeeded on the trading floor than I initially supposed. Some of the men who spoke to us were truly awful human beings. They sacked others to promote themselves. They harassed women. They didn't have customers. They had victims. Others were naturally extremely admirable. They inspired those around them. They treated their customers almost fairly. They were kind to trainees. The point is not that a Big Swinging Dick is intrinsically evil. The point is that it didn't matter one bit whether he was good or evil, as long as he continued to swing that big bat of his. Bad guys did not suffer their comeuppance in Act V on the 41st floor (though whether they succeeded *because* they were bad people, or because there was something about the business that naturally favoured them over the virtuous are separate questions). Goodness was not taken account of on the trading floor. It was neither rewarded nor punished. It just was. Or it wasn't.

(41) Because the 41st floor was the chosen home of the firm's most ambitious people, and because there were no rules governing the pursuit of profit and glory, the men who worked there, including the more bloodthirsty, had a hunted look about them. The place was governed by the simple understanding that the unbridled pursuit of perceived self-interest was healthy. Eat or be eaten. The men of the 41st worked with one eye cast over their shoulders to see whether someone was trying to do them in, for there was no telling what manner of man had levered himself to the rung below and was now hungry for your job. The range of acceptable conduct within Salomon Brothers was wide indeed. It said something about the ability of the free market-place to mould people's behaviour into a socially acceptable pattern. For this was capitalism at its most raw, and it was self-destructive.

(42) As a Salomon Brothers trainee, of course, you didn't worry too much about ethics. You were just trying to stay alive. You felt flattered to be on the same team as the people who kicked everyone's ass all the time. Like a kid mysteriously befriended by the playground bully, you tended to overlook the flaws of the bond people in exchange for their protection. I sat wide-eyed when these people came to speak to us, and observed a behavioural smorgasbord the likes of which I have never before encountered except in fiction. As a student, you had to start from the premise that each of these characters was immensely successful, then try to figure out why.

(43) The training programme wasn't a survival course, but sometimes a person came through who put the horrors of 41 into perspective. For me it was a young bond salesman, just a year out of the training programme and at work on 41, named Richard O'Grady. He began by telling us how he had come to Salomon. He had been one of the firm's lawyers. The firm's lawyers, when they see how good traders had it, often ended up as traders themselves. The firm had actually invited O'Grady

to apply. He interviewed on a Friday afternoon. His first meeting was with a managing director named Lee Kimmell. When O'Grady walked into Kimmell's office, Kimmell was reading his résumé. He looked up from the résumé and said, 'Amherst, Phi Beta Kappa, star athlete, Harvard Law School, you must get laid a lot.' O'Grady laughed (what else do you do?). 'What's so funny?' asked Kimmell. 'The thought that I get laid a lot,' said O'Grady. 'That's not funny,' said Kimmell, a viciousness coming into his voice. 'How much do you get laid?' 'That's none of your business,' said O'Grady. Kimmell slammed his fist on the desk. 'Don't give me that crap. If I want to know you tell me. Understand?'

(44) Somehow O'Grady squirmed through the interview and others, until, at the end of the day, he found himself facing the same man who had given me my job, Leo Corbett. 'So Dick,' said Corbett, 'what would you say if I offered you a job?' 'Well,' said O'Grady, 'I'd like to work at Salomon, but I'd also like to go home and think it over for a day or two.' 'You sound more like a lawyer than a trader,' said Corbett. 'Leo, I'm not making a trade; I'm making an investment,' said O'Grady. 'I don't want to hear any of that Harvard Law School clever bullshit,' said Corbett. 'I'm beginning to think you would be a real mistake . . . I'm going to walk out of here and come back in ten minutes and when I come back I want an answer.'

(45) O'Grady's first reaction, he said, was that he had just made a catastrophic error of judgement. Then he thought about it like a human being. Salomon had invited *him* to interview. Where did these butt-heads get off issuing ultimatums? O'Grady worked himself into an Irish rage. Corbett was gone far longer than he had promised, making O'Grady even angrier. 'Well . . .?' said Corbett upon his return. 'Well I wouldn't work here for all the money in the world,' said O'Grady. 'I have never met more assholes in my entire life. Take your job and stick it up your ass.' 'Now I am finally beginning to hear something I like', said Corbett. 'That's the first smart thing you've said all day.' O'Grady stormed out of Salomon Brothers and took a job with another Wall Street firm.

(46) But that was only the beginning of the story which, O'Grady said, resumed a year after he had told Leo Corbett where to stick his job offer. Salomon called him again. They had apologized for the way they had behaved. They had been smart to do so because O'Grady became not only an excellent bond salesman, but also a rare and much-needed example of goodness on the training floor. The surprise was not that Salomon called him, but that O'Grady had agreed to listen. O'Grady took a job with Salomon Brothers.

(47) And now he was about to tell us what we all wanted to know. 'So you want to know how to deal with assholes, don't you?' he said. Trainees sort of nodded their heads. O'Grady said he had discovered the secret earlier than most. When he was just starting out, he said, he had an experience which had taught him a lesson. He had been a flunkey for a senior bond salesman named Penn King, a tall blond Big Swinging Dick if ever there was one. One day, King told him to find prices on four bonds for a very large customer, Morgan Guaranty. O'Grady therefore asked the relevant trader for prices. When the trader saw him, however, he said, 'What the fuck do *you* want?' 'Just a few prices,' said O'Grady. 'I'm busy,' said the trader. Oh well, thought O'Grady, I'll see if I can find the prices on the Quotron machine.

(48) As O'Grady fiddled with the keyboard of the Quotron – it resembles a personal computer – Penn King demanded the prices for his customer. 'I told you to get the prices godammit,' he said. So O'Grady raced back to ask the trader again. 'Fuck it' said the trader, 'here, read it off the sheets,' and handed O'Grady a sheet listing bond prices. O'Grady returned to his desk only to find that while there were plenty of prices on the sheet, they weren't the prices he needed. 'Where are the goddam prices?' asked Penn. O'Grady explained what had transpired between himself and the trader to that point. 'Then this is what you do, you hear me?' said a completely pissed-off Penn King. 'You go over to that *asshole* and you say, "Look *asshole*, since you were so *fucking* helpful the first time I asked, maybe you could give me the goddam prices for Morgan Guaranty."'

(49) So O'Grady went back to the trader. He figured he could edit the request, you know, take out the part about the asshole and being fuckin' helpful. He had this sanitized version in his mind: 'Look I'm really sorry to be such a pain in the neck,' he was beginning to say, 'but Morgan Guaranty is one of our biggest customers and we need your help . . .' But when he reached the trader, the trader rose to his feet and screamed, 'What the fuck are you doing back here? I told you: *I . . . am . . . busy.*' 'Look *asshole*,' said O'Grady, forgetting the sanitized version, 'since you were so *fucking* helpful the first time I asked, maybe you would be so kind to give me the goddam prices *now*.' The trader fell back in his chair. Since O'Grady was about twice the size of the trader, he could threaten force. He stood over the trader and stared for about a minute. '*Asshole*' he shouted again, for effect.

(50) All of a sudden, the trader looked spooked. '*Pennnnn!*' he half-screamed, half-whined across the floor to O'Grady's boss. 'What the fuck is it with this guy?' Penn gave an innocent little shrug as if to say, he didn't have the faintest idea. O'Grady walked back to his seat to a standing ovation from three or four other bond salesmen who had watched the scene develop, and a big grin from Penn. Sure enough, not two minutes later, *the trader came to him with the prices.* 'And after that,' said O'Grady to a spellbound training programme, 'he didn't fuck with me again.'

Questions

General

1. Which type of Deal and Kennedy's 'corporate cultures' did Salomon Brothers have?

Anticipatory step of socialization process

During this phase, three important things happen. Review the case, and give examples of each of these.

2. What values, beliefs and behaviours are required by the neophyte, to enable them to survive and prosper in Salomon Brothers? How were they learned?

3. How were the graduate trainees 'sold' the organization, and encouraged to see themselves as members of an elite who had to pay the 'price of admission' which only a few could pay.

4. With what were the graduate trainees' old reference groups, roles and states replaced?

Initiation step of the socialization process

In this step, the 'new boy or girl' becomes the 'low man or woman'. The initiates form themselves into a training group in which the process of role acquisition begins. The effort to acquire a vast amount of technical information generates anxiety. This is compounded by a fear of failure and the possibility of rejection. The 'bosses' become the focus of a love–hate relationship. To survive, the group creates informal structures, status relationships and values. It takes over the job of indoctrinating other initiates. Give examples of these.

5. What informal training group structures were there?

6. How was social status assigned to members by the training group?

Assimilation step of the socialization process

In this step, the neophyte is taken into the work environment, and away from the relative safety of the training group, in order to be introduced to the complexities and dilemmas of the organization. He or she is introduced to the world of work families, each of which has their own territory, mandate, values and norms. These all operate but are hazy and difficult in the first instance to pick up.

7. Describe some of the processes of assimilation described in the case.

8. At which point in the case, did Lewis feel that he was becoming absorbed into the Salomon Brothers apparatus?

The case is taken from Michael Lewis's *Liar's Poker*, Hodder and Stoughton, London, 1989. Pages 42–89 have been abridged. Used with permission.

16.3 PREP: Role-set analysis and role conflict

Objectives

❑ To examine role conflict in an organizational setting.

❑ To clarify your position in an organization.

❑ To establish what demands and expectations are made of you in your role.

❑ To identify possible and actual areas of conflict arising from your role.

Introduction

One source of conflict in organizations is that which arises from the different expectations that those in particular roles have of each other. This activity helps you to examine this. The exercise is designed to be used by both undergraduates and experienced managers. The former may choose to consider their role as a student at the university. Significant members of the role set will include fellow students, course lecturers, personal tutors or advisers, weekend employers, parents, boy and girlfriends, and others. A class of managers will analyse their work role.

Procedure

Step 1   Before the class, use the blank space in your workbook, to write in the box, the title of the role that you occupy in an organization (e.g. student, nurse, operations manager).

Step 2   Around the box, enter in circles, the titles of all the other people who make significant demands upon you, and who have significant expectations of the role that you occupy (e.g. course lecturer, ward sister, departmental manager).

You will have reciprocal expectations and demands of these people. You should not forget members of other organizations (e.g. student union officer, nursing equipment representative, customer).

Those with whom your links are particularly strong should be located nearer the box at the centre of the page. Weaker-linked individual should be represented more on the periphery. Five such individuals should be identified by their job titles.

Step 3   Using the sheet overleaf, list in column A, the five members of your role-set who make the most demands upon you (i.e. those identified in the circles in your diagram).

For each, in turn, complete the other three columns.

Step 4   Finally, check your diagram and table by asking yourself:

1. How sure are you that you know what all the demands and expectations are that others have of you?

2. Would your expectations of them fit in with their perceptions? If asked, would they agree with what you have written?

3. Can you cite any specific examples of problems related to the conflict areas in column D? How have you tried to resolve these?

Bring these notes to the next class.

ME

A	B	C	D
Role-set member	Their demands/ expectations of me as:	My demands/ expectations of them as:	Possible conflict areas

1.

2.

3.

4.

5.

Step 5 *In class*, and in your groups, and using the role-set analysis that you have carried out as preparation:

1. Discuss the chart showing your network. Use this to check that you have included all significant relationships.

2. Identify how your network differs from those of other group members of your group. What are the reasons for this? What are the implications of this for the skills you need to develop?

3. Exchange information about the conflicts or difficulties shown up in column D. Suggest practical actions that might be taken to address two of these.

4. Prepare to report to the class as a whole, one specific example of a role conflict that a member of your group is experiencing and suggest how it might be resolved.

16.4 REV: Crossword

Objective

❑ To assess student familiarity with the language and concepts of *ORBIT*, Chapter 16.

Introduction

This test is based on Chapter 16 which considers bureaucracy.

Procedure

Complete the crossword.

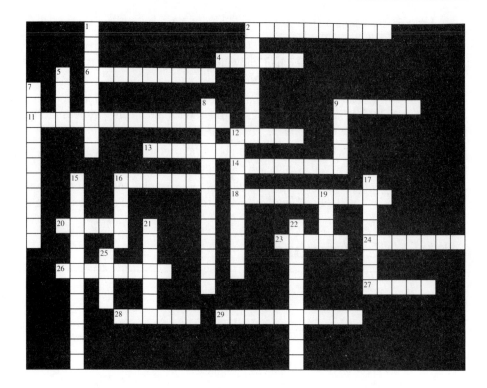

ACROSS

2. Loose, organic structures that permanently co-exist with bureaucracy (10)
4. Called bureaucracy 'a lifeless crutch that is no longer necessary' (6)
6. Few levels mean a flat _____ (9)
9. This conflict was Gilbert's responsibility (6)
11. Narrowness of an employee's job (14)
12. The specialist can only offer advice because of her relationship (5)
13. Perhaps he shouldn't touch an organizational objective (7)
14. As a form of organizational design, bureaucracy was both impersonal and _____ (8)
16. Decreasing the organizational levels reduces the span of _____ (6)
18. Authority based on the personal qualities of the individual (11)
20. He didn't invent bureaucracy (5)
23. Lifetime employment in Japan (5)
24. Argued that organizations damaged your personality's health (7)
26. Studied calcium sulphide extraction (8)
27. Believed Type Z organizations would predominate (5)
28. Project leader directs pranks on the rug, say (6)
29. In this relationship, the manager has to accept the advice (10)

DOWN

1. Commands perceived as legitimate are based on _____ power (9)
2. Roles pull one apart (8)
3. Obligation upon an occupier of position (14)
5. In this relationship, those above can direct those below (4)
7. Defines the key aspects of an individual's job (11)
8. Individuals 'learn the ropes' and how to behave in a company (12)
9. Role emulated in miniature (5)
12. Fox stressed this view of organizations (10)
15. Spirit in which the ideal official conducts his business (13)
16. Visually depicts authority and responsibility relationships.(5)
17. Felt that organizational roles imprisoned our behaviour (8)
19. Perhaps only turtles will identify with this bureaucracy! (4)
21. Not focal's roles, but the others' (7)
22. They operate to offer more basic guidelines about expected behaviour (10)
25. His employment agency subverted organizational aims (4)

Chapter 17
Classical management theory

17.1 LGA: Exodus 18:13–26

Objectives

❏ To introduce students to the purposes of organizational design.
❏ To give them practice in redesigning the structure of an organization.

Introduction

Throughout recorded history, whenever humankind has sought to achieve a major goal that has necessitated the contribution of many people, there has always been the need to apply the skills of management and organization. The construction of the Pyramids, starting in 2700 BC, involved the application of project management skills at the very highest level. It is true that these skills were not written down in the form of 'principles of management' until the beginning of the twentieth century. However, they were both known about and were communicated orally, and they have been applied for thousands of years.

This activity gives you the opportunity to become familiar with the idea of consciously designing an organization's structure and introduces you to some of the key concepts involved. Perhaps more importantly, however, it makes the point that as activities, management and organization, were not *invented* a hundred years ago, but have existed as long as human beings have banded together to achieve goals which they could not attain as individuals.

Procedure

Step 1 As briefed by your instructor, read the case, 'Exodus 18:13–26' and then answer the nine questions that follow.

Exodus 18:13–26

All through recorded history people have had to organize themselves so as to accomplish their objectives. Moses was faced with an organization that prevented him from achieving the more important goals that his Boss had set him. Luckily, Jethro, Moses' father-in-law, gave him some sound advice.

13. And it came to pass on the morrow, that Moses sat to judge the people; and the people stood by Moses from the morning unto the evening.

14. And when Moses' father-in-law saw all that he did to the people, he said, What is this thing that thou doest to the people? Why sittest thou thyself alone, and all the people stand by thee from morning unto even?

15. And Moses said unto his father-in-law, because the people come unto me to enquire of God:

16. When they have a matter, they come unto me; and I judge between one and another, and I do make them know the statutes of God, and his laws.

17. And Moses' father-in-law said unto him, the thing that thou doest is not good.

18. Thou wilt surely wear away, both thou, and this people that is with thee: for this thing is too heavy for thee; thou are not able to perform it thyself alone.

19. Hearken now unto my voice, I will give thee counsel, and God shall be with thee: Be thou for the people to God-ward, that thou mayest bring the causes unto God:

20. And thou shalt teach them ordinances and laws, and shalt shew them the way wherein they must walk, and the work that they must do.

21. Moreover thou shalt provide out of all the people able men, such as fear God, men of truth, hating covertness; and place such over them to be rulers of thousands, and rulers of hundreds, rulers of fifties and rulers of tens:

22. And let them judge the people at all seasons: and it shall be, that every great matter they shall bring unto thee, but every small matter they shall judge: so shall it be easier for thyself, and they shall bear the burden with thee.

23. If thou shalt do this thing, and God command thee so, then thou shalt be able to endure, and all this people shall also go to their place in peace.

24. So Moses hearkened to the voice of his father-in-law, and did all that he had said.

25. And Moses chose able men out of all Israel, and made them heads over the people, rulers of thousands, rulers of hundreds, rulers of fifties and rulers of tens.

26. And they judged the people at all seasons: the hard causes they brought unto Moses, but every small matter they judged themselves.

Numbers 1:44 mentions that the 'heads over the people' were twelve, one from each tribe. The total number of men of sword-bearing age (women not counting in the scheme of things, since Women's Lib was still far off) was slightly over 600,000.

Questions

1. Assuming each of the twelve tribes to be of the same size (although they weren't), draw an organizational chart of the Nation of Israel in the Wilderness. (You need only complete a chart for one tribe as we are assuming the others to be identical in size and structure).

2. What was Moses' span-of-control before the reorganization and after it?

3. How many levels of hierarchy were there below Moses?

4. Which tasks did Moses delegate to his subordinate managers? Speculate as to why he delegated these particular tasks?

5. Did Moses's father-in-law, Jethro, occupy a line or a staff position when he gave his advice to Moses? Why?

6. Did Moses occupy a line or a staff position? Why?

7. Who had the largest and smallest span-of-control?

8. In total, how many managers did Moses create to take over the duties he had previously done himself?

9. What effect do you think this reorganization had on Moses' ability to do his primary task of planning and leading the Nation of Israel to the Promised Land?

This activity is taken from R. M. Fulmer and T. T. Herbert, *Exploring the New Management: A Study Guide*, Macmillan Publishing Company, London, 1978, pp. 78–80. Used with permission.

17.2 SGA: Speedyprint Ltd

Objectives

❏ To contrast the formal and informal organizational structures in an organization.

❏ To examine the consequences when individuals have not been incorporated fully into the formal organizational structure.

Introduction

At the intellectual level, the distinction between the formal and the informal organization is easily grasped by students. So too, are the concepts of line and staff relationships, authority, accountability and responsibility. However, being asked to identify these in an organizational context, is perhaps more complex. This activity gives you a chance to examine these concepts, and their application, in a company setting.

Procedure

Step 1 Follow your instructor's briefing with respect to the preparation of the case, Speedyprint Ltd.

Step 2 In your groups, discuss the individual answers to the questions set.

Speedyprint Ltd

Trevor Horton inherited the managing directorship of Speedyprint eight years ago. The firm was established in the 1970s and was located in Flexborough, a town of 40,000 inhabitants. Demand for printing services expanded consistently, and appeared to be only marginally affected by the periods of recession which affected the other industries in the town. Horton's family owned the company, and he had been more-or-less forced into the job upon the death of his father. His sister had emigrated to Australia years ago with her husband. His own training and ambition was to be a musician. As a result he seemed to be more interested in his composing and playing, than in the success of the family business. He spent most of his time attending concerts and practising the piano.

Nevertheless, Mr Horton did take an interest in the firm to the extent that he frequently made personnel and work changes which he felt improved the immediate situation. These changes were mostly made on the spur-of-the-moment, and he rarely analysed the consequences of his decisions in terms of their possible effects on others. His manner with employees could be quite forceful. He showed clearly that he was the owner and boss, and accepted no arguments. He was assisted in his management tasks by Steven Philips, who was the general manager.

The organizational chart shows Horton and Philips and also Dennis Pringle, who was the chief accountant and office manager. Mr Pringle had been with firm for twenty years, ever since he had left school. Since joining, he had been given a varied range of responsibilities which he had carried out competently, if not with creativity. He had progressed, attaining his current situation of chief accountant and office manager, eight years ago. Pringle had an easygoing nature, supervised little, and only gave orders when specifically requested to. Because of his nature, he assumed an ever-increasing number of duties without making a fuss.

Toni Barlow was in her mid-twenties and had been hired by Horton earlier in the year. Toni had worked in the accounts department of an engineering company, but had left when her husband was offered a more senior job by his company. Her appointment was opportunistic. Toni and her husband were attending a local rotary club dinner at which Horton was present. Horton was introduced to Toni's husband through a mutual friend, and the three of them got talking. Finding out that she was an accountant and taking an instant liking to her (he said she reminded him of his sister), Horton offered her a job at Speedyprint.

Toni would have preferred to visit the firm and meet the employees with whom she would be working before deciding on the job offer. However, Horton's offer was attractive and she was currently between jobs. Horton seemed to want an immediate decision so, after discussing it with her husband during the meal, Toni accepted before Horton left that evening. Once Toni had accepted, Horton told his friend, 'I haven't talked this appointment over with my chief accountant, but I'm sure it will be OK.'

The office staff at Speedyprint consisted of six young women and eleven older women. They all got on satisfactorily with each other, although there were the inevitable frictions. Outside of the office, the older women often met each other, being members of the local church and Women's Institute. The younger women and girls frequented Flexborough's discos and pubs, and some attended the Wednesday evening aerobics class in the leisure centre. Most of them had come from school with some GCSEs, although there were a few who had been recruited through government youth training schemes. The older office employees had been with the company virtually all their working lives. Indeed, some of them had at been at Flexborough High School with Dennis Pringle, and had worked with him during the eight years that he had been chief accountant and office manager.

Speedyprint Ltd (partial organizational chart)

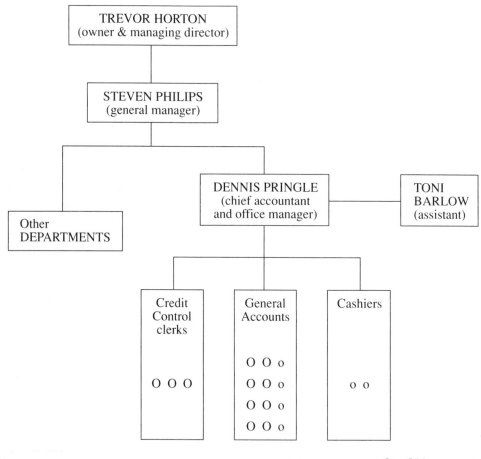

O = Older women
o = Younger women

Because of their length of service, their 'chumminess' in the office, and the comparative freedom in their jobs, the older women were satisfied to get somewhat less than the going local rate for the job. The younger women, in their turn, were pleased to have a job, and spent much of their break time talking about their boyfriends, engagements and imminent weddings. Turnover among this group of staff was high, but while they were with the company, they seemed to be happy. Their level of expertise and rapidity of departure meant that Pringle had trained them to do a limited number of very specific accounting tasks. Despite the repetitiveness of the work, the girls managed to achieve an acceptable level of accuracy.

The general office at Speedyprint was located on the first and second floors above the printing shop. The Credit Control department (three older women), Cashiers (two younger women) and Mr Pringle's office were on the first floor. The second floor housed the General Accounts office (eight older women, and four younger ones), and the offices of Mr Horton and Mr Philips.

FLOOR 1

| Credit Control | Cashiers | |
| O O O | o o | Mr Pringle |

FLOOR 2

General Accounts	Mr Horton
O O o	
O O o	Mr Philips
O O o	
O O o	Toni

Floor plan showing layout of offices

O = older women
o = younger women

The day after the Rotary Club dinner, Horton discussed Toni Barlow's arrival with most of the office staff. He arranged for a desk to be placed on the second floor. This would allow Toni to be near both the employees and the general accounting records which would be her main responsibility. Toni's main task would be to help Dennis Pringle in the preparation of daily, weekly and monthly accounting reports. Horton, as well as the general manager (Mr Philips) and the departmental managers, felt that the reports which they had been receiving from Pringle were of little use in controlling operations because they were out of date when they got them. Typically, they were received between one and four months after the period covered. Pringle acknowledged that these reports were issued late, but explained that he was too busy with day-to-day tasks to improve the situation.

On Toni's first day at the firm, she was taken on a tour of the printing works and the offices by Mr Horton, and was introduced to most of the employees including Dennis Pringle whom she would be assisting. He introduced Toni to the office staff and to the general managers with the comment, 'Toni is going to help us sort out the accounting office. Now we'll be able to get the reports out on time, at last!'

Toni spent most of her first day talking to the staff with whom she would be working. She also asked Mr Horton about the type of information that he and the other general managers needed. The staff were helpful, if a little reserved, and Toni felt that she would enjoy working with them once they had got to know her better. That evening, Toni and her husband were guests of Mr and Mrs Horton at a local restaurant as a 'welcome-to-the-firm' celebration. During the evening, Horton talked enthusiastically about music and what he was doing. Toni felt quite flattered when he said, 'I feel that I can confidently stay away from the office much more now, knowing that the reports to our managers will be coming out on time'.

Toni's first week involved going around with Pringle, and learning about the various accounting procedures. While finishing lunch one day, she noticed a group of the older women laughing and clapping at the far side of the canteen. Mr Pringle was among them. '. . . and we won't be paying her any extra' he shouted as he left what was clearly a social gathering. Seeing Toni, Pringle stopped by her table. 'Mary's just become a grandmother for the first time,' he explained, 'and they asked me to present their gift.'

Toni found Pringle very cordial and willing to help whenever she asked. This was a style that he adopted with other staff as well. Once, one of the girls from the Credit Control Department came up and asked, 'Mr Pringle, should we give United Machines thirty or sixty days credit?' He replied patiently, 'Sixty days Tracy, they're very good customers of ours. You'll find the credit rating of each of our customers in the green folder that I showed you. I update it at the end of each week.'

Over the next few weeks, Pringle and Toni became friends. As the months passed, the two with their spouses met for an evening of bridge. Toni respected Dennis Pringle's judgement and found him very obliging. Frequently, Pringle would say, 'Toni, you've really helped me out by taking the pressure of those reports off my shoulders. When Trevor isn't wrapped up in his music, he regularly grills me as to why they are so late'.

After a month, Toni became accustomed to the routine of her duties. She found herself working closely with most of the women in the two offices. All of them turned out to be involved, in varying degrees, in bookkeeping activities. Specifically, she was in daily contact with nine of the older women (eight on the second floor, and one on the first floor); and with three of the younger female employees (two on the second floor and one on the first floor). Using the statistical and accounting data produced by these women, Toni prepared her financial reports.

She worked on her tasks with great commitment because she wanted to succeed at the job. Within two months, she was able to get reports onto the desks of Mr Horton, Mr Philips and the departmental managers within the specified time. Toni was often called into senior departmental sales meetings to discuss the reports that she had prepared. Since her desk was located on the second floor, it was convenient for Mr Horton or Mr Philips, to call her in a loud voice, with a comment such as, 'Toni, could you come in here and help us with these reports?' Sometimes such requests occurred at the end of the day, and Toni's briefing finished at the wine bar across the road from the office.

Toni felt that she was doing a good job at Speedyprint. However, during the first six months she did have some minor problems. Three experiences were typical. First, while requesting data from one of the older women, Toni was asked, 'What's the hurry? Dennis never pressured us to supply the information by a deadline. We gave it to him when we were ready.' In response, Toni explained how the reports would be used and the need for their promptness. It seemed to her that her explanation only encouraged the woman to delay giving her the information even longer.

Second, one of the younger women from the General Accounts office on the second floor came to Toni and complained that the credit control clerks were making errors. In particular, on sales tickets, received invoices and packing slips. The girls frequently brought errors of this type to Toni's attention. As usual, she spoke tactfully and courteously to the clerks, and also to any of the other company employees who made errors. She pointed these out to them and explained how they affected the information that was needed. Some time later, Toni heard on the 'grapevine' that the employees whom she had corrected had complained that she was trying to 'run the firm'.

Finally, Mr Philips told Toni to instruct the women in the first and second floor offices not to stay in the canteen so long in the mornings. It had become the practice for all the younger women to gather in the canteen at 10.30. The older women took their 20-minute break at various times between 10 and 10.45, while Mr Pringle and Toni had coffee at their desks. Although a staggered coffee break for the younger women would have made more sense, the practice had existed for a number of years without any objection from management. However, it seemed to Mr Philips that frequently the girls stayed longer than their allotted twenty minutes. In response to Mr Philips's instructions, Toni said to the women in the offices, 'Mr Philips has asked me to ask you not to take such long coffee breaks in the morning'. She made the announcement to all the women as a group, on each floor, one afternoon as they were getting ready to go home.

Toni sometimes noticed resentment towards her among the older office women. She therefore tried to be especially nice to them. She was tactful and courteous in her requests for data, and was helpful whenever they requested anything from her. Despite her best efforts, the older women's actions, manner and words made Toni feel both uncomfortable and out of place.

One morning, about nine months after Toni joined, Mr Horton came into her office. He had not been coming into the office regularly for weeks because he was busy preparing for a recital. He said to her, 'I'd like you to do a couple of things for me as a kind of special project. First, revise our expenses code system. We need to expand our classification of expenses. The current one is out of date, it hasn't been changed for years. It'll mean staff having to memorize a new code, but I don't think they'll find it too difficult. And second, I want you to prepare a job analysis on each of the women in the office. Mr Philips suggested that you do this. It's never been done before, so I think it will be useful to find out just what each of the staff members is doing. Prepare one for the women on the first floor too, will you. Take your time on these projects, just work them in with your regular duties. Oh, by the way, tell Dennis you're doing this for me.' Toni agreed that she would try to do this. As Mr Horton left the office and Toni returned to her desk, she pondered how she would go about this new project.

Questions

1. (a) Prepare for contrast with the formal organizational chart, a chart that shows the informal organizational relationships that existed at Speedyprint Ltd.
   (b) Identify any significant differences between the formal and informal organizations.
   (c) Has management consciously encouraged these differences? How?

2. (a) What managerial and human relations errors were made in the process of hiring Toni Barlow and in introducing her into the organization?
   (b) Who made the errors?
   (c) What result did they have?

3. How did the following people affect Toni's successful performance of her duties:
   (a) Trevor Horton.
   (b) Steven Philips.
   (c) Dennis Pringle.

4. List the problems that Toni faced during her first nine months at Speedyprint Ltd. In what way, if any, should Toni have conducted herself differently?

5. What was Toni Barlow's role in the organization as perceived by:
   (a) Trevor Horton.
   (b) Steven Philips.
   (c) Dennis Pringle.
   (d) Younger office women.
   (e) Older office women.
   (f) Toni Barlow.

6. Did a satisfactory level of communication exist between the people described in the case? Explain.

7. How should Toni go about the project given to her at the end of the case? What particular problems does she now face?

8. Identify examples of change in Speedyprint. What are the effects of each? What is management's responsibility here?

This exercise was prepared with the assistance of Gemma Donnelly-Cox, Trinity College, Dublin.

17.3 PREP: Sanders and Murgatroyd, Accountants

Objectives

❑ To illustrate how different organizational perspectives can lead to differences in problem definition and solutions.

❑ To revise three major organizational behaviour perspectives.

Introduction

Organizational behaviour theory contains many different perspectives and approaches to problems which beset companies. Being predominantly based upon social science, many of the prescriptions compete with each other. To new students (especially those coming from scientific disciplines and backgrounds which offer, 'the one, right answer'), this may be both confusing and frustrating. Nevertheless, this situation has to be confronted. In this activity, the same case study is analysed through three different perspectives. It stresses that every OB approach has both strengths and weaknesses, and none is complete in itself.

Procedure

Step 1 Individually prepare the following assignment. Sanders and Murgatroyd's senior management has asked for:

1. An analysis of the reasons for the turnover of its trainee accountants.

2. A set of recommendations to solve the problem.

You are required to prepare three separate reports. These will analyse the problem and make recommendations from a:

1. Scientific management perspective (Frederick Taylor, *ORBIT*, Chapter 17).

2. Human relations perspective (Elton Mayo, *ORBIT*, Chapter 7).

3. Motivation perspective (Frederick Herzberg, *ORBIT*, Chapter 5).

Analyse the case as you think Frederick Taylor would, and then make recommendations based on his scientific management principles. Repeat the procedure for Elton Mayo and finally for Frederick Herzberg. Reread the textbook material before proceeding. *For each perspective*, your analysis should:

1. List the main principles or assertions.

2. Identify which of these appear to have been broken by the firm (as described in the case).

3. Recommend the steps to be taken by the firm (in line with the perspective's principles).

Sanders and Murgatroyd, Accountants

Phil was one of twenty-four Trainee Accountants (TA) who worked for Sanders and Murgatroyd, a large, international accounting firm. He had been with it for ten months ever since he completed his Bachelor of Accountancy degree at university. He was pleased to get a job with this prestigious firm since it recruited only from the top 10 per cent of each year's graduating class. His academic career had not been brilliant, but luckily his dad knew one of the senior partners in the firm. He said that it was a good, steady job. Most of the other graduates he met had only had a brief interview, and he was pleased that he was spared the psychological and problem-solving tests that university applicants to some of the other accounting firms were subjected to.

On his first day, he was shown into a small office in which he was to work. He had hoped to share it with a fellow TA but apparently these people were scattered in similar small offices throughout the large building. Phil discovered his job responsibilities in an *ad hoc* manner as different senior auditors briefed him on what he was to do. He had expected an introductory course, or at least some sessions on the company since it had recruited two dozen graduates that year. He was interested in knowing about the firm, what it did, the different departments in which one could work and so on. His university friends with jobs at some large firms had called these induction courses. Anyway, no one invited him to attend an induction course here.

In his post, Phil was responsible for gathering financial data and relevant information on each client to whom he was assigned. Having accumulated the information, he often had to supplement it with visits and interviews with the client's staff. Phil roughed out an outline of the report, which laid out the factors of importance in the client's financial standing.

Once he had got to grips with it, Phil found the job extremely tedious. It involved him wading through mountains of cost data, as well as tracing cost figures to determine if they were correctly allocated. Sometimes he would use the financial summaries provided by the clients, while at other times he referred to past data collected by S & M. Most of the time he did not bother to cross check the information because this practice was time-consuming.

However, when dealing with the accounts of certain clients, he did do this secondary analysis. Additionally, Phil had to ensure that all the categories of data were covered and appraised in his analysis. Once his research was completed, he passed it on to a Senior Auditor (SA) who wrote the final report based on Phil's work, correcting any minor errors. The SA then visited the client to give a verbal summary and to answer any questions. Meanwhile, Phil started another assignment.

This occurred irrespective of the complexity of the report. In some 60 per cent of cases, Phil found that the SA's final report differed very little from his own. The six senior auditors were divided into departments according to the type of organization they dealt with. When a job came in, they called upon a TA who was either between reports, or who was about to complete one. Sometimes finding one took a bit of time as the SA's secretaries had to ring around the TAs to find out who had finished what.

Looking at Phil's job in a little more detail, it involved specifying what raw material for the report was required (financial data); searching for and locating the raw material; classifying and sorting it; analysing and abstracting trends and patterns; and writing the outline for submission to the SA. After the first three months he had managed to get the hang of the techniques to be used. Many of them were similar to those he had picked up at university, and therefore required no new learning. He had hoped to be sent on a training course to develop the skills he had, but none of the senior auditors had suggested any training.

At times he found his progress was slowed by the fact that about 20 per cent of client records had not been computerized. When there was a query about an uncomputerized file, it took him a disproportionally long time to sort it out. In addition, the major computer installation in the company had occurred some four years ago during which time all the hardware and software had been updated. Since that time, technological improvements in computer power and developments in software had made the system dated and increasingly more difficult to use. It did not appear that any one manager had the remit to monitor developments in information technology and update the facilities as required.

Phil always looked forward to the lunch breaks in the dining room since it gave him the opportunity to talk to the other TAs who were scattered throughout the building. Most of them did similar work to his. What he found most interesting, was that some of them used different approaches to calculating things like return on investment and the value of an inventory. Phil remembered how he had once received a sharp rebuke from a SA for one of his outline submissions concerning the way he accounted for depreciation. However, when he submitted a report to another SA (using the same technique), he found he did not complain. Perhaps the first SA had had a bad day!

He was often surprised by the different amounts of time that it took his colleagues to complete similar tasks. The male trainees often bragged about how long they took to complete a piece of work, and how little effort they managed to put into it. Many of the senior accountants seemed reluctant to discuss the performance of the TAs and their reports. The female TAs seemed more conscientious but were reluctant to reveal how many reports they had completed for fear of being jeered at.

After these lunchbreaks, Phil came away feeling glad that the particular group of SAs for whom he prepared reports were happy to leave him to get on with it. In fact, he had very little to do with them other than receiving a briefing. He was once asked by one of them how he was getting on and whether he had any problems, That, however, had been an accidental meeting while both of them were waiting for the lift. He was thanked by the SA when submitting his report, but was rarely phoned up or seen again unless there was a problem.

The office itself was full of PCs and dated electronic hardware. At his induction day, he had been told that customized firm software would ensure a speedy analysis of data in a standardized format. At the end of the day, he had applied for a place on the computing course, but was still waiting to go. In talking to some people who had been on the course, it appeared that they were expected to deliver outline reports at a faster rate. Perhaps course attendance was not such a good idea after all.

Phil's time was charged to the account of the client for whom he was working. Since it represented a cost to the firm, it was important that Phil was as productive in his job as possible, and carried out the work carefully since there were numerous opportunities for error and bad judgement.

However, despite not having seen him for a few weeks, one of the SAs noted that at their last briefing, Phil's enthusiasm seemed to have worn off, and his productivity (in terms of the speed of completed assignments) had reduced. Perhaps most seriously, the quality of his work had dropped off recently, and several errors (one of them quite serious) had been discovered. However, this decline in performance was not restricted to Phil but had been noted among the other Trainee Accountants who had been recruited at the start of the year. Reviewing last year's staff turnover figures, the head of administration discovered that the figure for trainee accountants was 50 per cent above the average. Some had resigned, while others were dismissed for unsatisfactory work performance.

This activity is developed from the exercise, 'Analysing a problem through management links', in R. M. Fulmer and T. T. Herbert, *Exploring the New Management: A Study Guide with Cases, Readings, Incidents and Exercises*, Macmillan, New York, 1978, 2nd edition, pp. 29–30.

17.4 REV: Reorganizing the Allied Paint Company

Objective

❑ To apply the principles of effective structural design in order to identify potential organizational design problems.

Procedure

Review the organization chart of Allied Paint Company. The organization of the company has grown over the years without very much planning or reflection. There are now a number of problems. Examine the organization chart in detail, focusing on job titles, seniority of positions, unity of command and spans of control. Identify the fifteen problems and suggest possible solutions (e.g. Should jobs be retitled? Layers removed? Posts transferred? Which ones? Why?).

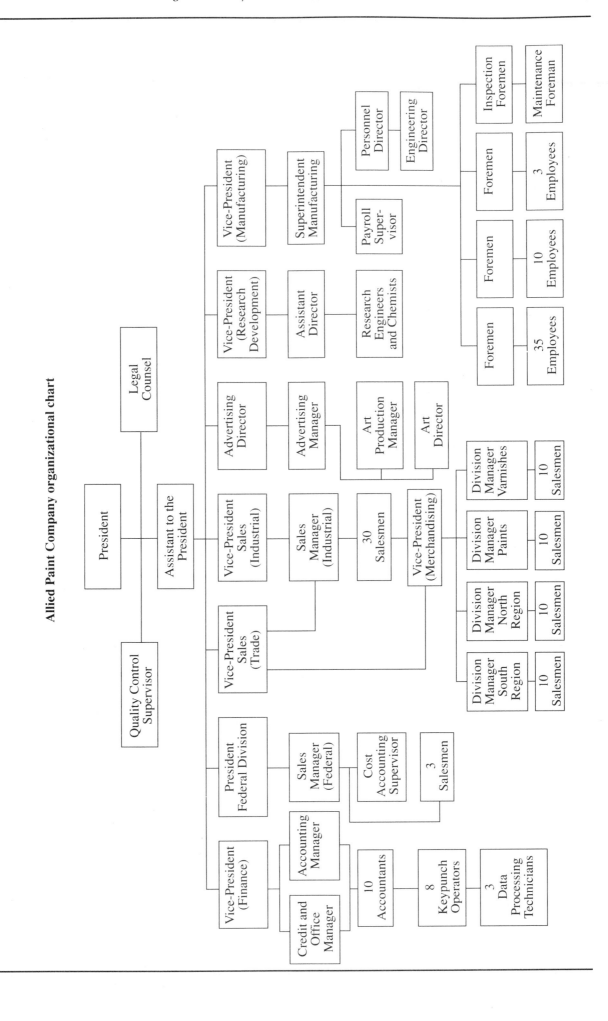

Allied Paint Company organizational chart

1. Problem:

   Solution:

---

2. Problem:

   Solution:

---

3. Problem:

   Solution:

---

4. Problem:

   Solution:

---

5. Problem:

   Solution:

---

6. Problem:

   Solution:

---

7. Problem:

   Solution:

---

8. Problem:

   Solution:

9. Problem:

   Solution:

10. Problem:

    Solution:

11. Problem:

    Solution:

12. Problem:

    Solution:

13. Problem:

    Solution:

14. Problem:

    Solution:

15. Problem:

    Solution:

Chapter 18
Contingency approach

18.1 LGA: Identifying my preferred organizational structure

Objectives

❑ To allow students to distinguish between two different types of organizational structure.

❑ To explore their preferences for working in one or the other.

❑ To reflect on the possible effects of different organizational structures on the motivation of the employees within them.

Introduction

The type of organizational structure in which people work can greatly affect their motivation and productivity. Structure involves the number of levels in a hierarchy, the span of control, the extent to which jobs are defined in detail, and the number and types of rules. Some people operate most effectively in very hierarchical organizations with narrow spans of control, where each job is defined in detail and where ample rules exist to guide actions and avoid ambiguity. Other people would find such structural arrangements excessively stifling, and would prefer more autonomy to make their own decisions. This activity will introduce two different organizational forms, and help students to decide in which they would prefer to work.

Procedure

Step 1 Individually, complete your *Organizational structure questionnaire*.

Step 2 Listen to your instructor's lecture on the different features of mechanistic and organic organizational structures.

Step 3 Score your questionnaire using the key in your workbook, and then read the score interpretations.

Step 4 With the person next to you, use your score interpretations and understanding of the differences between the two organizational structures to discuss the four questions below:

1. Which organizational structure do you prefer? Why?

2. What problems might result from a conflict between a new employee's expectations of a company's structure, and its actual structure?

3. Can you give an example of a 'pure' organic or mechanistic system? On what evidence would you label it as one or the other?

4. Which type of organizational structure would motivate today's workforce? Which personal needs might each structure best satisfy?

Organizational structure questionnaire

Think of the type of organization for which you would like to work. Then read the fifteen A and B statements below, and score each using the following scale:

> If statement A is totally descriptive of your ideal organization, give yourself 5 points.

> If statement A is more descriptive of your ideal organization than statement B, give yourself 4 points.

> If statement A is slightly more descriptive of your ideal organization than statement B, give yourself 3 points.

> If statement B is slightly more descriptive of your ideal organization than statement A, give yourself 2 points.

> If statement B is much more descriptive of your ideal organization than statement A, give yourself 1 point.

> If statement B is totally descriptive of your ideal organization, give yourself 0 points.

Write your points score for each of the fifteen questions in the space adjacent to the question number:

1. _____

A. Job descriptions should be detailed and complete so that personnel know precisely what they are supposed to be doing, and exactly how their performance is being assessed.
B. Job descriptions are not really necessary. A general verbal description of the work to be done will get the personnel into the ballpark, and that should be enough to allow them to develop their role themselves.

2. _____

A. Organizational charts should be constructed for every unit and department as well as for the company as a whole, so that everyone knows where they fit in the total structure and who reports to whom.
B. Organization charts are unnecessary. At best they merely serve to provide a general scheme of things, but since operations are in a continual state of flux, they really never reflect things as they truly are.

3. _____

A. Authority should be reflected in position, ensuring that decisions are made at the appropriate level of seniority. Those in higher-level positions should have authority over those in lower-level positions.
B. Authority should be a function of knowledge. Regardless of formal job descriptions or seniority, the person who knows most about the problem or solution, should be the one who decides what is to be done.

4. _____

A. Since only senior management can possess a long-term view of a firm's direction, goal setting should be top-down, with managers setting objectives for their people.
B. Goal setting should be a participative process, with both managers and subordinates getting together to set objectives for the company.

5. _____

A. The general nature of the work to be done should be routine and repetitive.

B. The general nature of the work to be performed should be non-routine and challenging.

6. _____

A. The focus of the planning process should be on the formulation and implementation of long-term goals.
B. The focus of the planning process should be on the formulation and implementation of short-term goals.

7. _____

A. The environment in which the organization operates should be a predictable one.
B. The environment in which the organization operates should contain a great deal of uncertainty.

8. _____

A. The relations between company employees should be formal in nature.
B. The relations between employees should be informal.

9. _____

A. Motivation to work should come basically in the form of extrinsic rewards, e.g. increases in pay, promotions, company cars.
B. Motivation to work should come basically in the form of intrinsic rewards related to features of the job itself, e.g. responsibility, recognition, sense of achievement.

10. _____

A. The technology used by the company should be stable and not subject to much change.
B. The company's technology should be dynamic and take advantage of new developments and improvements.

11. _____

A. The general nature of the industry should be calm with predictable, evolutionary changes.
B. The general nature of the industry should be turbulent, with frequent, unexpected challenges to be met.

12. _____

A. The procedures used to make the behaviour of employees predictable should be primarily impersonal in nature, e.g. rules, regulations, procedure manuals.
B. Control procedures should be predominantly interpersonal in nature, e.g. personal requests, group pressure.

13. _____

A. The values of the company should stress efficiency, predictability and security.
B. The pervading values of the organization should be effectiveness, adaptability and risk-taking.

14. _____

A. The decision-making process should entail only standard, routine decisions.
B. The decision-making process should include many non-standard and non-routine decisions.

15. _____
   A. The organizational emphasis should be on effectiveness, efficiency and profitability.
   B. The organizational emphasis should be on problem-solving.

Scoring

Insert each of your fifteen answers and total them.

1. ____	9. ____
2. ____	10. ____
3. ____	11. ____
4. ____	12. ____
5. ____	13. ____
6. ____	14. ____
7. ____	15. ____
8. ____	Total: _____

Interpretation

0–15   You would feel most comfortable working in an organization that is highly organic.

16–30   You would feel most comfortable working in an organization that is basically organic.

31–45   You would feel most comfortable working in an organization that is a blend of organic and mechanistic characteristics.

46–60   You would feel most comfortable working in an organization that is basically mechanistic.

61–75   You would feel most comfortable working in an organization that is highly mechanistic.

The source of this exercise is unknown.

18.2 SGA: Company AD 2005 plc

Objectives

❑ To help students identify those aspects of the environment which are likely to affect organizational performance in the future.

❑ To consider the implications of these factors on organizational design.

Introduction

Organizations exist in a social, political, economic and technological milieu. What happens outside them has implications for what goes on inside. The most successful companies not only adapt to external changes, but also anticipate such changes. This activity focuses on such crystal-ball gazing. It asks you to identify some possible (non-technological) external change stimuli that may affect an industry that all of you are familiar with. It then asks you to go further and consider the implications of these external changes on the organizational structure and management of firms in that industry.

Procedure

Step 1   Imagine that you are a management consultant. You have been approached by the directors of a multinational company which manufactures and distributes non-alcoholic drinks. The company's product range includes soft drinks (e.g. natural orange juice); carbonated soft drinks (e.g. fizzy orange); colas and mixers (e.g. tonic water).

You have been called in because the company's senior management are reviewing strategy through to the year AD 2005. They want your team's ideas about the factors which they will need to take into account with respect to their market, and to the internal organization of production. They have already been briefed on the key technological issues. They now want to consider the future more broadly. Their remit to you is:

- To identify the social, economic and political developments in Britain and the rest of Europe which are likely to impact upon their consumers and suppliers, and will thus affect what they sell, how they sell it, and how they manufacture and distribute it.

- To speculate on the organizational and management changes that these are likely to necessitate.

Step 2   Working individually for fifteen minutes, note down any trends or developments which you think are likely to be important in this business. You are to use your experience as a consumer, newspaper reader and student. You are encouraged to be creative and you should go for quantity of suggestions rather than quality. Next to each development, note any possible organizational or managerial implications.

Step 3   In your group, review, sort and organize the items of individuals into a single group list (external factors on the left, organizational and managerial implications on the right).

Each group will be provided with a flipchart/overhead transparency foil and pen with which to summarize their main conclusions. It should nominate one group member to give a 3-minute presentation of the group's ideas. Your group has twenty-five to thirty minutes for this task including the charting of the points.

18.3 PREP: Organizational structure analysis

Objectives

❑ To identify the strategic direction of your organization.

❑ To analyse its current organizational structure.

❑ To evaluate the suitability of the current structure in terms of current and future organizational objectives.

❑ To recommend changes which would allow the structure better to support strategic goals.

Introduction

The purpose of this exercise is to encourage you to identify systematically the demands that are made on a department's structure (in terms of its key result areas, objectives, future changes, future objectives and individual objectives) and to assess the suitability of that structure (in terms of roles, rules, authority, responsibility, job descriptions) for the organizational goals.

Procedure

Step 1   Prepare notes in line with the questions in the *Organizational structure analysis questionnaire* before coming to class.

Step 2   In groups, on the basis of both your responses to the preparatory questions and with your knowledge of structural options, you should assess:

1. How adequate the existing organizational structure is in meeting current and future departmental objectives.

2. Is the achievement of objectives helped or hindered by the way that departmental responsibilities are divided and allocated to individual jobs?

3. How might the departmental structure be improved?

4. Are the performance expectations up-to-date, and do they tie in with the organization's structure of the department?

5. Are employees in the department meeting the performance expectations associated with their current jobs?

6. Are they aware of whether or not they are fulfilling the company's performance requirements?

Organizational structure analysis questionnaire

1. Review the present structure of an organizational department that you are familiar with in relation to the organizational goals. Your review should be in terms of:
   (a) number of levels of hierarchy;
   (b) relationships between roles;
   (c) procedures and systems that exist;
   (d) nature of the controls that are exercised.

2. What are the key result areas in the department? What five or six things, if well done, will have the most beneficial results for the company, e.g. 90 per cent plant utilization?
   (a) List them in order of importance.
   (b) Specify those which are not being met and why this failure is occurring.

3. What are the department's objectives? The achievement of objectives contributes to high organizational performance in the key result areas, e.g. regular machine maintenance, few machine breakdowns.
   (a) Examine the departmental objectives.
   (b) Are the objectives realistic?
   (c) Are they being met?
   (d) List any shortfalls.

4. Future changes. What changes (in new products, new procedures, new responsibilities, new systems, changes in technology, manufacturing processes, equipment, outside markets, customer behaviour, internal, external and political environments) are likely?
   Assess how these might affect your department.

5. Individual objectives. The aims, ambitions, hopes and aspirations of staff are an important factor in the achievement of the department's key result areas.
   (a) Do you know the objectives of the individuals in your department?
   (b) Do you know how they feel about their work at present?

This activity works best when you have an in-depth knowledge of a real organization. Thus, managers attending the course on a part-time basis will have no difficulty. If you are a full-time student or have limited work experience, take the role of a management consultant and interview a relation or acquaintance who holds a managerial position. Use the checklist of questions provided. Check that your interviewee is in a position to answer these questions. Bring the responses with you to the session.

18.4 REV: Crossword

Objective

❏ To assess student familiarity with the language and concepts of *ORBIT*, Part IV.

Introduction

This test is based upon Chapters 15–17 of the textbook which consider the structural influences on behaviour.

Procedure

Complete the crossword.

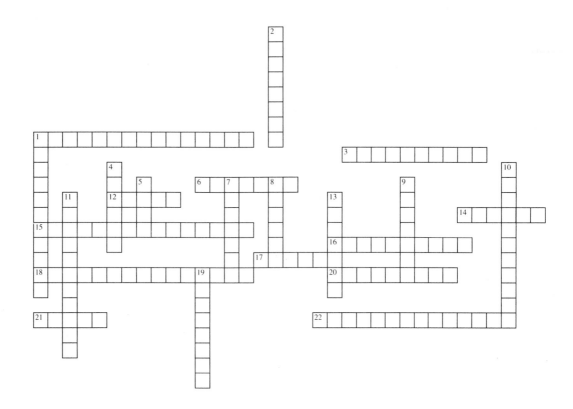

ACROSS

1. Lawrence and Lorsch's division of work [15]
3. One of the four classes of activities to be found in an organization [10]
6. For Woodward, continuous flow production was an example of this technological category [7]
12. He considered organizational design to be a political process [5]
14. He considered corporate culture to be a way of socializing organizational members [6]
15. Macrae's confederations of worker groups [15]
16. The range of environmental activities that are relevant to organizational actions [10]
17. British propagandist for classical management [6]
18. Notion that organizational structure is a management decision [9, 6]
20. Principle that delegation should be maximised with decisions being taken at the lowest level possible [9]
21. '_____ of command' is a classical management principle [5]
22. For Perrow, the _____ of work decided the organizational structure [14]

DOWN

1. Belief that certain variables independently cause changes in organizational structure [11]
2. Deal and Kennedy's culture that is high on risk and quick on feedback [5, 3]
4. Chef's guide to industry wisdom?
5. You can't go wrong with this dramatic, cultural activity! [4]
7. Environmentally friendly electronics company [7]
8. Concept which views organization as a group of grades arranged in a sequence [7]
9. Female classical theorist [7]
10. Refers to the degree to which a company's environment changes [11]
11. Level to which work units are linked together [11]
13. He predicted that organizational size would follow function [7]
19. To fulfil the 16 'Administrative Duties'

Latecomer A

General information

You are one of the student members of the Departmental Course Committee (DCC). Each member represents one of the tutorial groups from the year class. The DCC meets regularly to hear student complaints and receive suggestions for improvements. It is attended by the course director, members of the departmental lecturing staff, and the head of department.

You and your fellow student members hold preliminary meetings, to set the agenda and agree an approach, before bringing matters to DCC. In the past, your group has brought up matters at the DCC which have been swiftly resolved by the course director. At other times, your group has got into unproductive and acrimonious discussions on trivial matters, while important issues were neglected. You and your colleagues have looked silly in front of the teaching staff, and you have been criticized by those whom you represent.

You and your fellow student representatives are meeting today to decide whether or not to invite the course director to your future preliminary meetings (ahead of the DCC). You need a consensus before an invitation can be issued.

Specific information

You have been a member of the DCC from the start of the year, and will be more than happy to give the job to someone else. You don't like the other committee members and have no respect for them. They appear to be a bunch of barrack-room lawyers, seemingly practising to take on student union jobs. They seem to be more interested in themselves, and in how they argue their cases, than in getting the problems of other students sorted out. At the last meeting, two of them got so carried away with their own oratory, they disagreed among themselves in front of the course director, head of department and other departmental staff. Apart from looking silly, the discussion got bogged down, and some serious student problems never even got discussed.

Here's yet another DCC meeting that's going to be a waste of time. You dislike these events so much, you leave it till the last minute to go. Often, like today it means you arrive late. Your own view is that current practice SHOULD be changed, and the course director be invited to future meetings, Your reasons are noted below. Feel free to consult your notes during the role play.

1. You are sceptical whether student members of the DCC can in fact sort out their differences beforehand. Inviting the course director to preliminary meetings at least makes future fiascos less public.

2. The DCC is a problem-solving forum where student difficulties are discussed and resolved. It is not a court of law or a trade union–management negotiation situation (even though some student reps may see it as such).

3. If student members are incapable of sorting out the trivial from the important issues, then they should not be on the DCC.

4. Sorting out the trivial issues with the course director will leave more time to prepare and discuss important matters with teaching staff and the head of department.

5. By discussing only important items at the DCC, teaching staff will come to see these events as valuable, and not just 'student moan sessions about trivia'.

PART V
MANAGEMENT IN THE ORGANIZATION

Chapter 19

Leadership and management style

19.1	Large group activity:	The Apia Harbour incident
19.2	Small group activity:	Choose your style
19.3	Prepared task:	The shelf-fillers
19.4	Review:	Leadership training

19.1 LGA: The Apia Harbour incident

Objectives

❑ To identify the characteristics of incompetent leaders.

❑ To consider explanations of leadership behaviour.

❑ To consider the attributes of competent leaders.

Introduction

What makes a good leader? One way in which to approach this issue is to look at poor leadership, and that is what you are invited to do in this exercise. The incident report which follows reports an actual event, and is not fictitious. The behaviour reported is both extraordinary and tragic. How can such behaviour – so obviously inappropriate at the time and with hindsight – be explained? One set of explanations lies in the personal attributes of leaders – their skills, knowledge and personalities. It is, however, necessary to look beyond personality and to look at the context in which leaders operate. The context reported in this particular incident is also unusual.

Procedure

Step 1 Read *The Apia Harbour incident*, on your own, without discussing it with colleagues.

Step 2 Make personal notes in response to the four questions following the case, again without discussing these issues with colleagues.

Step 3 Now compare your thinking and your notes with colleagues in buzz groups of two to four members (depending on your seating arrangements).

Step 4 Share your thinking with your instructor, according to his or her wishes.

The Apia Harbour incident

The place is Samoa and the date 1889. Seven warships – three American, three German and one British – are lying at anchor in the harbour of Apia. They are there as a naval and military presence to watch over the interests of their various Governments in the political upheavals that are taking place ashore. Accordingly they anchor in what has been described as one of the most dangerous anchorages in the world, for to call Apia a harbour at all is at best an unfortunate euphemism. Largely occupied by coral reefs, this saucer-shaped indentation lies wide open to the north, whence the great Pacific rollers come sweeping in. In fair weather, Apia provides an uneasy resting-place for no more than four medium-sized ships. For seven large ships and numerous smaller craft, under adverse conditions, it is a death-trap.

This was the situation in which the seven men-of-war witnessed the first bleak portents of an approaching typhoon. Even to a landsman a rapidly darkening sky and falling glass, squally gusts of wind, and then a lull, would bode ill. For seven naval captains the signs were unmistakable. They knew they were in a region of the world peculiarly subject to typhoons, which, in a matter of minutes, could lash the sea into a furious hell of boiling water. They knew that such storms generate winds travelling at upwards of a hundred knots, gusts that could snap masts like carrots, reduce deck-fittings to matchwood and throw ships on to their beam ends. They knew that it was the worst month of the year and they also knew that only three years before every ship in Apia had been sunk by such a storm. In short . . . their stored information coupled with present input pointed to only one decision: to get up and get out. And, as if this was not enough, the urgency of weighing anchor and putting to sea was respectfully suggested by subordinate officers.

But the captains of the warships were also naval officers and so they denied the undeniable and stayed where they were. Their behaviour has been described as 'an error of judgement that will for ever remain a paradox in human psychology'.

When the typhoon struck, its effects were tragic and inevitable. Without sea room, their anchors dragging under the pressure of mountainous seas, their hulls and rigging crushed by the fury of the wind, three of the warships collided before being swept on to the jagged reefs of coral. Another sank in deep water; two more were wrecked upon the beach. Of all the ships in the harbour the only survivor was a British corvette, which, thanks to its powerful engines and superb seamanship, squeaked through to the open sea.

The Apia Harbour incident: Analysis

1. Using this incident as a guide, and drawing on your own experience, draw up a list of *rules for incompetent leaders* – rules which would help senior organizational figures to make sure that blunders like this happened more often.

2. What aspects of the *situation* or *context* in which the captains found themselves could explain their error of judgement?

3. We are not told much in this incident report about the naval captains as individuals. However, from the available evidence what can we guess about the *personality traits* of those captains?

4. You are a seaman on board one of the warships in Apia Harbour in 1889. Identify the five main *leadership qualities* of the person you would most like to be the captain of the vessel on which you serve.

This exercise is based on an incident reported in Norman F. Dixon's *On The Psychology of Military Incompetence*, Futura Publications, London, 1976, pp. 34–5. For a fascinating (but not flattering) assessment of the behaviour of one individual military leader, see Denis Winter's *Haig's Command: A Reassessment*, Penguin Books, London, 1991.

19.2 SGA: Choose your style

Objectives

❑ To illustrate the use of different leadership styles.

❑ To demonstrate the issues that arise from the advice that leaders change their style to suit the circumstances.

Introduction

Situational leadership is an approach to determining the most effective style of influencing which takes into account the amounts of direction and support the leader gives, and the readiness of followers to perform a particular task. Paul Hersey and Ken Blanchard identify four leadership styles:

Telling: in which the leader gives direct instructions and supervises performance closely.

Selling: in which the leader takes care to explain decisions and gives subordinates an opportunity to check their understanding.

Participating: in which the leader shares ideas and involves subordinates in decision-making.

Delegating: in which the leader gives responsibility for decision-making and implementation to subordinates.

These styles thus vary in the attention given to task behaviour or guidance on the one hand, and relationships behaviour or support on the other. As with other similar approaches to leadership, Hersey and Blanchard argue that the leader must adapt the style to fit the context. One of the main elements in the context, they argue, is the readiness or willingness of subordinates to carry out the task in hand.

To use this approach effectively, the leader has to change style according to the situation, participating with some subordinates, for example, and perhaps telling others. But most of us don't change the way in which we interact with other people. We each have our own 'comfort zone' or preferred ways of behaving, and we do not typically make conscious choices about how to speak to this person, how to speak with that other person. So, what is involved in making conscious choices about behavioural style and potentially moving outside our comfort zone? This exercise offers an opportunity to experience those choices and the outcomes.

Procedure

Step 1   Familiarize yourself with the situational leadership approach of Hersey and Blanchard and as explained in Chapter 19 of *ORBIT* (pp. 506–8). Make sure that you know what each of the four styles means in terms of your behaviour as a leader.

Step 2   Divide into groups of three, and label each other A, B and C at random. We are going to set up a series of three interviews; on each run of the series, one person will take the role of the superior, one will take the role of the subordinate and the third will act as observer. The series looks like this:

		Run	
Role	1	2	3
Superior	A	B	C
Subordinate	B	C	A
Observer	C	A	B

So on the first run through, A interviews B with C observing. Then B interviews C with A observing and so on.

Step 3   Read the briefs for run 1. Give the superior and subordinate time to 'think themselves' into the role they are being invited to play, and give the superior in particular an opportunity to decide how they are going to tackle the interview.

Step 4   Run your first interview for about five to seven minutes, then give the observer five minutes to provide feedback. Each interview run should take from ten to fifteen minutes; remember that between each run, each of the participants needs a little time to familiarize themselves with their new role.

Step 5   Repeat the process for run 2; five to seven minutes for the interview and five minutes' observer feedback.

Step 6   Repeat the process finally for run 3.

Step 7   Return to plenary session. Key learning points can be captured on OHP or whiteboard or flipchart.

Choose your style

Run 1: Superior's briefing (A)

You are Pat Lowry, the office supervisor. One of your clerks, Bill Taylor, seems to spend a lot of time on the job socializing, talking with the secretaries and regularly coming back late from lunch. As a result, a lot of the clerical work does not get done on time, and you can see the work of others being disrupted. You have asked Bill to come and see you because you want to see what can be done about this.

How are you going to handle this conversation? In particular, what *style* are you going to use: telling, selling, participating or delegating? You could choose a style (or styles) that you feel would be appropriate in a situation like this, or you could on the other hand choose a style that you feel you would not normally use – to see how it feels to behave in that way.

When you have decided on your style or styles, decide how you are going to open the conversation, how you are going to progress it, what questions you might ask and in what sequence, what responses you expect to get and how you hope to end the conversation. When you have completed your preparation, write the name of your chosen style on a scrap piece of paper and hand it to your observer. There is a knock on your door and your subordinate comes in.

Run 2: Superior's briefing (B)

You are Chris Peacock, the manager of the sales department. One of your staff, Peter Albrow, has started coming to work late over the past couple of months. He can arrive anything between ten and thirty minutes after the normal starting time. This is annoying other people on the staff, as well as yourself, and you have asked him to come and see you about it so that you can try to persuade him to come in on time.

How are you going to handle this conversation? In particular, what *style* are you going to use: telling, selling, participating or delegating? You could choose a style (or styles) that you feel would be appropriate in a situation like this, or you could on the other hand choose a style that you feel you would not normally use – to see how it feels to behave in that way.

When you have decided on your style or styles, decide how you are going to open the conversation, how you are going to progress it, what questions you might ask and in what sequence, what responses you expect to get and how you hope to end the conversation. When you have completed your preparation, write the name of your chosen style on a scrap piece of paper and hand it to your observer. There is a knock on your door and your subordinate comes in.

Run 3: Superior's briefing (C)

You are Les Johnson, head of the computing department. Peter Long, one of your subordinates, has special computing skills and is at present deeply involved in a major project. Something urgent has come up, an exciting software development programme for a major customer, and you have asked him to come and see you, to give him this extra work on top of his existing work load which cannot be passed on to anybody else.

How are you going to handle this conversation? In particular, what *style* are you going to use: telling, selling, participating or delegating? You could choose a style (or styles) that you feel would be appropriate in a situation like this, or you could on the other hand choose a style that you feel you would not normally use – to see how it feels to behave in that way.

When you have decided on your style or styles, decide how you are going to open the conversation, how you are going to progress it, what questions you might ask and in what sequence, what responses you expect to get and how you hope to end the conversation. When you have completed your preparation, write the name of your chosen style on a scrap piece of paper and hand it to your observer. There is a knock on your door and your subordinate comes in.

Run 1: Subordinate's briefing (B)

You are Bill Taylor, a clerk in the general office. Your job is pretty mundane and routine, and you don't see it as much of a challenge. Nevertheless, you enjoy the job. The people you work with are nice, and you enjoy talking to them as you go round to collect the mail and other paperwork. Sometimes you all go to the pub for lunch, and are sometimes late in getting back. Your boss, Pat Lowry, has asked you to come for a talk today. You are not sure what it is about, but you suspect that it might have something to do with these long lunches.

You knock on the door and enter.

Run 2: Subordinate's briefing (C)

You are Peter Albrow, and you have worked in the sales department for some time. You have recently moved to a new apartment which is further away from the office. If you miss the bus–train connection, which has a reputation for being unreliable, you can be late for work. This has happened a few times recently. Your boss, Chris Peacock, has asked to see you today. You are not sure what it is about, but you suspect that it might be about your timekeeping.

You knock on the door and enter.

Run 3: Subordinate's briefing (A)

You are Peter Long and you work in the computing department. At present, you are up to your eyes in a major programming project, which is interesting and requires skills that nobody else in the department has. Your boss, Les Johnson, has set up a meeting with you today. You are not sure what this meeting is about, but you think that it might mean more (unwelcome) work for you.

You knock on the door and enter.

Observers' briefing: Run 1 (C), Run 2 (A), Run 3 (B)

You are about to observe a meeting between a manager and his or her subordinate. The meeting has been called because the manager has a specific issue to discuss with the subordinate, perhaps to reach a decision or to resolve a problem. Before the meeting starts, the manager will let you know what style he or she has decided to adopt in the meeting.

Your first task is to make sure that the meeting does not run beyond the 7-minute maximum, or whatever other limit your instructor sets for this exercise.

Your second task is to make brief personal notes during the meeting on how the manager handles the conversation and how the subordinate is responding. Points to note might include:

- The way in which the meeting began.
- How the manager introduced the topic.
- How the manager controlled the conversation.
- The way in which the subordinate responded.
- Problems that arise and how they are dealt with.
- How conflicts or disagreements are handled.
- How the issues are resolved.
- How the conversation is closed.

Your final task is to give the manager feedback after the meeting, for about five minutes, before moving on to the next stage of the exercise. Your feedback should cover:

- At least one weakness in the manager's approach, one aspect of the style or a behaviour that you felt could have been avoided or handled better.

- At least one strength in the manager's approach, one aspect of the style or a behaviour that you felt worked well and could be repeated in future.
- General observations about the conduct of the meeting and the subordinate's response.

19.3 PREP: The shelf-fillers

Objectives

❑ To demonstrate the application of concepts from Chapter 19 in *ORBIT* concerning leadership and management style to a specific organizational setting.

❑ To offer students experience of peer assessment of assigned work.

Introduction

The area of leadership and management style is rich with theories and concepts. These are topics that have attracted a lot of academic and management attention and changes in thinking and understanding in this area are still taking place. However, can these concepts and theories be applied to practical organizational settings? That is the question that we wish to raise in this exercise. Also in this exercise we would like to suggest that, instead of your instructor assessing, commenting on and grading your preparation, you exchange your work with somebody else in your class or group and grade each other's submissions.

Procedure

Step 1 Working out of class time, read *The shelf-fillers* organizational description which follows.

Step 2 Still working out of class time, make brief, and precise notes in response to the questions which follow the case description.

Step 3 Bring your responses with you to class as instructed and exchange your work in groups of three; A gives their material to B who gives their material to C who gives their material to A. (You may be left with one pair who simply exchange between them.)

Step 4 Assess, and grade the work that you have received, checking the answers against your own understanding, and by referring back to the textbook (if you really feel that you must). Give the work a percentage grade, out of 100, and write a brief comment explaining what you see as the main strengths and weaknesses in the work.

Step 5 Return the work to the author in your group of three. Identify, discuss and seek to resolve any disagreements or disputes among the members of your group. Adjust your grades if necessary. If you are unable to reach agreement, consult your instructor.

Step 6 Discuss with your instructor any general points arising from this exercise, either about the leadership style issues which have arisen, or about the peer assessment and grading approach.

The shelf-fillers

Malcolm worked on the backshift at Sainsway Supermarket in Ashlock (7.00 p.m. until 10.30 p.m.). He was one of twenty of the store's employees who worked these hours. The store manager often had to plead with staff to work overtime but, as this was not compulsory, he rarely got any volunteers.

The shelf-filling job cannot be described as creative or as a route to self-actualization or as a means of self-expression. Having said that, a section of shelving, stocked correctly, can look very impressive. The monotonous simplicity of the job means that only minimal skill is required and that skill is easy to pick up. Indeed, the less active your mind, the more likely you are to enjoy the job.

Boredom can lead to inefficient working and can reduce productivity. The store manager believed that productivity was reduced when the shelf-fillers spent time talking to each other. So he prohibited them from talking to each other. The boredom also encouraged staff to stick rigidly to their contracted working hours. Although staff were supposed to take a 15-minute tea-break after four hours on shift, they were rarely allowed to have this.

Apart from the store manager, Ashlock Sainsway had a grocery manager, a backshift manager, a shop-floor manager and a warehouse manager. You were either a 'chief' or an 'indian'. There were no intermediate levels. The managers distanced themselves from the 'common' workers and were rarely seen on the shop-floor after they had given their orders. The organization structure looked like this:

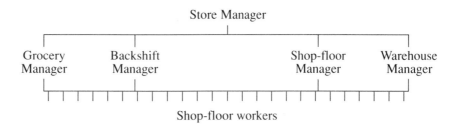

Managers continually shouted at and harassed staff in an effort to make them work faster. Management would introduce new ideas, but no sooner had staff been told to do a job one way, they were told by somebody else to do it differently. On the whole, the store manager's comments to staff tended to be negative, critical and derogatory. The staff reciprocated by holding managers in contempt. One week, three visiting inspectors came from head office to check on the store. As they sauntered around, one of them stopped behind Malcolm who was stacking a bottom shelf, put his hand on his shoulder and said, 'Well done son, keep up the good work'. So unused to praise, Malcolm nearly fainted from shock.

The wage rates on offer were not high enough to encourage workers to work late, especially since overtime was paid at the normal hourly rate. A frequent cause of resentment among the backshift staff was the receipt of a smaller paycheque than they were entitled to. It was common knowledge that even if you did work overtime, you were unlikely to get the full benefit. It was thought that the store manager deleted hours from the record of overtime. This made his figures look better in the eyes of head office, and it saved the company money. The staff were moved around the different display sections, and were constantly reallocated to different parts of the store. About the only thing that remained constant were the hours worked.

One afternoon, the store received a large delivery. When asked, only five of the twenty workers were willing to work overtime. Malcolm was one of them. Because of the lack of volunteers, the small team of five did not finish the task of shelf-filling and rubbish compacting until 6 o'clock the next morning. The store manager complained that the trouble with young people today was that they had no loyalty or commitment to their employer.

The Ashlock Sainsway questions

1. Problem-solving is often simplified if we can distinguish causes from symptoms. However, establishing that distinction is not always straightforward. Identify three main symptoms of the problem facing management in the Ashlock Sainsway store, and three main causes.

2. If you were able to get the managers in this store to complete Edwin Fleishman's Leadership Behaviour Description Questionnaire, how would you expect them to rate on the two dimensions? Give specific examples of store management behaviour that support your conclusion.

3. John French and Bertram Raven identify five main bases of power. On which base or bases do the managers in Ashlock Sainsway exercise power? Which bases would

you recommend they use in addition to or instead of those currently in use?

4. Rensis Likert, University of Michigan, identified four 'leadership systems' or leadership styles. In Likert's terminology, which leadership system is in use in this store? Cite specific management behaviours to support your answer.

5. In terms of Fred Fiedler's theory of leadership behaviour, in which 'condition' are the store managers operating? What are the implications of this analysis for the store managers?

6. The most effective style in a *situational* leadership approach depends on subordinate readiness or maturity. How would you rate the readiness or maturity of subordinates in the Ashlock Sainsway? What are the implications of this rating for management?

19.4 REV: Leadership training

Objectives

❑ To review understanding of leadership concepts and theories.

❑ To assess ability to apply leadership theories and concepts to a specific practical task.

Introduction

If you have completed the previous exercise, 19.3 PREP, you have had experience in analysing and criticizing leadership behaviour. The result of that analysis is a series of suggestions about how management in that particular setting should behave. However, people will not always change their behaviour just because you tell them to. They may wish to know why they should do so. They may want to understand your reasoning, your theories, your concepts. They may want to understand better the options which they face, and the different consequences of different choices. So, the way in which you tell them and what you tell them will influence the extent to which your message is effective. One way to enhance the effectiveness of your message is to run a training programme. In this exercise, you are invited to design a training programme for the store managers in Ashlock Sainsway, following your critical analysis of their behaviour in the previous exercise. Some training course design hints are offered, but your starting point is a good understanding of the concepts and theories in Chapter 19 of *ORBIT* on management and leadership style.

As any organizational behaviour instructor will tell you, one way to improve your understanding of the subject is to try to teach it to somebody else. (This applies to any subject, of course.) Here, then, is your opportunity to decide how you would teach the subject of leadership to a specific management group.

Procedure

Step 1 Read the following brief on *Leadership training*.

Step 2 Design a course following the instructions and suggestions provided. Write this up in report form and/or prepare an oral presentation of your design, depending on the wishes and aims of your instructor.

Step 3 Submit or present your design for critical review and comment.

Leadership training brief

The store manager at Ashlock Sainsway is depressed. He has known for some time that relationships in the store are not as good as they should be. He also feels that there are faults on both sides – management and shop-floor. However, he also accepts that this is ultimately a management responsibility. Having heard your analysis of the problems arising from the management style used in the store, he has asked you to design a 5-day, residential training programme in leadership skills. There are, of course, only five managers at Ashlock, so he has persuaded two other stores in the region to send their managers on this course too, giving you a group of fifteen people. Not surprisingly, the other two store managers feel that they share many of the same problems. Special arrangements have been made to cover the management absence for the week, so nobody will have to disappear suddenly to cope with an emergency during your training programme. Why *would* anyone want to leave during the week? Well, the store managers may have accepted your analysis of their difficulties and your recommendations about what should be done, but some of their other managers think that this could all be a waste of time because the *real* problems lie with lazy and incompetent staff. After all, you don't get university and college graduates looking for careers as shelf fillers!

The company has booked a comfortable and well-equipped four-star hotel where you and the fifteen managers will spend the week. They will arrive on the Sunday evening, before dinner time, and plan to finish with lunch the following Friday. Your task is to design a training programme that will help to address the leadership and management style problems identified in the analysis of the previous exercise. Here are some hints to help you:

1. Write a statement of the *objectives* of your training programme.

2. Divide your programme into a series of discrete morning, afternoon and evening sessions. Do you want to be working *all* the time? You could, for example, use one or more evenings for social events.

3. Use a range of different methods and techniques to give your programme variety and to sustain the interest of your group. In addition to lecture inputs, you could think of using exercises of the type found in this manual (role plays, questionnaires, group discussion and so on).

4. Remember that some of your participants are sceptical of the value of this exercise, and may dismiss your arguments about managerial styles and behaviours. What methods will you use to overcome this resistance?

5. You may wish initially to base your planning on the contents of Chapter 19 in *ORBIT* on leadership style. However, there are other ideas, concepts, theories, frameworks and techniques from other chapters that could usefully be added; give this some thought.

6. Make your training programme interesting, memorable and challenging. Do you need to spend the whole week working inside the hotel? Can you make creative use of some of the hotel's facilities?

Chapter 20
Managing change

20.1 Large group activity: **Managing change – good practice**
20.2 Small group activity: **Causes of resistance**
20.3 Prepared task: **Force field analysis**
20.4 Review: **Methods rating**

20.1 LGA: Managing change – good practice

Objectives

- ❑ To establish from experience guidelines for good management practice in the implementation of change.
- ❑ To develop understanding of the wide range of individual, organizational and managerial issues involved in implementing change effectively.

Introduction

We have all experienced change, in different forms and settings. We are frequently reminded by media commentary that increasingly rapid and complex change is a central facet of our modern lifestyles. What factors influence our reactions to change? Do we, as many will argue, have a 'natural' resistance to change? Or do we get bored with routine and seek fresh experiences from time to time? The argument that we would like to advance here is that our reactions to change and the outcomes of change depend to a large extent on how change is *managed*. How *should* change be managed, to avoid or overcome resistance, and to ensure that the implementation is smooth and effective? In this exercise we would like to invite you to consider your own experiences of change, positive and negative, and to identify 'rules' for good management practice.

Procedure

Step 1 Working on your own, consider your own experiences of change in organizations. This should ideally concern recent personal experience. However, if you have so far avoided such an experience, perhaps you know what relatives and friends have experienced. Or perhaps you have a good understanding of change issues from media and other accounts.

Step 2 Make notes for your own use on what you would regard as characteristics of effective change management. What should management do to ensure smooth and effective change?

Step 3 Still working on your own, make notes on what you would advise management to *avoid* in attempting to implement change effectively.

Step 4 Working in buzz groups of three or four members – depending on your seating arrangements – compare notes and produce a master list of management 'best practice', and of things to avoid with respect to effective change implementation. Nominate a spokesperson to feed back your lists of 'dos' and 'don'ts' to your Instructor.

Step 5 Feedback and discussion, according to your instructor's wishes.

20.2 SGA: Causes of resistance

Objectives

❑ To establish the possible causes of resistance to change in organizations.

❑ To identify approaches to overcoming resistance to change in organizations.

Introduction

Many managers regard resistance to change as one of the main barriers to organizational development and technological innovation. The expectation that change will be resisted thus influences the way in which changes are introduced in the first place. Resistance is often taken for granted. Solutions to organizational problems are naturally based on what we assume or know to be the cause of those problems. If our assumptions are correct, our knowledge sound, then our proposed solutions are more likely to be effective. We would like to invite you in this exercise to consider – and possibly to refine – your own personal assumptions about resistance to change and also about how it can be overcome or avoided. If we want to solve the problem of resistance to change, we need to know what causes it; we will therefore begin by looking at some actual instances of resistance to change and at the causes of that behaviour.

Procedure

Step 1 Working on your own, complete the *Resistance to change analysis sheet* which follows. Give particular attention to the *why?* question; what caused the resistance in this case? Remember that there may be more than one cause.

Step 2 Working in syndicates each with three members, go round the group sharing the examples which you have each generated. Note similarities in and differences between the accounts. Note any *patterns* that seem to emerge from these accounts. As you listen to the other accounts, ask questions to ensure that you understand *why* the change was resisted in that example.

Step 3 Instructor issues a separate *Explanations for resistance* (1) sheet. Read the list and, for each of the examples of resistance to change represented in your syndicate group, *identify the reason or reasons* that apply. Note the item number or numbers of the explanations that apply in each example. This checklist may not cover all the reasons in the cases under discussion. Note any additional explanations you would want to add to the checklist.

Step 4 Instructor takes a 'popularity poll' by asking each person in turn simply to reveal the number or numbers of the explanations that apply to their examples of resistance to change. When the poll is complete, you will have a count against each of the ten items (and possibly for a few additional explanations as well).

Step 5 Instructor issues a separate *Explanations for resistance* (2) sheet. Comparing the results of your popularity poll with the *Resistance* (2) sheet, what conclusions can you reach about the causes of resistance to change, and thus about the most appropriate forms of solution to this problem?

Resistance to change analysis sheet

Think of a specific example of resistance to change. This could involve new organization structures, systems or working practices, or it could involve new technology, or it could involve a combination of such factors. Choose if you can a specific instance you have experienced personally. If that is not appropriate, there may be instances you can recall from the accounts of friends or relatives, or media accounts. Use the spaces to make notes, initially for your own purpose, in response to the following questions:

What did the change or changes involve?

Who resisted?

Why did they resist?

What *form* did the resistance take?

How was the matter resolved?

Explanations for resistance (1)

Resistance to change in an organization can be caused by a number of factors. Identify which of the following *possible* explanations apply to the case or cases you have been considering. What follows is simply a *checklist of possibilities*; there may explanations here with which you disagree, and there may be explanations that you feel have been missed out. Several of these items may apply to the explanation of resistance in one given setting. Check within your syndicate group that you are each clear about the explanation or explanations that apply in each case.

1. People have a natural resistance to all change.

2. Older people are more likely to resist change.

3. Users of new technology resist the introduction of equipment and systems that are poorly designed.

4. Users of new technology resist the introduction of equipment and systems that have poor ergonomic features, such as seating, and the positioning of controls and lighting.

5. Users of new technology resist the introduction of equipment and systems that are complicated and difficult to learn and use.

6. People resist changes that interfere with their established ways of working with others in the organization.

7. People resist changes that disturb the distribution of tasks and responsibilities across the organization.

8. People resist changes that interfere with their autonomy and decision-making.

9. People resist changes that interfere with their access to information and discretion over how it is being used.

10. People resist changes that reduce their ability to influence and control other people and events in the organization.

Explanations for resistance (2)

There are four broad types of explanation.

1. People-focused

Here the fault, or blame, or cause of resistance lies with the individuals involved, their personalities, their attitudes, values, preferences and so on.

2. Systems-focused

Here the fault lies with system designers and with equipment characteristics such as 'user friendliness', complexity, ergonomic features, access for maintenance and so on.

3. Organization-focused

Here the cause of resistance lies with the perceived lack of 'fit' between the change and its organizational context. The key factor here concerns *allocation of responsibility.* New technology, for example, or a 'total quality management' package, typically involves new patterns of working, and changes to social interaction in the organization. This may cut across traditional cultures and established 'ways of doing things'. Can also affect real and presumed status differentials.

4. Politics-focused

Here the cause of resistance again lies with the interaction between changes and context. But the key factor under this heading is *distribution of power.* New ways of working alter the 'ownership' of information, alter patterns of access to information and affect established patterns of decision-making and the exercise of influence by individuals and groups.

On the checklist of possible options,

> items 1 and 2 are people-focused
> items 3 to 5 are systems-focused
> items 6 to 8 are organization-focused
> items 9 and 10 are politics focused

Item 8 could relate to either of the last two sets of explanations. This depends on why people are resisting interference with their autonomy.

This exercise and the classification of explanations is based on M. L. Markus, 'Power, politics and MIS implementation', *Communications of the ACM*, 1983, vol. 26, no. 6, pp. 430–44.

   The practical implications for the change agent in what Markus calls, 'the political variant', are explored in David Buchanan and David Boddy, *The Expertise of the Change Agent: Public Performance and Backstage Activity*, Prentice Hall International, Hemel Hempstead, 1992.

20.3 PREP: Force field analysis

Objectives

❑ To develop understanding of the technique of force field analysis.

❑ To develop ability to translate such an analysis into a practical action plan.

Introduction

If you have completed the previous two exercises in this section, you will be fully aware of the multi-variate, multi-dimensional, multi-faceted nature of organizational change. Put more crudely, there are an awful lot of factors to take into account. Planning and implementing change can, therefore, be a complex, untidy, messy business. Particularly so when the factors affecting the change are in conflict, with some dimensions favourable, and some not. In such circumstances, it is helpful to find and to use methods that bring order to chaos, and that bring systematic structure to complex and contradictory information. One such 'ordering and systematizing' method is *force field analysis*, developed by the social psychologist Kurt Lewin in the 1960s and now widely cited and used. In this exercise, we plan to:

● Introduce the technique.

● Ask students to conduct an analysis of the force field related to a specific change.

● Work that analysis through to a practical action plan.

● Present that action plan for critical appraisal.

The need for clarity of objectives is frequently mentioned as an element in the effective implementation of change. If you do not know the destination, it is difficult to determine the direction of travel. Before we begin this exercise, therefore, we would like to ask you to reflect on a specific organizational change that you would like to introduce. This proposed change should have a number of criteria. It should be relevant to your current experience and be visible to you. It should be specified in precise terms, either with respect to events, behaviours or outcomes or some combination of these factors. It should be realistic, in terms of practical implementation, timescale and resource implications. Organizational changes that could meet these criteria could include the introduction of a new committee structure for the local students' union, the introduction of revised organizational behaviour course examination and feedback procedures, the introduction of improved student evaluation of teaching performance mechanisms, the implementation of a new scheme of social and sports club membership and fee charges and so on.

There will be specific local issues of relevance to you and to fellow students; choose a *target situation* that is of some immediate relevance and significance, and one that would be interesting to work on for this assignment.

Procedure

Step 1 Identify an appropriate *target situation* for this assignment, using the criteria set out in the Introduction. Your target situation should be capable of precise and unambiguous definition, and should not be stated in vague and generalized terms.

Step 2 Conduct a *force field analysis* using the guidance sheet which follows, identifying and rating as instructed the driving and the resisting forces.

Step 3 Write a short and realistic assessment of how the forces balance, and of the probability of success should you proceed with the proposal.

Step 4 Produce a practical action plan in accordance with the advice and instruction set out on the *Components of an action plan*.

Step 5 Produce a realistic assessment of your action plan against the criteria identified, and up to three additional criteria that you find relevant.

Step 6 Submit your force field analysis, your action plan and your action plan assessment in accordance with the directions of your instructor.

Force field analysis

Main steps:

1. Define your target situation in terms of events, outcomes or behaviours.
2. Identify all the driving forces you can think of.
3. Identify all the resisting forces you can think of.
4. Drivers and resistors can include people (key individuals and groups), aspects of the context, and arguments for which there is support and evidence. Do not be surprised if some drivers appear in a modified form as resistors, and vice versa.
5. Rate each of the driving and resisting forces in terms of *strength*: high, medium or low.
6. Give the *strength* ratings numerical values: 5 for high, 3 for medium, and 1 for low; you can now calculate totals for the driving and resisting forces to help you assess the balance.
7. Rate each of the driving and resisting forces in terms of how *easily influenced* they are: high, medium, low (this is independent of the *strength* of each force).
8. HINT: identify the *strong* forces that are *easily influenced*. These are the ones on which you may wish to concentrate when formulating a practical action plan. However, these are not necessarily the only factors to be considered at that stage.

The target situation is: _____

Components of an action plan

To translate your force field analysis into a practical action plan designed to achieve the target situation, you need to consider the following items:

*   Definition of the problem or issue to be resolved.
*   Specification of the target situation, outcomes and results.
*   Practical actions:
    first steps
    next steps
    what next
    what then
*   Any preconditions for the above?
*   Any options or contingencies to mention, should things go wrong?
*   Specified milestones and deadlines.
*   Specific responsibilities – who's going to do all this?
*   Timing of events.

Put your proposed action plan into the form of a summary report. In deciding on action to increase driving forces, introduce new driving forces; and to reduce or eliminate resisting forces, consider in particular the advice offered in Chapter 20 in *ORBIT* with respect to 'rules for overcoming resistance', 'techniques for blocking interference', 'effective project definition' and 'causes of resistance'. There may be other research-based ideas you can incorporate too.

Force field analysis

Driving forces	Resisting forces

Action plan assessment

Having produced a practical action plan to achieve your desired target situation, how should you evaluate the plan? Once again, there are perhaps a large number of dimensions on which such a plan can be assessed, and it would be helpful if we could structure or systematize this assessment.

One commonly applied technique is *cost-benefit analysis*. This can be a sophisticated evaluation methodology, but it can also be applied with effect in a simplified form. Try this approach:

- List the main *costs* of your proposed action plan. These costs can be financial, material and psychological (money, resources, time, frustration and so on).
- Rate each cost, subjectively, in terms of its *strength* – high cost, medium cost, low cost.
- List the main *benefits* of your proposed action plan.
- Rate the strength of each benefit.
- You do not need to attach numbers to the strength ratings to get a reasonably good feel as to whether one set of outcomes outweighs the other, or whether the costs and benefits balance each other out. If the benefits outweigh the costs, or if the costs and benefits evenly balance, would you wish to give up – or would you try to find additional benefits and new ways to reduce the costs?
- Indicate how you would amend your action plan (if at all) in the light of your cost-benefit analysis.

There are other criteria on which you can assess your action plan. These should include:

Impact – will this action make a significant difference to the organization and its performance?

Can-do – will this action plan really work in practice?

Appeal – will this action plan 'strike a chord' and attract the attention of those who will contribute to its success?

Timing (1) – is this the right time to be doing something like this?

Timing (2) – are the stages of the action plan timed in an appropriate and realistic way?

Optional: Identify up to three additional criteria on which you feel it appropriate to assess your action plan.

20.4 REV: Methods rating

Objectives

❏ To test understanding of different approaches to the effective management of organizational change.

❏ To compare the strengths and weaknesses and relative appropriateness of different change management methods.

Introduction

In Chapter 20 of *ORBIT*, in the section on 'Managing organizational change', six specific methods for dealing with resistance to change are explained. These are derived from the work of J. P. Kotter and L. A. Schlesinger and appear on pages 540–3. Just knowing the labels of the six methods and what each involves is inadequate. In what kinds of organizational settings are these approaches suitable? What are the advantages of each of these methods? What are the disadvantages and weaknesses of each of these methods? We need answers to these questions if the techniques are to be used in ways that are both appropriate and effective. The answers to these critical questions can be found in the material of Chapter 20 (and not just in the managing change section) and in your own experience.

Procedure

Step 1 Remind yourself of the six methods for managing resistance to change as advocated by Kotter and Schlesinger.

Step 2 Complete the grid which follows where you are asked to identify:

- The organizational circumstances in which that method would be appropriate.
- The strengths of that approach.
- The limitations or weaknesses in that approach.

Step 3 Submit your analysis for assessment, according to the wishes of your instructor.

Methods for managing resistance to change

Approach	Commonly used in situations where	Advantages	Drawbacks
Education + communication			
Participation + involvement			
Facilitation + support			
Negotiation + agreement			
Manipulation + cooptation			
Explicit + implicit coercion			

Chapter 21
Managing conflict

21.1 LGA: My conflict management style

Objectives

❏ To introduce students to the different ways in which conflict can be managed.
❏ To allow students to identify which conflict management mode they typically use.

Introduction

Each individual possesses a particular way of dealing with conflict situations. This exercise seeks to raise students' awareness of what alternative management styles are available and which one(s) they typically use.

Procedure

Step 1 Individually, complete the *Thomas–Kilmann conflict instrument*.

Step 2 Score the questionnaire as directed by your instructor.

Step 3 Compare your scores with the two people sitting on either side of you, and with the comparison scores of middle and senior managers.

Thomas–Kilmann conflict questionnaire

Consider work or non-work situations in which you find that your wishes differ from those of another person. How do you usually respond to such situations? Below are several pairs of statements describing possible behavioural responses. For each pair, please *circle* the 'A' or 'B' statement which is most characteristic of your own behaviour. In many cases, neither the 'A' nor the 'B' statement may be very typical of your behaviour, but please select the response which you would be more likely to use.

1. A There are times when I let others take responsibility for solving the problem.
    B Rather than negotiate the things on which we disagree, I try to stress those things upon which we both agree.

2. A I try to find a compromise solution.
    B I attempt to deal with all of my, and the other person's concerns.

3. A I am usually firm in pursuing my goals.
    B I might try to soothe the other's feelings and preserve our relationship.

4. A I try to find a compromise solution.
    B I sometimes sacrifice my own wishes for the wishes of the other person.

5. A I consistently seek the other's help in working out a solution.
    B I try to do what is necessary to avoid useless tensions.

6. A I try to avoid creating unpleasantness for myself.
   B I try to win my position.

7. A I try to postpone the issue until I have had some time to think it over.
   B I give up some points in exchange for others.

8. A I am usually firm in pursuing my goals
   B I attempt to get all concerns and issues immediately out into the open.

9. A I feel that differences are not always worth worrying about.
   B I make some effort to get my way.

10. A I am firm in pursuing my goals.
    B I try to find a compromise solution.

11. A I attempt to get all concerns and issues immediately out into the open.
    B I might try to soothe the other's feelings and preserve our relationship.

12. A I sometimes avoid taking positions which would create controversy.
    B I will let the other person have some of their positions if they let me have some of mine.

13. A I propose a middle ground.
    B I press to get my points made.

14. A I tell the other person my ideas and ask them for theirs.
    B I try to show them the logic and benefits of my position.

15. A I might try to soothe the other's feelings and preserve our relationship.
    B I try to do what is necessary to avoid tensions.

16. A I try not to hurt the other's feelings.
    B I try to convince the other person of the merits of my position.

17. A I am usually firm in pursuing my goals.
    B I try to do what is necessary to avoid useless tensions.

18. A If it makes the other person happy, I might let them maintain their views.
    B I will let them have some of their positions if they let me have some of mine.

19. A I attempt to get all concerns and issues immediately out in the open.
    B I try to postpone the issue until I have had some time to think it over.

20. A I attempt to work immediately through our difficulties.
    B I try to find a fair combination of gains and losses for both of us.

21. A In approaching negotiations, I try to be considerate of the other person's wishes.
    B I always lean towards a direct discussion of the problem.

22. A I try to find a position that is intermediate between the other person's and mine.
    B I assert my wishes.

23. A I am very often concerned with satisfying all our wishes.
    B There are times when I let others take responsibility for solving the problem.

24. A If the other person's position seems very important to them, I would try to meet their wishes.
    B I try to get them to settle for a compromise.

25. A I try to show the other person the logic and benefits of my position.
    B In approaching negotiations, I try to be considerate of the other person's wishes.

26. A I propose a middle ground
    B I am nearly always concerned with satisfying all our wishes.

27. A I sometimes avoid taking positions that would create controversy.
    B If it makes the other person happy, I might let them maintain their views.

28. A I am usually firm in pursuing my goals.

B   I usually seek the other's help in working out a solution.

29. A   I propose a middle ground.
    B   I feel that differences are not always worth worrying about.

30. A   I try not to hurt the other's feelings.
    B   I always share the problem with the other person so that we can work it out.

Scoring sheet: Thomas–Kilmann conflict questionnaire

Circle the letters below which you circled on each item of the questionnaire. Then add up the total for each of the five columns.

Insert style label	I	II	III	IV	V
1.				A	B
2.		B	A		
3.	A				B
4.			A		B
5.		A		B	
6.	B			A	
7.			B	A	
8.	A	B			
9.	B			A	
10.	A		B		
11.		A			B
12.			B	A	
13.	B		A		
14.	B	A			
15.				B	A
16.	B				A
17.	A			B	
18.			B		A
19.		A		B	
20.		A	B		
21.		B			A
22.	B		A		
23.		A		B	
24.			B		A
25.	A				B
26.		B	A		
27.				A	B
28.	A	B			
29.			A	B	
30.		B			A
Total	_____	_____	_____	_____	_____

Comparison sheet: middle and senior managers

Insert style label	I	II	III	IV	V
High (25%)	8–12	10–12	9–12	8–12	7–12
Middle (50%)	4–7	6–9	5–8	5–7	4–6
Low (25%)	0–3	0–5	0–4	0–4	0–3

The model of conflict managing behaviour is described in Kenneth Thomas, 'Conflict and conflict management', in M. Dunnette, *The Handbook of Industrial and Social Psychology*, Rand McNally, Chicago, 1976.

21.2 SGA: Using conflict management styles

Objectives

❑ To revise the various ways of dealing with interpersonal, group and organizational conflict.

❑ To identify when a particular conflict management style is most appropriate.

❑ To give students experience of group decision-making.

Introduction

There are three steps to managing conflict effectively. First, you learn the five different management styles that exist – competition, collaboration, avoidance, accommodation and compromise. Second, you become aware of the one or two styles that you habitually use, and then develop your skill and confidence in using the others. Finally, armed with a repertoire of these five different styles, you teach yourself to select the most appropriate one for a given situation. This activity seeks to develop your ability in this last area.

Procedure

Step 1 Turn to the page in your workbook containing the *Conflict management style worksheet*. Complete it individually, and insert your answers in the first column on the left-hand side of the page (headed I). You have fifteen minutes in which to do this.

Step 2 Form into groups as instructed.

You are to complete the same worksheet again, but this time *as a group*. You are to note down your group decisions in the second column on the left-hand side of the worksheet page (headed G).

All groups should avoid conflict-reducing techniques such as voting; and differences of opinion should be treated as constructive.

Make your rankings *as a group* (do not just arithmetically translate the rankings of individual group members into a group ranking). Use logic and mutual understanding to arrive at a group decision.

All the groups have forty-five minutes to complete the task.

Step 3 Once time is up, your observer will deliver a report upon the *group decision process*.

Conflict management styles worksheet

Instructions: Below are four different cases. Each one is followed by five alternative courses of action (options). Your task is to rank all the five options (A–E) using '1' to indicate the most appropriate or desirable; '2' for the next most desirable, and so on through to '5' for the least appropriate or desirable. All five rankings should be made for each case, and these should be placed in the first column (headed I) on the left-hand side of the page.

Case 1

Pete is a lead operator of a plastic moulding machine. Recently he has noticed that one of the men from another machine has been coming over to his machine and talking to one of his men (not in break time). The efficiency of Pete's operator seems to be falling off, and there have been some rejects due to his inattention. Pete thinks he detects some resentment among the rest of the team. If you were Pete, what would you do?

I G

__ __ A. Talk to your man and tell him to limit his conversations during on-the-job time.

__ __ B. Ask your foreman to tell the lead operator of the other machine to keep his operators in line.

__ __ C. Confront both men the next time that you see them talking together (as well as the other lead operator, if necessary), find out what they are up to, and tell them what you expect of your operators.

__ __ D. Say nothing now; it would be silly to make something big out of something so insignificant.

__ __ E. Try to put the rest of the team at ease; it is important that they should all work together well.

Case 2

Sally is the senior quality-control (QC) inspector and has been appointed group leader of the QC people on her team. On separate occasions, two of her people have come to her with different suggestions for reporting test results to the machine operators. Paul wants to send the test results to the foreman and then to the machine operator, since the foreman is the person ultimately responsible for production output. Jim thinks that the results should go directly to the lead operator on the machine in question, since he is the one who must take corrective action as soon as possible. Both ideas seem good, and Sally can find no definitive rules in the department on who should receive the reports first. *If you were Sally, what would you do?*

I G

__ __ A. Decide on the suggestion you prefer and ask the other person to agree to your decision (perhaps implement it as a written procedure).

__ __ B. Wait and see; the best solution will become apparent.

__ __ C. Tell both Paul and Jim not to get so het up about their disagreement; it is not that important!

__ __ D. Get Paul and Jim together and examine both of their ideas closely.

__ __ E. Decide to send the reports to the foreman, with a copy to the lead operator (even though it might mean a little bit more photocopying for QC).

Case 3

Ralph is a module leader. His module consists of four very complex and expensive machines and five team members. The work is exacting and any inattention, or the use of improper procedures could result in a costly mistake or a serious injury. Ralph suspects that one of his men is taking drugs on the job, or at least is turning up for work under the influence of drugs. Ralph feels that he has some strong indications, but he knows that he does not have a solid case against the operator. *If you were Ralph, what would you do?*

I   G

__ __ A. Confront the man outright, tell him what you suspect and why, and that you are concerned for him and safety, and the safety of the team.

__ __ B. Ask that the suspected offender keep his habit off the job. What he does while on the job is part of your business.

__ __ C. Not confront the individual just at the moment. This might either 'turn him off' or drive him underground.

__ __ D. Give the man 'the facts of life'. Tell him it is illegal and unsafe, and that if he gets caught, you will do everything you can to see that he is fired.

__ __ E. Keep a close eye on the man to see that he is not endangering others.

Case 4

John is the foreman of a production team. From time to time in the past, the Product Development section has 'tapped' the production teams for operators to augment their own operator personnel to run test products on special machines. In the past this has put little strain on the production teams, as the demands have been small, temporary and infrequent. Recently, however, there seems to have been an almost constant demand for four production operators. The remaining members of the production teams have to fill in for the missing people, usually by working harder and by taking shorter breaks. *If you were John, what would you do about this?*

I   G

__ __ A. Let it go for now. The crisis will probably be over soon.

__ __ B. Try to smooth things with your own team members and with the development foreman. We all have our own jobs to do and can't afford a conflict.

__ __ C. Let Product Development have two of the four operators they requested.

__ __ D. Go to the Product Development foreman, and discuss with him how these demands for additional operators can best be met so as not to cause problems for your own department.

__ __ E. Go to your own boss, and get him to stop the Product Development department borrowing your operators.

Make a note below of the conflict management style that your group discussion suggests would be most likely to be appropriate or desirable in the circumstances:

Case 1. _____ Case 2. _____ Case 3. _____ Case 4. _____

Further reading

Reread Chapter 21 of the *ORBIT* textbook, especially the part dealing with the Thomas research on the different conflict management styles and when these should be used.

Group observer sheet

Your task as observer is to watch your group as it deals with the task of agreeing a ranking order for the options in each of the four cases. Focus exclusively on which conflict management styles are demonstrated by which group members. Do not concern yourself with the content of their deliberations.

The scoring sheet below contains a list of the five conflict management styles and spaces for you to enter the names of group members. Each time a member uses a style, put a tick adjacent to the style category under their name.

Listen carefully for the verbal clues given by group members.

Style	Summary	Group member				
Competition	Highly assertive regarding own goals; furthers own views; adopts a battling style					
Collaboration	Problem-solving approach; differences confronted; ideas and information shared					
Avoidance	Differences suppressed, member withdraws, silent to avoid confrontation.					
Accommodation	Member 'gives in' to others so as to appease them.					
Compromise	Bargaining as each member trades off desires to reach agreement.					

Other comments about group:

This exercise format is based upon D. T. Simpson's, 'Conflict styles: organizational decision-making', *The 1977 Annual Handbook for Group Facilitators*, University Associates, La Jolla, California, which was developed by A. A. Zoll and appeared in *Explorations in Managing*, Addison Wesley, Reading, MA, 1974.

21.3 PREP: Strikebreaker

Objectives

- ❏ To analyse a conflict situation using a conflict resolution process.
- ❏ To evaluate the process in terms of its strengths and weaknesses, and limitations and possibilities.
- ❏ To assess which conflict management styles could be used in this situation, and what their likely outcomes are likely to be.

Introduction

Of the five available conflict management styles, many management consultants favour collaboration, or failing that, compromise. When collaborating to solve a problem jointly, the two parties work together to create a solution that they can both value. If this is not possible, compromise, often arrived at by bargaining and 'splitting the difference', produces a solution that, while it is less than ideal, is nevertheless perceived as fair, and is accepted by both parties.

These two styles ensure that the two parties at least maintain, and possibly even enhance a positive working relationship into the future. The use of the other styles – accommodation, avoidance and competition, while it may be unavoidable because of circumstances, can produce explicit hostility or internal resentment among one or both parties.

The CUDSA process provides a set of steps that can lead to the resolution of a conflict situation collaboratively. Although the two parties described in the case did not use it, students can apply it to test its feasibility and assess its possibilities and limitations.

Procedure

Step 1 Before the class, familiarize yourselves with the five steps of the CUDSA process.

Step 2 Then read Isaac Isamov's short story, *Strikebreaker*.

Step 3 Apply the CUDSA process by making individual notes in response to the series of questions associated with each of its five steps. For the purpose of the analysis, Steven Lamorak and Blei should be treated as representing the Council,

CUDSA process

Step 1: Confront the conflict

Decide whether the conflict is sufficiently important to both parties to be confronted openly. Confrontation involves three factors. First, self-awareness – preparedness to acknowledge the existence of conflict in your relationship. Second, confronting the other party, that is, assertively stating positively your wants, wishes and preferences, and letting the other person(s) know how you want their behaviour to be altered. Third, if the conflict is not resolved amicably and quickly by being discussed, persuading the other person to collaborate with you to solve the problem to your mutual benefit.

Step 2: Understanding each other's position

Expending effort to understand the other's position ensures that you check that there is a real conflict (and not just a misunderstanding or misperception); demonstrating a commitment to a collaborative approach to managing the conflict; and showing respect for the other person. This may defuse the situation by having the situation stated and having each party's feelings ventilated, and allowing real (rather than imaginary) issues to be identified. In this step, the parties offer their own definitions of the problem.

Step 3: Define the problem

This involves arriving at a mutually acceptable definition of the problem. This must avoid a power struggle in which one party is labelled positively and the other negatively. Also avoid power-plays which are attempts to control, exploit or manipulate another against their will. Examples of these include using 'You-blame' language; engaging in character assassination; using threats that engender security; using passive-aggressive tactics such as attacking under the guise of being a victim; sulking and emotional withdrawal; using intimidation in your conversation to inhibit the other.

Step 4: Search for and evaluate alternative solutions

This involves collaboratively searching for mutually acceptable solutions. This two-step process begins with the generation of numerous solutions followed by their evaluation. Brainstorming is used. The parties focus on their mutually owned problem and together communicate their suggestions clearly to each other, and together develop one or two workable solutions. In deciding on a solution, a combative approach involves each party looking only for their own advantage, while a collaborative approach looks for solutions that meet the needs of both. The latter solution is that which maximizes the fulfilment or happiness of both whilst leaving neither feeling violated or taken advantage . of.

Step 5: Agree upon and implement the best solution(s)

Following an evaluation of the best solution in terms of which suits both parties, those adopting a collaborative approach make an agreement. Agreements are contracts (sometimes written) which clearly define each party's rights and obligations. If, for whatever reason, one party to the original agreement cannot keep it, it is preferable to try to renegotiate it than to break it unilaterally.

CUDSA questions

1. Confront the conflict.

   Write out Ragusnik's and Council's wants, wishes and preferences in this conflict situation.

2. Understand each other's position.

   (a) What does Ragusnik think and feel about the conflict?
   (b) How does Ragusnik perceive the Council's feelings and thoughts about the conflict?

3. Define the problem.

   To what extent are the prescriptions of this step of the CUDSA process being implemented by the two parties?

   (a) Are there any hidden agendas?
   (b) Which needs of each party are to be satisfied?
   (c) Define the problem as succinctly as possible.
   (d) Specify Blei's contribution to sustaining the problem.

4. Search for and evaluate alternative solutions.
   (a) From the information given in the story, write out as many possible solutions to the problem as you can think of without evaluating any of them (10 mins).
   (b) Evaluate the advantages and disadvantages of the TWO most appealing solutions.
   (c) Decide what kind of solution you decide need (competitive, collaborative, accommodating, compromising or avoidance).

5. Agree upon and implement the best solution(s)
   How might your suggested solution be implemented?

Strikebreaker

I

(1) Elvis Blei rubbed his plump hands and said, 'self-containment is the word'. He smiled uneasily as he helped Steven Lamorak of Earth to a light. There was uneasiness all over his smooth face with its small wide-set eyes.

   Lamorak puffed smoke appreciatively and crossed his lanky legs.

   His hair was powdered with grey and he had a large and powerful jawbone. 'Home grown?', he asked, staring critically at the cigarette. He tried to hide his own disturbance at the other's tension.

'Quite,' said Blei.

'I wonder,' said Lamorak, 'that you have room on your small world for such luxuries.'

(Lamorak thought of his first view of Elsevere from the spaceship visiplate. It was a jagged, airless planetoid, some hundred miles in diameter – just a dust-grey, rough-hewn rock, glimmering dully in the light of its sun, 200,000,000 miles distant. It was the only object more than a mile in diameter that circled that sun, and now men had burrowed into that miniature world and constructed a society in it. And he himself, as a sociologist, had come to study the world and see how humanity had made itself fit into that queerly specialized niche.)

(2) Blei's polite fixed smile expanded a hair. He said, 'We are not a small world, Dr Lamorak; you judge us by two-dimensional standards. The surface area of Elsevere is only three-quarters that of the State of New York, but that's irrelevant. Remember, we can occupy, if we wish, the entire interior of Elsevere. A sphere of 50 miles radius has a volume well over half a million cubic miles. If all Elsevere were occupied by levels 50 feet apart, the total surface area within the planetoid would be 56,000,000 square miles, and that is equal to the total land area of Earth. And none of these square miles, Doctor, would be unproductive.'

Lamorak said, 'Good Lord', and stared blankly for a moment. 'Yes, of course, you're right. Strange I never thought of it that way. But then Elsevere is the only thoroughly exploited asteroid world in the Galaxy; the rest of us simply can't get away from thinking of two-dimensional surfaces, as you pointed out. Well, I'm more than ever glad that your Council has been so cooperative as to give me a free hand in this investigation of mine.'

Blei nodded convulsively at that.

Lamorak frowned slightly and thought: He acts for all the world as though he wished I had not come. Something's wrong.

(3) Blei said, 'Of course, you understand that we are actually much smaller than we could be; only minor portions of Elsevere have as yet been hollowed out and occupied. Nor are we particularly anxious to expand, except very slowly. To a certain extent we are limited by the capacity of our pseudo-gravity engines and Solar energy converters.'

'I understand. But tell me Councillor Blei – as a matter of personal curiosity, and not because it is of prime importance to my project – could I view some of your farming and herding levels first? I am fascinated by the thought of fields of wheat and herds of cattle inside a planetoid.'

'You'll find the cattle small by your standards, Doctor, and we don't have much wheat. We grow yeast to a much greater extent. But there will be some wheat to show you. Some cotton and rice, too. Even fruit trees.'

'Wonderful. As you say, self-containment. You recirculate everything, I imagine.'

Lamorak's sharp eyes did not miss the fact that this last remark twinged Blei. The Elseverian's eyes narrowed to slits that held his expression.

He said, 'We must recirculate, yes. Air, water, food, minerals – everything that is used up – must be restored to its original state; waste products are reconverted to raw materials. All that is needed is energy, and we have enough of that. We don't manage with 100 per cent efficiency of course, there is a certain seepage. We import a small amount of water each year; and if our needs grow, we may have to import some coal and oxygen.'

Lamorak said, 'When can we start our tour, Councillor Blei?'

Blei's smile lost some of its tangible warmth. 'As soon as we can, Doctor. There are some routine matters that must be arranged.'

Lamorak nodded, and having finished his cigarette, stubbed it out. Routine matters? There was none of this hesitancy during the preliminary correspondence. Elsevere had seemed proud that its unique asteroid existence had attracted the attention of the Galaxy.

(4) He said, 'I realize I would be a disturbing influence in a tightly-knit society', and watched grimly as Blei leaped at the explanation and made it his own.

'Yes,' he said, 'we feel marked off from the rest of the Galaxy. We have our own customs. Each individual Elseverian fits into a comfortable niche. The appearance of a stranger without fixed caste is unsettling.'

'The caste system does involve a certain inflexibility.'

'Granted,' said Blei quickly; 'but there is also a certain self-assurance. We have firm rules of intermarriage and rigid inheritance of occupation. Each man woman and child knows his place, accepts it, and is accepted in it; we have virtually no neurosis or mental illness.'

'And there are no misfits?' asked Lamorak.

Blei shaped his mouth as though to say no, then clamped it suddenly shut, biting the word into silence; a frown deepened on his forehead. He said, at length, 'I will arrange for the tour, Doctor. Meanwhile, I imagine you would welcome a chance to freshen up and to sleep.'

They rose together and left the room, Blei politely motioning the Earthman to precede him out of the door.

II

(5)   Lamorak felt oppressed by the vague feeling of crisis that had pervaded his discussion with Blei.

The newspaper reinforced that feeling. He read it carefully before getting into bed, with what was at first merely clinical interest. It was an 8-page tabloid of synthetic paper. One quarter of its items consisted of 'personals': births, marriages, deaths, record quotas, expanding habitable volume (not area! three dimensions!). The remainder included scholarly essays, educational material and fiction. Of news, in the sense to which Lamorak was accustomed, there was virtually nothing.

One item only could be so considered and that was chilling in its incompleteness.

It said, under a small headline: DEMANDS UNCHANGED: *There has been no change in his attitude of yesterday. The Chief Councillor, after a second interview, announced that his demands remain completely unreasonable and cannot be met under any circumstances.*

Then, in parentheses, and in a different type, there was the statement: *The editors of this paper agree that Elsevere cannot and will not jump to his whistle, come what may.*

Lamorak read it over three times. *His* attitude. *His* demands. *His* whistle.

Whose?

He slept uneasily that night.

III

(6)   He had no time for newspapers in the days that followed; but spasmodically, the matter returned to his thoughts.

Blei, who remained his guide and companion for most of the tour, grew ever more withdrawn.

On the third day (quite artificially clock-set in an Earthlike 24-hour pattern), Blei stopped at one point, and said, 'Now this level is devoted entirely to chemical industries. That section is not important – '

But he turned away a shade too rapidly, and Lamorak seized his arm. 'What are the products of that section?'

'Fertilizers. Certain organics,' said Blei stiffly.

Lamorak held him back, looking for what sight Blei might be evading. His gaze swept over the close-by horizons of lined rock and the buildings squeezed and layered between the levels.

Lamorak said, 'Isn't that a private residence there?'

Blei did not look in the indicated direction.

Lamorak said, 'I think that's the largest one I've seen yet. Why is it here on a factory level?' That alone made it noteworthy. He had already seen that the levels in Elsevere were divided rigidly among the residential, the agricultural and the industrial.

He looked back and called, 'Councillor Blei'.

The councillor was walking away and Lamorak pursued him with hasty steps. 'Is there something wrong, sir?'

Blei muttered, 'I am rude. I know. I am sorry. There are matters that prey on my mind – ' He kept up his rapid pace.

'Concerning *his* demands?'

Blei came to a full halt. 'What do *you* know about that?'

'No more than I've read in the newspaper.'

Blei muttered something to himself.

Lamorak said, 'Ragusnik? What's that?'

Blei sighed heavily. 'I suppose you ought to be told. It's humiliating, deeply embarrassing. The Council thought that matters would certainly be arranged shortly and that your visit need not be interfered with, that you need not know or be concerned. But it is almost a week now. I don't know what will happen and, appearances notwithstanding, it might be the best for you to leave. No reason for an Outworlder to risk death.'

(7) The Earthman smiled incredulously. 'Risk death? In this little world, so peaceful and busy. I can't believe it.'

The Elseverian councillor said, 'I can explain. I think it best I should.' He turned his head away. 'As I told you, everything on Elsevere must recirculate. You understand that.'

'Yes.'

'That includes – uh, human wastes.'

'I assumed so', said Lamorak.

'Water is reclaimed from it by distillation and absorption. What remains is converted into fertilizer for yeast use; some of it is used as a source of fine organics and other by-products. These factories you see are devoted to this.'

'Well?' Lamorak had experienced a certain difficulty in the drinking of water when he first landed on Elsevere, because he had been realistic enough to know what it must be reclaimed from; but he had conquered the feeling easily enough. Even on Earth, water was reclaimed by natural processes from all sorts of unpalatable substances.

Blei, with increasing difficulty, said, 'Igor Ragusnik is the man who is in charge of the industrial process immediately involving the wastes. The position has been in his family since Elsevere was first colonized. One of the original settlers was Mikhail Ragusnik and he –, he –'

'Was in charge of waste reclamation.'

'Yes. Now that residence you singled out is the Ragusnik residence; it is the best and most elaborate on the asteroid. Ragusnik gets many privileges the rest of us do not have; but, after all – .' Passion entered the Councillor's voice with great suddenness, 'We cannot *speak* to him.'

'What?'

'He demands full social equity. He wants his children to mingle with ours, and our wives to visit – Oh!' It was a groan of utter disgust.

Lamorak thought of the newspaper item that could not even bring itself to mention Ragusnik's name in print, or to say anything specific about his demands. He said, 'I take it he's an outcast because of his job.'

'Naturally. Human wastes and – ', words failed Blei. After a pause, he said more quietly, 'As an Earthman, I suppose you don't understand.'

'As a sociologist, I think I do.' Lamorak thought of the Untouchables in ancient India, the ones who handled corpses. He thought of the position of swineherds in ancient Judea.

He went on, 'I gather Elsevere will not give in to those demands.'

'Never,' said Blei, energetically. 'Never.'

'And so?'

'Ragusnik has threatened to cease operations.'

'Go on strike, in other words.'

'Yes.'

'Would that be serious?'

'We have enough food and water to last quite a while; reclamation is not essential in that sense. But the wastes would accumulate, they would infect the asteroid. After generations of careful disease control, we have low natural resistance to germ diseases. Once an epidemic started – and one would – we would drop by the hundred.'

'Is Ragusnik aware of this?'

'Yes, of course.'

'Do you think he is likely to go through with his threat, then?'

'He is mad. He has already stopped working; there has been no waste reclamation since the day before you landed.' Blei's bulbous nose sniffed at the air as though it had already caught the whiff of excrement.

Lamorak sniffed mechanically at that, but smelled nothing.

Blei said, 'So you see why it might be wise for you to leave. We are humiliated, of course, to have to suggest it.'

But Lamorak said, 'Wait, not just yet. Good Lord, this is a matter of great interest to me professionally. May I speak to the Ragusnik?'

'On no account,' said Blei alarmed.

'But I would like to understand the situation. The sociological conditions here are unique and not to be duplicated elsewhere. In the name of science – '

'How do you mean, speak? Would image-reception do?'

'Yes.'

'I will ask the Council,' muttered Blei.

IV

(8)   They sat about Lamorak uneasily, their austere and dignified expressions badly marred with anxiety. Blei, seated in the midst of them, studiously avoided the Earthman's eyes.

The chief counsellor, grey-haired, his face harshly wrinkled, his neck scrawny, said in a soft voice, 'If in any way you can persuade him, sir, out of your own convictions, we will welcome that. In no case, however, are you to imply that we will, in any way yield.'

A gauzy curtain fell between the Council and Lamorak. He could make out the individual councillors still, but now he turned sharply towards the receiver before him. It glowed to life.

A head appeared in it, in natural colour and with great realism. A strong dark head, with massive chin faintly stubbled, and thick, red lips set into a firm horizontal line.

The image said, suspiciously, 'Who are you?'

Lamorak said, 'My name is Steve Lamorak. I am an Earthman.'

'An Outworlder?'

'That's right. I am visiting Elsevere. You are Ragusnik?'

'Igor Ragusnik, at your service,' said the image, mockingly. 'Except that there is no service, and there will be none until my family and I are treated like human beings.'

Lamorak said, 'Do you realize the danger that Elsevere is in? The possibility of epidemic disease?'

'In twenty-four hours the situation can be made normal, if they allow me humanity. The situation is theirs to correct.'

'You sound like an educated man, Ragusnik.'

'So?'

'I am told you're denied no material comforts. You are housed and clothed and fed better than anyone else on Elsevere. Your children are the best educated.'

'Granted. But all by servo-mechanism. And motherless girl-babies are sent us to care for until they grow up to be our wives. And they die young for loneliness. Why?' There was a sudden passion in his voice. 'Why must we live in isolation as if we were all monsters, unfit for human beings to be near? Aren't we human beings like others, with the same needs, and desires and feelings. Don't we perform an honourable and useful function –?'

(9) There was a rustling of sighs from behind Lamorak. Ragusnik heard it, and raised his voice. 'I see you of the Council behind there. Answer me: Isn't it an honourable and useful function? It is *your* waste made into food for *you*. Is the man who purifies corruption worse than the man who produces it? – Listen, Councillors, I will *not* give in. Let all of Elsevere die of disease – including myself and my son, if necessary – but I will not give in. My family will be better dead of disease, than living as now.'

Lamorak interrupted. 'You've led this life since birth, haven't you?'

'And if I have?'

'Surely you're used to it.'

'Never. Resigned, perhaps. My father was resigned, and I was resigned for a while; but I have watched my son, my only son, with no other boy to play with. My brother and I had each other, but my son will never have anyone, and I am no longer resigned. I am through with Elsevere and through with talking.'

The receiver went dead.

The Chief Councillor's face had paled to an aged yellow. He and Blei were the only ones of the group left with Lamorak. The Chief Councillor said, 'The man is deranged. I don't know how to force him.'

He had a glass of wine at his side; as he lifted it to his lips, he spilled a few drops that stained his white trousers with purple splotches.

(10) Lamorak said, 'Are his demands so unreasonable? Why can't he be accepted into society?'

There was momentary rage in Blei's eyes. 'A dealer in excrement.'

Then he shrugged. 'You are from Earth.'

Incongruously, Lamorak thought of another unacceptable, one of the numerous classic creations of the medieval cartoonist, Al Capp. The variously-named, 'inside man at the skonk works'.

He said, 'Does Ragusnik really deal with excrement? I mean, is there physical contact? Surely, it is all handled by machinery.'

'Of course,' said the Chief Councillor.

'Then what exactly is Ragusnik's function?'

'He manually adjusts the various controls that assure the proper functioning of the machinery. He shifts units to allow repairs to be made; he alters functional rates with the time of day; he varies end production with demand.' He added sadly, 'If we had the space to make the machinery ten times as complex, all this could be done automatically; but that would be such needless waste.'

'But even so,' insisted Lamorak, 'all Ragusnik does, he does simply by pressing buttons or closing contacts or things like that.'

'Yes.'

'Then his work is no different from any Elseverian's.'

Blei said, stiffly, 'You don't understand.'

'And for that you will risk the death of your children?'

'We have no other choice,' said Blei. There was enough agony in his voice to assure Lamorak that the situation was torture for him, but that he had no other choice indeed.

Lamorak shrugged in disgust. 'Then break the strike to force him.'

'How?' said the Chief Councillor. 'Who would touch him or go near him? And if we kill him by blasting from a distance, how will that help us?'

(11) Lamorak said, thoughtfully, 'Would you know how to run his machinery?'

The Chief Councillor came to his feet. 'I?' he howled.

'I don't mean *you*,' cried Lamorak at once. 'I used the pronoun in its indefinite sense. Could *someone* learn how to handle Ragusnik's machinery?'

Slowly, the passion drained out of the Chief Councillor. 'It is in the handbooks, I am certain – though I assure you I have never concerned myself with it.'

'Then couldn't someone learn the procedure and substitute for Ragusnik until the man gives in?'

Blei said, 'Who would agree to do such a thing? Not I, under any circumstances.'

Lamorak thought fleetingly of Earthly taboos that might be almost as strong. He thought of cannibalism, incest, a pious man cursing God. He said, 'But you must have made provision for vacancy in the Ragusnik job. Suppose he died.'

'Then his son would automatically succeed to his job, or his nearest other relative,' said Blei.

'What if he had no adult relatives? What if all his family died at once?'

'That has never happened; it will never happen.'

The Chief Councillor added, 'If there was a danger of it, we might, perhaps place a baby or two with the Ragusniks and have it raised to the profession.'

'Ah. And how would you choose that baby?'

'From among children of mothers who had died in childbirth, as we chose the future Ragusnik bride.'

'Then choose a substitute Ragusnik now, by lot,' said Lamorak.

The Chief Councillor said, 'No! Impossible! How can you suggest that? If we select a baby, that baby is brought up to the life, it knows no other. At this point, it would be necessary to chose an adult and subject him to Ragusnik-hood. No, Dr Lamorak, we are neither monsters nor abandoned brutes.'

No use, thought Lamorak, no use, unless –

V

(12) That night, Lamorak slept scarcely at all. Ragusnik asked for only the basic elements of humanity. But opposing that were 30,000 Elseverians who faced death.

The welfare of 30,000 on one side; the just demands of one family on the other. Could one say that 30,000 who would support such injustice deserved to die? Injustice by what standards? Earth's? Elsevere's? And who was Lamorak that he could judge?

And Ragusnik? He was willing to let 30,000 die, including men and women who merely accepted a situation they had been taught to accept and could not change if they wished to. And children who had nothing at all to do with it.

Thirty thousand on one side; a single family on the other.

VI

(13) Lamorak made his decision in something that was almost despair; in the morning he called the Chief Counsellor.

He said, 'Sir, if you can find a substitute, Ragusnik will see that he has lost all chance to force a decision in his favour and will return to work.'

'There can be no substitute,' sighed the Chief Counsellor. 'I have explained that.'

'No substitute among the Elseverians, but I am not an Elseverian; it doesn't matter to me. *I* will substitute.'

VII

(14) They were excited, much more excited than Lamorak himself. A dozen times they asked him if he was serious.

Lamorak had not shaved, and he felt sick, 'Certainly, I'm serious. And any time Ragusnik acts like this, you can always import a substitute. No other world has the taboo and there will always be plenty of temporary substitutes available if you pay enough.'

(He was betraying a brutally exploited man, and he knew it. But he told himself desperately: *Except for ostracism, he's very well treated. Very well.*)

They gave him the handbooks and he spent six hours, reading and re-reading. There was no use asking questions. None of the Elseverians knew anything about the job, except for what was in the handbook; and all seemed uncomfortable if the details were as much as mentioned.

'Maintain zero reading of galvanometer A-2 at all times during red signal of the Lunge-howler,' read Lamorak. 'Now what's a Lunge-howler?'

'There will be a sign,' muttered Blei, and the Elseverians looked at each other hang-dog and bent their heads to stare at their fingerends.

VIII

(15) They left him long before he reached the small rooms that were the central headquarters of generations of working Ragusniks, serving their world. He had specific instructions concerning which turnings to take and what level to reach, but they hung back and let him proceed alone.

He went through the rooms painstakingly, identifying the instruments and controls, following the schematic diagrams in the handbook.

There's a Lunge-howler, he thought, with gloomy satisfaction. The sign did indeed say so. It had a semi-circular face bitten into holes that were obviously designed to glow in separate colours. Why a 'howler' then?

He didn't know.

Somewhere, thought Lamorak, *somewhere wastes are accumulating, pushing against gears and exits, pipelines and stills, waiting to be handled in half a hundred ways. Now they just accumulate.*

Not without a tremor, he pulled the first switch as indicated by the handbook in its directions for 'Initiation'. A gentle murmur of life made itself felt through the floors and walls. He turned a knob and lights went on.

At each step he consulted the handbook, though he knew it by heart; and with each step, the rooms brightened and the dial indicators sprang into motion and a humming grew louder.

Somewhere deep in the factories, the accumulated wastes were being drawn into the proper channels.

IX

(16) A high-pitched signal sounded and startled Lamorak out of his painful concentration. It was the communications signal and Lamorak fumbled his receiver into action.

Ragusnik's head showed, startled; then slowly, the incredulity and outright shock faded from his eyes. '*That's* how it is, then.'

'I'm not an Elseverian, Ragusnik; I don't mind doing this.'

'But what business is it of yours? Why do you interfere?'

'I'm on your side, Ragusnik, but I must do this.'

'Why, if you're on my side? Do they treat people on your world as they treat me here?'

'Not any longer. But even if you are right, there are 30,000 people on Elsevere to be considered.'

'They would have given in, you've ruined my only chance.'

'They would *not* have given in. And in a way you've won; they know now that you're dissatisfied. Until now, they never dreamed a Ragusnik could be unhappy, that he could make trouble.'

'What if they know? Now all they have to do is hire an Outworlder anytime.'

Lamorak shook his head violently. He had thought this through in these last bitter hours. 'The fact that they know means that the Elseverians will begin to think about you; some will begin to wonder if it's right to treat a human so. And if Outworlders are hired, they'll spread the word that this goes on upon Elsevere and Galactic public opinion will be in your favour.'

'And?'

'Things will improve. In your son's time, things will be much better.'

'In my son's time,' said Ragusnik, his cheeks sagging. 'I might have had it now. Well, I lose. I'll go back to the job.'

Lamorak felt an overwhelming relief. 'If you'll come down here now, sir, you may have your job and I'll consider it an honour to shake your hand.'

Ragusnik's head snapped up and filled with gloomy pride. 'You call me "sir" and offer to shake my hand. Go about your business, Earthman, and leave me to my work, for I would not shake yours.'

X

(17)   Lamorak returned the way he had come, relieved that the crisis was over, and profoundly depressed, too.

He stopped in surprise when he found a section of corridor cordoned off, so he could not pass. He looked around for alternative routes, and was startled at a magnified voice above his head. 'Dr Lamorak, do you hear me? This is Councillor Blei.'

Lamorak looked up. The voice came over some sort of public address system, but he saw no sign of an outlet.

He called out, 'Is anything wrong? Can you hear me?'

'I hear you.'

Instinctively, Lamorak was shouting, 'Is anything wrong? There seems to be a block here. Are there complications with Ragusnik?'

'Ragusnik has gone to work,' came Blei's voice. 'The crisis is over, and you must make ready to leave.'

'Leave?'

'Leave Elsevere; a ship is being made ready for you now.'

'But wait a bit,' Lamorak was confused by this sudden leap of events. 'I haven't completed my gathering of data.'

Blei's voice said, 'This cannot be helped. You will be directed to the ship and your belongings will be sent after you by servo-mechanisms. We trust – we trust –'

Something was becoming clear to Lamorak. 'You trust *what*?'

'We trust you will make no attempt to see or speak directly to any Elseverian. And of course we hope you will avoid embarrassment by not attempting to return to Elsevere at any time in the future. A colleague of yours would be welcome if further data concerning us is needed.'

'I understand,' said Lamorak, tonelessly. Obviously, he had himself become a Ragusnik. He had handled the controls that in turn had handled the wastes; he was ostracized. He was a corpse-handler, a swineherd, an inside man at the skonk works.

He said, 'Goodbye.'

Blei's voice said, 'Before we direct you, Dr Lamorak –. On behalf of the Council of Elsevere, I thank you for your help in this crisis.'

'You're welcome,' said Lamorak, bitterly.

This short story was written by Isaac Asimov in 1957. It appears in *The Best Science Fiction of Isaac Asimov*, Grafton Books, London, 1987, pp. 258–71. Used with permission.

21.4 REV: Chapter search

Objective

❑   To encourage students to revise the key facts and concepts associated with the management of conflict.

Introduction

The purpose of this test is to ensure that you have read and understood the chapter thoroughly, and are fully conversant with its content. On this occasion, your instructor will brief you on what is required prior to the start of the test. Write this down in the space provided.

Procedure

Note the test instructions as they are read out by your instructor:

_____

_____

Test

	A	B

1. Name given to employees who steal in groups, according to agreed rules, and through a well-defined division of labour.

2. Name given by Mars to the dimension which differentiates workers' jobs in terms of the degree of autonomy that they give their job-holders to organize their work.

3. Name given by Thomas to the dimension which differentiates the degree of forcefulness with which individuals pursue their goals in a conflict situation.

4. A conflict situation whose existence can be identified by the prevalence of sabotage, absenteeism, labour turnover and industrial theft.

5. A perspective on conflict which sees it as a natural phenomenon that is found in all organizations and groups.

6. Thomas' conflict-handling orientation in which both parties try to satisfy their own goals and concerns.

7. An approach in conflict theory and research identified by Beaumont which sees it as central, inevitable and desirable.

8. Hofstede's culture type in which nationals have a tendency to work together for the common goal.

9. Thomas' conflict-handling orientation that is most appropriate in a situation in which the individual does not possess the right answer, and has to learn.

10. Marx's analysis of societal conflict focused on the intentions and actions of the working classes which he called the _____?

Latecomer B

General information

You are one of the student members of the Departmental Course Committee (DCC). Each member represents one of the tutorial groups from the year class. The DCC meets regularly to hear student complaints and receive suggestions for improvements. It is attended by the course director, members of the departmental lecturing staff and the head of department.

You and your fellow student members hold preliminary meetings, to set the agenda and agree an approach, before bringing matters to DCC. In the past, your group has brought up matters at the DCC which have been swiftly resolved by the course director. At other times, your group has got into unproductive and acrimonious discussions on trivial matters, while important issues were neglected. You and your colleagues have looked silly in front of the teaching staff, and you have been criticized by those whom you represent.

You and your fellow student representatives are meeting today to decide whether or not to invite the course director to your future preliminary meetings (ahead of the DCC). You need a consensus before an invitation can be issued.

Specific information

You have been a student member of the DCC from the start of the year, and have enjoyed taking part. You value the status that the membership of this group gives you, and you personally like the other student reps. Due to an unscheduled tutorial meeting, you are a little late today.

You were personally embarrassed at the last DCC meeting when two of the student members started arguing among themselves about an issue which could have been easily resolved with a simple timetable change. This unnecessary and extended discussion meant that the question of student finance problems was not even discussed.

Your own view is that current practice SHOULD be changed, and the course director be invited to future meetings. Your reasons are as shown below. Feel free to refer to your notes during the role play.

1. You are sceptical whether student members of the DCC can in fact sort out their differences beforehand. Inviting the course director to preliminary meetings at least makes future fiascos less public.

2. The DCC is a problem-solving forum where student difficulties are discussed and resolved. It is not a court of law or a trade union–management negotiation situation (even though some student reps may see it as such).

3. If student members are incapable of sorting out the trivial from the important issues, then they should not be on the DCC.

4. Sorting out the trivial issues with the course director, will leave more time to prepare and discuss important matters with teaching staff and the head of department.

5. By discussing only important items at the DCC, teaching staff will come to see these events as valuable, and not just 'student moan sessions about trivia'.

Management control

22.1 LGA: The need to control

Objectives

❏ To introduce the behaviour pattern known as *Machiavellianism*.

❏ To assess individual differences in *Machiavellianism*.

❏ To develop understanding of how such behaviours are related to job performance.

Introduction

Chapter 22 of *ORBIT* introduces the *authoritarian* personality. This collection of traits implies intellectual rigidity, resistance to change, deference to authority, and a preoccupation with power and status. Authoritarians can thus be expected to perform badly in jobs that require sensitivity, tact, flexibility and the ability to deal with complexity and change. However, where the task is stable, and performance requires strict adherence to rules and procedures, an authoritarian may perform well.

In this exercise we wish to introduce the related personality construct of *Machiavellianism*, and give you an opportunity to find out how Machiavellian you are yourself. The authoritarian respects authority and shows deference to those who possess it. The Machiavellian, in contrast, seeks power with which to manipulate and control others. This personality construct is named after the sixteenth-century writer Niccolo Machiavelli from whose book *The Prince* some of the initial thinking around this idea was drawn. What traits does someone with a strong Machiavellian personality possess? What behaviours do these traits imply? In what ways can the desire to manipulate and control others affect job performance? What moral or ethical issues are raised by Machiavellian behaviour? Here is an opportunity to relate these questions to your own personality, by first assessing your Machiavellianism score.

Procedure

Step 1 Working on your own and without discussion with colleagues, complete the *Control orientation test* that follows.

Step 2 In buzz groups of about three members, compare your answers to the test. Note and discuss differences.

Step 3 Turn to the scoring instructions and work out your score.

Step 4 In buzz groups of about three members, share and compare your thinking in response to the two sets of analysis questions.

Step 5 Feedback optional, according to instructor's wishes.

Control orientation test

This is a test of your orientation towards the manipulation and control of others. In response to each statement, circle the number that most closely represents your attitude.

Statement:	DISAGREE a lot	a little	neutral	AGREE a little	a lot
1. The best way to handle people is to tell them what they want to hear.	1	2	3	4	5
2. When you ask someone to do something for you, it is best to give the real reason for wanting it rather than giving reasons that might carry more weight.	1	2	3	4	5
3. Anyone who completely trusts anyone else is asking for trouble.	1	2	3	4	5
4. It is hard to get ahead without cutting corners here and there.	1	2	3	4	5
5. It is safest to assume that all people have a vicious streak, and it will come out when they are given a chance.	1	2	3	4	5
6. One should take action only when it is morally right.	1	2	3	4	5
7. Most people are basically good and kind.	1	2	3	4	5
8. There is no excuse for lying to someone else.	1	2	3	4	5
9. Most people forget more easily the death of their father than the loss of their property.	1	2	3	4	5
10. Generally speaking, people won't work hard unless they're forced to do so.	1	2	3	4	5

Source: from R. Christie and F. L. Geis (eds), *Studies in Machiavellianism*, Academic Press, New York, 1970.

Control orientation test: scoring instructions

This test is designed to assess your Machiavellianism score. To score your answers, first add the numbers that you have circled on these items:

Item	Score
1.	_____
3.	_____
4.	_____
5.	_____
9.	_____
10.	_____
Subtotal:	_____

Then for the other four items, add the *reverse* scores, giving yourself a 5 if you circled 1, a 4 if you checked 2, and vice versa; a 3 stays a 3.

Item	Score
2.	_____
6.	_____
7.	_____
8.	_____

Subtotal: _____

Final score: _____

The average score is 25.

Analysis

First, some personal issues. Is your score much as you expected – consistent with your own self assessment? Would you like your score to be lower or higher, given what this would mean about your behaviour with respect to other people? Why? Share and compare your thinking on these points with your immediate colleagues.

Second, some organizational issues. Should we dismiss Machiavellianism out of hand as unethical and therefore inappropriate? Or should we take a more balanced stance: in what organizational settings would Machiavellian behaviour be appropriate and effective? Once again, share and compare your thinking on these issues with your immediate colleagues.

22.2 SGA: Design your control system

Objectives

❑ To identify the procedures and problems of designing an effective organizational control system.

❑ To explore the nature and characteristics of *dysfunctional* controls.

Introduction

The STOP! exercise on page 580 of Chapter 22 of *ORBIT* invites you to consider how your behaviour and performance on your organizational behaviour course are controlled. Here is an opportunity to turn the spotlight on your instructors, to consider their performance, and to consider how it in turn is controlled. However, we can take this analysis at least one step further; let us consider the design and implementation of controls on organizational behaviour instructors in order to improve performance on specific, predefined, criteria.

In approaching this exercise, and in tackling any similar control problem in an organizational setting, there is one fundamental aspect of controls on people that must be remembered. *We respond as individuals to the measures on which we will be appraised.* The corollary of this observation is that we are unlikely to attend to aspects of behaviour and performance that are *not* measured. Consider the apparently straightforward example of a machine operator. We want the operator to produce as many items as possible during an 8-hour working shift, or to produce to and exceed a quota. It is easy to count the number of items produced, and also easy to tie financial reward through a 'piece rate' to the output. However, this situation is *not* straightforward if there is a negative correlation between output and quality (in other words, if quality is likely to suffer as the volume of items produced increases, as the operator gets careless in an attempt to boost earnings). The control on volume of output in this case is *dysfunctional*, because it can lead to behaviours opposite to those actually required (i.e. it can lead to the production of defective items).

The 'simple' solution, of course, is to introduce a quality control; only count the good items. However, somebody now has to check quality. Can you trust the machine operator to do that? Will you employ specialist inspectors to do this, with the extra costs this will involve? What controls on the performance of the inspectors will be required? What began as a simple control problem turns out to have other costs and organizational complexities. Effective control system design must therefore take into account the likely responses of those to be controlled, the dysfunctional nature of some controls, and the need to look beyond what may be 'ideal' in any given setting and to design a *cost-effective* control system.

Academic promotion in many universities is dependent on volume (and perhaps quality) of published output from scholarship and research. To the extent that this control diverts attention away from other aspects of the academic task, that control may also be seen as dysfunctional. An educational institution that links academic salary progression to the educational level of its staff's teaching activities may find that 'low level' and vocational course innovation slows or stops, while staff creatively introduce innovative new 'high level' courses at degree and postgraduate level. To the extent that the mission of such an institution is to offer a broad range of vocational and academic courses, such a control on staff earnings is dysfunctional in that through time the portfolio of courses will be biased towards those which contribute most effectively to staff salaries. In some payment systems, a component of management salary is linked to the number of staff for whom that manager is responsible. This too can be a dysfunctional control, encouraging and rewarding behaviour inconsistent with the interests of the organization. Why? Because a manager in this situation is rewarded for recruiting more staff, regardless of the actual workload of the section concerned.

With these considerations in mind, we would like to invite you to consider the design of a cost-effective control system to maintain and perhaps improve your Instructor's teaching performance.

Procedure

Step 1 Working on your own, read the following *Control system design* brief and make preliminary notes on how you plan to tackle this assignment.

Step 2 Working in syndicate groups of three to five members, design a control system that meets the specified criteria.

Step 3 Produce a realistic assessment of your control system, concentrating in particular on how cost-effective it is, identifying any dysfunctional aspects.

Step 4 Nominate a spokesperson to present your design and its assessment to the class as a whole.

Control system design

The problem facing you is how to control the teaching performance of your organizational behaviour instructor. Your institution may already have some mechanisms in place that seek to achieve this – student feedback questionnaires, or a staff development unit that carries out classroom observation, perhaps. However, surely you can improve on what is already there, and you can always build existing controls into your new design.

You will recall that control is a process that involves setting standards, measuring performance, comparing actual with standard and determining as necessary any corrective action. Applied to the control of teaching performance, you will need to consider the following issues:

1. How are you going to define the standard of teaching performance expected of your Instructor? Will you use one measure or several? Can you define these measures clearly and unambiguously? In setting this standard, or these standards, do you wish to stay with current levels of performance, or to set 'stretch goals' that will improve standards of performance?

2. How are you going to measure your instructor's actual performance against your

standard or standards? You need to specify not only how this will be done, but also who will do it, and how often.

3. How are you going to compare the actual performance measures with your standards? Once again, you need to specify how this will be done, by whom, and when.

4. What will happen if performance is not up to the standard or standards required? Specify the actions that will unfold in this instance.

5. Now that you have designed your control system, give some thought as to how cost effective it will be in operation. What would be ideal, and what will work as intended, may not be the same, and could have significantly different cost implications.

6. Now consider whether any of the controls you have introduced are dysfunctional and will lead to behaviours opposite to or different from those you desire. Will your system encourage rigid bureaucratic behaviour or information distortion, and will any aspect of your system threaten need satisfaction and create hostility and lack of cooperation?

7. Prepare a presentation of your design and assessment to your instructor and the assembled class in plenary session.

22.3 PREP: Control to commitment

Objectives

❏ To develop understanding of the practical implications of Richard Walton's argument for a shift from cultures of control to cultures of commitment.

❏ To apply this argument to a specific organization.

Introduction

Richard Walton (*ORBIT*, p. 604) argued in 1985 that managers have to choose between a strategy based on imposing control and a strategy based on eliciting commitment. If you are not already familiar with this argument, turn to it now and read it through. The summary provided in the textbook is comprehensive but, of course, can never be as good as the real thing. If you have the time and opportunity, you could find it helpful and interesting to track down the original in *Harvard Business Review* which should not be a difficult journal to trace. The argument revolves around notions of high-involvement management, participation and empowerment, and it offers an account of a desirable organizational culture that can be difficult to criticize. It is a relatively simple matter to specify a desirable organizational culture on a sheet of paper. However, it may not be so easy to take an existing organization and introduce the changes required to move the culture in that direction. In addition, the existing culture may already contain elements of the 'ideal'. There may be aspects of the organization's environment or of its business which discourage the full implementation of a commitment culture. To establish the problems of taking advice such as Walton's and putting it into practice, it is necessary to try and do just that – with respect to a particular organization. That is what we would like to invite you to do in this prepared assignment.

Procedure

Step 1 Make sure that you are familiar with the arguments in the Assessment section of Chapter 22 of *ORBIT*, beginning on page 603. Pay particular attention to the work of Richard Walton, and note that similar arguments have appeared earlier in the book.

Step 2 Read the *Task briefing* which follows.

Step 3 Carry out whatever field research you feel is necessary to complete this assignment.

Step 4   Write a report which describes the current organization culture with respect to Walton's framework. Indicate the nature and extent of the gap between current practice and what Walton identifies as ideal.

Step 5   Formulate recommendations for the organization with respect to the management action required to move the organization closer to the ideal. Be as specific and detailed in your recommendations as you feel it necessary.

Step 6   Feedback according to your Instructor's wishes.

Task briefing

You have two tasks in this assignment.

Your first task is to establish the extent to which your educational institution has a commitment culture as opposed to a control culture. Having identified any 'gap' between current reality and Richard Walton's ideal, your second task is to develop a set of recommendations for the development of a commitment culture in your institution.

To carry out this analysis, you will need to speak to at least a small number of people who work for the organization. You will need to decide what questions you want to ask them. You could, for example, show them Walton's two specifications and ask them to comment under each heading (job design, performance expectations and so on) where they feel their organization lies at present. It might take you some time to explain Walton's material in enough detail to enable your respondents to give you ready answers, so you could instead work out an interview schedule to get you the information you need. You must decide what approach to use; there are practical research methods problems to resolve here, and you may find the content of Chapter 2 of use in that respect. However, when writing up the report of what you have found, indicate clearly how you gathered the information on which your analysis and recommendations are based. Remember that one particularly valuable source of practical recommendations lies in your informants; after all, they work here.

When planning the fieldwork for this assignment, note that your educational institution employs people in capacities other than lecturers. You may find it instructive for the purposes of this assignment to speak to secretaries and to administrative and library staff as well as to academic personnel. Don't expect their perspectives on the culture of the organization to be consistent. If there are significant differences in perceptions, what does this tell you about the culture of the organization?

Your final report should have the following broad structure:

1. *Executive summary:* a single-page outline of the main findings and recommendations.

2. *Introduction:* a short statement of the aims of your report, explaining also the background to your analysis in the work of Richard Walton.

3. *Methodology:* a summary of how you gathered the data for this assignment, with a candid assessment of the strengths and limitations of your approach.

4. *Gap analysis:* the heart of the report in which you present a structured assessment of the extent to which the organization matches the 'ideal' commitment culture.

5. *Recommendations:* where you set out proposals, based on your gap analysis, for changing the culture or aspects of it from a control orientation to a commitment orientation.

22.4 REV: Eulogy and invective

Objectives

❑ To expose the contradictions in perspectives on control in organizations.

❑ To develop skills in summarizing arguments concisely.

Introduction

Students of any age or background coming to the study of organizational behaviour looking for the correct answer, the best way, the weight of evidence that points a clear finger, will often find only disappointment. The study of any social scientific domain will produce the same frustration. Disappointment and frustration, however, are a product at least in part of anticipation. If you don't expect to find clarity and lack of ambiguity, if instead you expect to find ambiguity and contradictions, then you will not be disappointed. The ambiguities and contradictions typical of those found in the study of organizational behaviour can be found in Chapter 22 in *ORBIT* in the domain of management control. Here we find that control is critical and beneficial; here we also find that control is insidious and damaging. How are we ever to strike a balance between these extremes? Are these *really* opposing views, or is there in practice less of a problem reconciling this apparent conflict? In this final review exercise, you are invited to 'get closer' to the arguments by producing concise summaries of the two apparently opposing views. This will help in developing and retaining an understanding of the main lines of argument. This review can be completed as an individual assignment. It is more fun, however, if time and facilities allow, to complete this assignment in class in a competitive team setting. The instructions which follow concern the latter approach.

Procedure

Step 1   Divide the class into teams of four or five members. Half the teams will be *eulogy* teams and the other half will be *invective* teams.

Step 2   Each team constructs its assigned presentation in accordance with either one of the two briefs which follow. The presentation should be produced either on an overhead projector foil, or on a sheet of flipchart paper, for subsequent presentation to the group as a whole. Each team must nominate a spokesperson to lead the presentation; other team members may take part in the presentation if they wish.

Step 3   When ready, two *invective* teams present, with time for questions and discussion, and for other *invective* teams to add to the arguments offered.

Step 4   Then two *eulogy* teams present, again followed by questions and discussion with additional input from other *eulogy* teams.

Step 5   The instructor conducts a vote to establish which perspective has attracted the most sympathy.

Eulogy team briefing

A eulogy is a speech or writing in praise; to eulogize is to extol the virtues or positive attributes of someone or something. Your team task in this assignment is to prepare a eulogy for control in an organizational setting. Your eulogy, which you may be invited to present to your whole class, should meet the following simple criteria:

1. It must open with a concise statement of the position you wish to support and defend.

2. The heart of your eulogy must consist of 'one-line' statements that offer argument and evidence to back your line of reasoning.

3. To the extent possible within these constraints, your eulogy must be delivered with passion and conviction.

4.   You have one overhead projector foil or sheet of flipchart paper on which to summarize the main points of your presentation.

Invective team briefing

An invective is a severe or reproachful accusation, an attack with words, possibly with satire, sarcasm and abuse. Your team task in this assignment is to prepare an invective against control in an organizational setting. Your invective, which you may be invited to present to your whole class, should meet the following simple criteria:

1.   It must open with a concise statement of the position you wish to support and defend.

2.   The heart of your invective must consist of 'one-line' statements that offer argument and evidence to back your line of reasoning.

3.   To the extent possible within these constraints, your invective must be delivered with force and conviction.

4.   You have one overhead projector foil or sheet of flipchart paper on which to summarize the main points of your presentation.